DIFFICULT TIMES: A FRESH LOOK AT DEMOCRACY IN MODERN AMERICA

Revised Edition

By Thomas Lemberg

Revised Edition 2017

© 2010-17

DEDICATION

I dedicate this book to my grandchildren Zack, Aerin, Lexa and Jamie in the hope that they live in a world impede with the American Dream.

PART ONE: SOMETHING'S HAPPENING HERE   2

CHAPTER ONE: A TIME OUT OF JOINT   7
CHAPTER TWO: AMERICANS: LIKE A ROLLING STONE   12

PART TWO: LIVING IN MODERN TIMES: WHAT'S PUSHING AND PULLING AMERICA   30

SECTION ONE: "USING IDEAS AS OUR MAPS"   33

CHAPTER THREE: "NOT MUCH IS REALLY SACRED" IN OUR SECULAR MATERIAL WORLD   36
   A. The Spiritual, Christian World of the Middle Ages   36
   B. The Modern World-View of Secular Materialism   39

CHAPTER FOUR: "I STAND ALONE WITHOUT BELIEFS": SECULAR MATERIALIST LIFE   43
   A. Boons and Burdens of Secular Materialism   43
   B. Secular Materialism in America   49
   C. The Unsettling Effects of Secular Materialism   50
   D. The Future of Secular Materialism   59

CHAPTER FIVE: "I, ME, MINE": INDIVIDUALISM AND THE PURSUIT OF SELF-INTEREST   61
   A. The Emergence of American Individualism   61
   B. Contemporary American Individualism   62
   C. Costs of Our Contemporary Individualism   67

CHAPTER SIX: "ANYTHING GOES": ERODED VALUES   70
   A. Modernity's Impact on Values   70
   B. The Erosion of Traditional Values   71
   C. The Effects of Moral Erosion   78

SECTION TWO: ECONOMIC AND SOCIAL FORCES: "SOMEONE'S IN MY HEAD BUT IT'S NOT ME"   83

CHAPTER SEVEN: "DID YOU THINK THAT MONEY WAS HEAVEN SENT?": OUR ECONOMY AND THE AMERICAN DREAM   84
   A. The Seeming Triumph of Unbridled Capitalism   86
   B. Free Market Imperfections and Regulation   89
   C. Inequality: Economics and Ordinary Americans   103

D. Advancement in the Contemporary Economy 114

CHAPTER EIGHT: LONELY LIFE IN MODERN SOCIETY 121
A. Contemporary America 121
B. Mass Culture and Politics in Modern America 126
C. The Social Psychology of Mass Culture 130
D. The Speed of Change and the Pace of Life 136

CHAPTER NINE: EMPTY AND ACHING FOR LOST COMMUNITY 139
A. Atomistic Thinking and Individualism 139
B. Loss of Local Community 140
C. The National Community 143

SECTION THREE: OUR POLITICAL WORLD 147

CHAPTER TEN: OUR POLITICAL SCENE: REPUBLICANS AND DEMOCRATS, CONSERVATIVES AND LIBERALS 148
A. The Republican Move to the Right 148
B. The Politics of American Liberalism 158

CHAPTER ELEVEN: AMERICA'S POLITICAL UGLY SIDE 174
A. The Politics of Polarization 174
B. Political Discourse in Modern America 178
C. American Government Today 181

PART THREE: STORMS AND HARBORS 190

CHAPTER TWELVE: THINKING PAST OUR DOGMAS 195
A. From Secular Materialism To Spirituality 196
B. Communitarian Ideas and Capabilities 203
C. Values and the Grounds of Ethics 208

CHAPTER THIRTEEN: DEMOCRACY FOR THE USA 211
A. What Kind of a Country Do We Want? 211
B. Some Thoughts About Policies 213

CHAPTER FOURTEEN: DEMOCRACY CAN FAIL: ARE WE WILLING TO PAY THE COST OF FREEDOM? 221
A. What a Strong, Democratic Nation Needs 222
B. Dangers Facing America 226

CHAPTER FIFTEEN: HOPE 232
A. Prognosis 232
B. Getting to Success 234

A WORD ON THE REVISED EDITION

I wrote the first edition of Difficult Times while Barack Obama was President. It was inconceivable to me, and to most other Americans, that he would be succeeded by Donald Trump. Though Trump the President was utterly unexpected, the book described, and sought to explain, a citizenry so deeply angry, unhappy and dissatisfied that, in retrospect, this seeming revolution in American politics was there to be foreseen.

This edition makes substantial revisions to reduce duplication and streamline the text. It makes four brief additions to reflect ideas in recent books which add depth and support to the theses here. It brings the work into the Presidency of Trump, which requires updating but no substantive changes. And, it removes quite a bit of the last quarter of the first edition discussing solutions. It now limits that discussion to general principles, to sharpen the focus on why all this is happening.

"But we have to make an effort in the United States, we have to make an effort to understand, to get beyond, or go beyond these rather difficult times....

What we need in the United States is not division; what we need in the United States is not hatred; what we need in the United States is not violence and lawlessness, but is love and wisdom, and compassion toward one another, and a feeling of justice towards those who still suffer within our country, whether they be white or whether they be black.

So I ask you tonight to return home, to say a prayer for the family of Martin Luther King — yes, it's true — but more importantly to say a prayer for our own country, which all of us love — a prayer for understanding and that compassion of which I spoke.

We can do well in this country. We will have difficult times. We've had difficult times in the past, but we — and we will have difficult times in the future. It is not the end of violence; it is not the end of lawlessness; and it's not the end of disorder.

But the vast majority of white people and the vast majority of black people in this country want to live together, want to improve the quality of our life, and want justice for all human beings that abide in our land.

And let's dedicate ourselves to what the Greeks wrote so many years ago: to tame the savageness of man and make gentle the life of this world. Let us dedicate ourselves to that, and say a prayer for our country and for our people."

Robert Kennedy, April 4, 1968, telling the crowd in the Indianapolis ghetto that Martin Luther King had just been assassinated.

PART ONE: SOMETHING'S HAPPENING HERE

This is a book on why America is so distressed, angry and divided and why our politics are so badly broken. I took the title *Difficult Times* from a phrase in Robert Kennedy's great speech telling the black crowd in Indianapolis that Martin Luther King had just been murdered.

America is, in Robert Kennedy's phrase, living in difficult times. We are not, have long not been, a happy people. Americans are angry, insecure, decreasingly tolerant, increasingly dogmatic and torn asunder. The nation has real issues we must solve: an environmental crisis which threatens healthy human life, our drift into a divided class society, health care costs threatening to bankrupt the country, massive deficits, educational inadequacies, immigration, crumbling infrastructure. Experts say these problems are fixable, if we have the political will. Which, so far, we have not. Instead, our national government is gridlocked. Unless, that is, the newly minted Trump Administration and Republican Congress eventually are able to do as they wish and make our problems much the worse.

America has always been a nation of doers, undaunted by problems, determined to fix what's broken. Through the travails of history, most Americans had an underlying optimism that this great nation could, would, do the necessary. Not now. Why? Why can we not get to solving our major problems? Why are our politics so dysfunctional? Why are Americans so out of sorts? We need to know: you can't fix what you don't understand. But, we have not understood what ails democracy in modern America.

To quote one of the anthems of the Sixties:

> "There's something happening here.
> What it is ain't exactly clear....
> There's battle lines being drawn
> Nobody's right if everybody's wrong....
> A thousand people in the street
> Singing songs and carrying signs
> Mostly say, hooray for our side
> It's time we stop, hey, what's that sound
> Everybody look what's going down...
> Paranoia strikes deep
> Into your life it will creep
> It starts when you're always afraid
> You step out of line, the man come and take you away."[1]

We must take a fresh look at how and why we have gotten here. We must, now, seek the underlying causes of our national malaise. Which is what this book tries to do, to understand the forces angering, dividing and paralyzing us. Albert Einstein said, "We can't solve problems by using the same kind of thinking we used when we created them." To solve our problems, we must look for causes not just on, but beneath and above, the surface.

Most of us fume at the venom and futility of our politics. We get angry at terrible words and deeds while big problems continue to fester neglected. Our rancor and dysfunction have profound causes beyond cynical political manipulation to gain advantage, though as always in history, that is abundantly present.

The book is motivated by hope and compassion. The hope is that understanding can help us find our way. The compassion is to grasp why we are so distressed, to discern how aspects of the modern world so deeply malaise Americans on all parts of the political spectrum. We

---

[1] Stephen Stills "For What It's Worth" ©1966

can't get at what's wrong if we don't, in that old phrase, "feel their pain".

It's often been said, "The only way to cure an illness is to diagnose it."[2] This book offers a fresh look at the causes of America's disorder. America's problems are severe and their causes deep and interconnected. While some of those causes have been the subject of civic discourse, many have not reached the public eye; and, so far as I know, they have not been put together. Part One looks at the symptoms of the dysfunctions of our democracy and the anguish of Americans which are diseasing our nation. Part Two, the heart of the book, uncovers the causes. Part Three speaks about ideas, policy directions and politics which would make things better.

Briefly said, what ails modern America are the interlocking effects of the ideas, economy, culture and politics of the modern world. Some of these are on the surface and evident: others need to be teased out to become visible. There are three sets of causes, each powerful, and all the more so as, like some chemicals in a test tube, they are more explosive in combination.

The first set of causes are the dominant ideas of the modern world-view. These are secular materialism and the extreme contemporary form of individualism. Together with their handmaiden, free market ideology, they have wounded the psyches and, if one may boldly use the word, the souls of many Americans. Secular materialism is at odds with faith, spirituality and religion. Contemporary individualism makes it easy to avoid personal responsibility and self-reliance. These ideas have alienated and angered many traditional and religious Americans and have left holes in the hearts of many who are not. They have led to divisive changes in the old national moral code.

These have been abetted in the past several decades by the triumph of the worship of the free market. America and the rest of the West have been capitalist societies for centuries. What is new is that our dominant

---

[2] Recently said by Barack Obama.

economic ideology has removed the restraints on unbridled avarice that have served for all that time to regulate and deplore unrestrained. The result is that now we worship and encourage unbridled rapacity.

The second set of causes come from the forces of modern mass society and culture. For a majority of Americans, even before the Great Crash, the American economy was not working well. Growing disparities in levels of income and wealth have created a class society in which the American dream has receded for the un-well-off. We feel at sea in the gales of mass culture and in the rapid change and pace of the present. We are diminished by lost community. It's hard to be the active citizens the Founders considered the bedrock of their created republic when public affairs are dominated by mass media and money, and the connections of local and national community have badly frayed.

The third set of causes is what has happened to American politics. We are discomfited because our democracy is working poorly: our politics polarized and angry, our government not working well; the Republicans captured by the hard Right as liberalism has alienated a large part of the country, including much of its old constituency. The nation's major problems are solvable with political will and skill, but our political system seems incapable to address them. Our politics and government have become dangerously dysfunctional. The forces which have bedeviled us as people and citizens have corroded the quality and democratic nature of our government.

This work is no jeremiad. America has vast assets and immense strengths with which to remedy its ailments. If Americans can better understand each other, we can communicate better, return dialogue, tolerance, empathy and insight to the national discourse, find goodwill and re-open our minds and hearts. Americans then will be able to, as we've often done, "move forward", as Robert Kennedy liked to say and "do well in this country". There is no need to stay mired in our collective disquiet, no need outside ourselves to let our problems control our destiny. No need to let our great nation decline into weakness.

CHAPTER ONE: A TIME OUT OF JOINT

"Let us then, fellow citizens, unite with one heart and one mind. Let us restore to social intercourse that harmony and affection without which liberty and even life itself are but dreary things... Every difference of opinion is not a difference of principle." Thomas Jefferson, "First Inaugural Address", March 4, 1801.

America is, as Hamlet said, in a time out of joint. Patriots all, we Americans are angry about our country.[3] We disagree, vehemently, about what's wrong, what's been lost and who and what actions and policies are responsible. The disagreements are political because social emotions in a democracy are expressed in the public square.

American politics and government have become dangerously dysfunctional. The forces bedeviling Americans have corroded the quality and democratic nature of our government. We have dangerously drifted far from Lincoln's ideal — our ideal — of "government of the people, by the people and for the people". We have serious problems but seem paralyzed at getting at them.

The American Congress is hopelessly deadlocked: ugly partisan rhetoric has pushed out dialogue. One party refuses to compromise. More than before, members seem to value re-election and getting "pork" to their voters (and, often, enrichment to themselves) much more than public service. Congress has plenty of vitriol and stasis but little cooperation and accomplishment.

The executive side of the national government is serving the nation poorly. Most government agencies are big bureaucratic organizations, impersonal, inefficient and inflexible in accomplishing their missions and serving the public. When Theodore Roosevelt took office in 1901, the Presidency was a weak office. TR and other strong Presidents since

---

[3] We're like what Leonard Cohen said, "I love the country but I can't stand the scene." "Democracy" © 1992

built up a robust executive to get things done. While Presidents can do little to solve major problems when Congress will not act, they have developed vast unchecked powers (think of the Administration of the younger Bush) out of control of Congress, let alone of the "the people".

American public discourse has become as rancid as a garbage dump in a heat wave. The nation is angrily divided. The conservatives despise the liberals, who return the compliment. Each side blames the other for the mess. The traditionalists in the "culture wars" are furious at the loss of standards and what they decry as permissiveness about the likes of abortion ("baby killing"), divorce, homosexuality, pornography and open sex. The secularists are furious at the traditionalists' attacks on social freedoms. On issue after issue, each side treats the other as if they are, because of their beliefs, the scum of the earth.[4] Though it may have seemed impossible for the level of discourse to have fallen from what it was a few years ago, Donald Trump has demonstrated that we didn't, that short time ago, realize how low low can be.

Pubic discourse is driven by irrationality and the basest emotions. Compromise has become, for many, a dirty word; and the ability to craft one is a dying art. So is the ability to accept as legitimate compromise when made. Instead of dialogue, we hear angry, hating shouting. Consider the reaction of the late Reverend Jerry Falwell, a prominent leader of the Christian Right, to Nine Eleven:

> "I really believe that the pagans, and the abortionists, and the feminists, and the gays and the lesbians who are actively trying to make that an alternative lifestyle, the ACLU, People For the American Way — all of them who have tried to secularize America — I point the finger in their face and say 'you helped this happen.' "[5]

---

[4] Republicans are particularly fond of abusing fellow Republicans who cross the party line, as over immigration reform.

[5] Telecast on September 13, 2001.

Such rhetoric is now common, especially from the Right, and now, from President Trump.

The atmosphere is nurtured by television, an expensive medium best at appealing to emotions. The power of television has enabled politics to be driven by the sound bite instead of discourse, by negative attack ads and by the ability to raise immense sums of money. Ordinary citizens can almost never get the attention of the media to be heard.

The Founding Fathers believed that active citizenship of the American people was the necessary condition for the success of their great experiment to create a national republic. But, the sense of a citizen's duty has much waned. So has the sense of a common weal, with shared responsibility to each other as fellow citizens. We are much less willing than our forebears to sacrifice for the common good, to give up a benefit or pay a tax because that is what the country needs.

The sense of national community of earlier times seems gone. The nation is increasingly divided economically, as the well-off get richer and everyone else is left behind. Americans say they care deeply about the future, but have so far displayed virtually no willingness to "walk the talk" by agreeing to policies which would avoid a crisis tomorrow at some cost today.

America has naturally been a moderately conservative country. But, the brand of conservatism which has dominated for forty years is different. Though it much supports the rich, it has little else in common with the politically sluggish Gilded Age or the Roaring Twenties. Nor does it have much in common with the quiescent moderate conservatism of Eisenhower and the Fifties. It is angry, aggressive and determined to change America, big time. It is the main source of the fury, polarization, deadlock and dysfunction bedeviling our land.

Why is this so? The fact is that America has always heretofore made strong progressive reforms when the times demanded, as they do now. The distribution of income and wealth, which thanks to the New Deal had much narrowed from the Depression until about 1970, has widened to extreme levels not seen since the Twenties, to become the most extreme among major nations. The Republicans are ever promoting tax cuts and other policies which benefit the rich, the most notorious being George W. Bush's immense tax cuts for the very wealthy. Mitt Romney's plan (remember him?) and the Paul Ryan budget would be even more pro-super-wealthy than what W did. Donald Trump's proposed tax cuts for the wealthy are radically worse than even those of the younger Bush.

W's Administration drove the American car off the cliff and was, by the time he left office widely reviled. And, yet, within a short time of the election of Barack Obama, the angry, polarizing Right had re-taken control of the political agenda and won an enormous triumph in November 2010. Despite the Democrats' victory in 2012, the far Right GOP kept control of the House. Now, after the elections of 2014 and 2016, the hard Right controls the House, the Senate and the White House (and the Supreme Court).

The sum of it all is the present unhappy state of American democracy. America is politically paralyzed, immobile to solve pressing, solvable problems. Though a democracy in name, it has drifted dangerously far from being "of, by and for" the people.

Alexis de Tocqueville wrote *Democracy in America* about the nation he observed in the 1830s. As we shall see, he was full of acute insights into what makes democracy work and what could turn it to despotism. Reading Tocqueville in light of the present state of the American polity is frightening.

Americans of all persuasions are patriotic. They believe with John Winthrop, governor of the early Puritans, that "we must consider that we shall be as a City upon a hill. The eyes of all people are upon us."[6] They believe that their nation is a special place, blessed by nature with great bounty and endowed by history, divinely chosen or otherwise fated to serve its people and the world as the well-spring of liberty and

---

[6] From the sermon "A Model of Christian Charity", 1630.

human dignity. A nation unique in history in the promise it gives its people, a beacon of freedom and justice to guide the world to a shiny future.

And, yet, here we are, the American democracy having become dysfunctional. Why has this happened? How have Americans become so politically divided and incapacitated? The next step in understanding is to look at the distress of the American people.

CHAPTER TWO: AMERICANS: LIKE A ROLLING STONE

"How does it feel, how does it feel
To be without a home
Like a complete unknown
Like a rolling stone?"
Bob Dylan, "Like A Rolling Stone" © 1965

The American people have gotten in a bad way. We haven't been this divided since the Civil War. People feel lost and betrayed, bewildered by what's happening to their beloved country, enraged and pained it has lost its way. They feel precious little of that happiness, whose pursuit is celebrated in the Declaration of Independence.

The ideas which dominate the modern world have, in different ways for different people, put us badly out of sorts. For more than forty-five years, the vaunted economy has not delivered to most Americans on its ancient, central promise. We feel at sea in the contemporary gales of mass culture, rapid change and lost community. We despise our rancidly unproductive politics and inability to address serious problems. Enough of us are so distressed that we've elected as President an unqualified, uninformed, unthinking demagogue with a most un-Presidential temperament.

We wonder: What is going on in our beloved country? Where did we lose our ballast? Why are we so angry, disaffected and sour? Where are we heading? We generally blame the other guys.

Conservatives think the problem is that liberals' moral relativism, horrible policies and big government have ruined the country. Liberals have the opposite opinion: it's the hard Right and its venom, dogma, intolerance and callousness, with Congressional Republicans blocking needed reforms. They wonder if a brainwashing virus explains why all those un-wealthy voters vote Republican much against their interest. People in the middle are upset too: can't we be reasonable and address our problems? Like the movie character from the Eighties, everyone seems "mad as hell and not going to take it any more."[7]

It's emotionally satisfying to blame the other guy. If only the conservatives, the liberals, the extremes on each side would stop being so obstinate, contrary, intolerant, bigoted, self-seeking and obtuse. If only they'd put national needs ahead of partisanship. If only they weren't so rotten. If only they were more like me. Ah, then, the country would get back on track.

The blame game is like losing one's temper: emotionally satisfying for a moment and useless in solving problems. In fact, there are ample reasons why progressives believe as they do, why millions of Americans have turned to conservative politics and evangelical religion. The reasons for the common disquiet, disaffection and distress include but are much deeper than politics.

It will help to understand the state of the nation to look through the eyes of four types of people whose experiences and feelings are characteristic of many other Americans: Mrs. Evangelical, Mr. Reagan Democrat, Ms. Working Mom and Mr. Meritocrat. Getting into their shoes to see what makes them tick is a good way to begin to grasp the forces and circumstances abroad in modern America.

Mrs. Evangelical

Mrs. Evangelical is a mother in her early forties with three children, ten, eight and six. She works as a doctor's aide, and her husband sells insurance. They live in a new suburb far from the city they rarely visit. Their life is centered on the evangelical church where they met and the children's school, the local Christian academy.

Her parents had been traditional Methodists, and centered their small town life on Jesus and Christian ethics. Her parents joined the Moral Majority in the early seventies, disgusted at the "sex, drugs and rock-n-roll" of those days. Still, her parents didn't vote all that often until

---

[7] From *Network*, written by Paddy Chayevsky and directed by Sidney Lumet.

Ronald Reagan's Presidency. Then, energized by Reagan and their preacher, they started to take politics seriously.

Mr. and Mrs. E are active in local Republican politics, canvassing and getting out the vote for conservative candidates. Mrs. E likes to say, "We've got to throw those darn liberals out and get this country back where it used to be. We need to take back our freedoms from Government and stop coddling criminals and deviants."

Mrs. E was shaken by the experience of her favorite aunt. Her aunt became convinced in college that there is no God. She remembers her parents and aunt having fierce arguments, which did nothing to change her aunt's mind that the world is made by science's laws, that the idea of a God or a soul or an afterlife is poppycock and all those Bible stories just so much fiction.

Her aunt said she was happy being liberated, but Mrs. E thought otherwise. She seemed angry and cynical and, Mrs. E felt an emptiness at her aunt's core. The reason was clear: she had abandoned God. It scared Mrs. E: she didn't want that for herself. So, when she encountered atheism at college and heard people debunk spirituality, she realized that she wanted, needed, a very active faith. If the professors' favorite word "reason" was supposed to substitute for God, well, it was not for her. The kind of faith she wanted was available back home in the new evangelical megachurch. It was just what she sought: more emotional, more fundamentalist, more fervent even than the church of her childhood.

Soon after joining the Church, she had a profound experience. She felt Jesus had come to her, touched her and blessed her. She felt imbued with Divine Grace. She wasn't going to talk about it, until others spoke in Church of their own meetings with Jesus or Mary.

The pastor is of the new breed of politically active preachers, sermonizing against the evils abroad in the land. Sex is a flash point, as it is for Mrs. E: he rails at promiscuous sex, homosexuality, abortion and divorce. Another flash point is the loss of personal responsibility, especially among the pampered poor living off the largesse paid for by the taxes of good, hard-working Americans.[8]

Mrs. E says "I'm no racist, but these black slum-dwellers don't have the gumption to take care of themselves. They just want us to fix their problems. Bill (her husband) and I are tired of paying taxes to support them and their drug habits when if they'd only take responsibility for their lives, they'd be fine." She's angry at the liberals: "I don't cuss, so I should stop using that word." She often erupts in anger when a liberal politician speaks on television.

It upset her when her aunt asked if she didn't feel "Christian compassion" for people living in the slums. Her answer was "God helps those who help themselves." She got angry that when she railed against Government, her aunt pointed out that federal subsidies to the mining business in town enabled it to employ lots of people. "That's different," she insisted. "That's to help the economy. This good community has a right to that sort of thing."

Her preacher pushed Mr. and Mrs. E into active politics. They eagerly became active in a very conservative Christian family group and through that in the local Republican Party where they support the most conservative candidates. They're angry about America: about the destruction of the old morality by liberals and the Establishment; about Big Government's swallowing their freedoms as it swallows all those taxes it exacts; about liberals' lack of patriotism, indulging criminals and fags (as they call them) as they ooze contempt for solid Americans.

She's afraid for the future. Afraid of Muslim terrorists, afraid that China will take over the world, afraid that the devil is taking over America, just as her preacher said, afraid that the great freedoms enshrined in the Constitution are being destroyed, that people outside her church don't much tell the truth any more. She feels she's living in an age of Satan. She sees that America has no will to solve its

---

[8] This, though the welfare system was largely dismantled in the Nineties.

immense problems — none bigger than the enormous deficit. She worries what kind of world they will leave their children. Every day her resolve that something has to be done to take this great country back from the Godless liberals becomes stronger.

Some of her worries are economic. She and Bill struggle to make ends meet. They have enough — for now. But, Bill's business selling insurance took a big dip in the Great Recession and he has lost clients as small businesses close or are bought by large companies. Quite a few of her fellow congregants have been laid off and others forced to move far away just to keep a pay check coming in. She worries deeply about whether they'll have enough when she and Bill are older and, more, about the future of her children. They love the Christian academy, but few of its graduates get into the better colleges, and they're anxious about whether their kids will get good jobs. They certainly aren't being prepared to work for the likes of Google or Apple. What's happened to the American Dream that hard work would bring success and children do better than their parents?

Though many Americans are getting rich, her family, friends and neighbors are not. Until the Great Crash, her adult years were mostly boom times, but precious little of the wealth found its way into her community. The only thing Democrats say that makes any sense is that too much goes to the rich and the rich pay too few taxes. But, really, she knows, the problem is big government and high taxes. And, all those companies trying to rip everyone off.

She is content in her faith and much comforted. But. She's lost her hope that the future will be better. She finds herself resigned that the country, her children's world, will ever again be what they should. And, she is sad to be cynical about leaders — except the people you can trust on the Christian Right. She has contempt for "those darned Ivy League elitists hating the likes of us and ruining this country."

She is nostalgic for the Fifties her parents loved, watching Fifties TV reruns from before she was born and listening to Sinatra and Perry Como croon. She feels sad missing what her parents described as the shared sense of national identity back then: sure, there were political differences, but the country seemed one. What a great loss: another fault of those darned, contrary liberals.

And, then, there was the scandal of the preacher at a nearby evangelical church. My, what a powerful preacher! Full of the fire and brimstone sexual sinners deserved. But, then he was caught consorting with prostitutes. Are we humans just a depraved sort? Is life on Earth condemned to all this badness? Do we really have to wait for heaven or the Second Coming for people to be good?

She believes her marriage is strong, but it's lost its excitement. To her shock, she was tempted when a man from church suggested an affair, saying his wife was through with sex. Mrs. E said "no" at once, but then had a sleepless night of soul-searching about whether she should say "yes". She loves Bill, of course. But, had she done right? She knows of acquaintances — in her church — who are "doing things" and still being with God, staying married. After all, people are doomed to be sinners. Maybe next time she's tempted — oh, my, what if she never were? — she'd give in. She hopes not, she thinks, feeling conflicted, uncertain and bad.

She feels graced by Jesus and God, but still unsettled. She feels diminished by the loss of so much that was familiar and comfortable and doesn't have the time and energy to keep up with everything new. Her church and town are as stable as any place she knows, but so many people keep moving away. Still, she realizes how blessed she is to have the roots they've put down, especially in the church. Several of her girlhood and school friends live in suburbs and belong to churches that don't feel to them like a real community.

And, yet, she often feels she's adrift. She hopes she's living a good life but isn't sure. Is she doing what her fellow congregants expect of her? Why does she feel as if she has so little ability to affect her life, to pave the way for her children? Why does she feel disappointed, even though she has God's and Jesus' blessings and her family and church?

Why does she still, on some long, dark nights when she can't sleep, feel as if somehow she doesn't belong?

She deplores Donald Trump's personal life, his abuse of women and lack of Christian virtue. Though all that was greatly exaggerated by the liberal media. Still, she voted for him with enthusiasm. She despises Democrats and none more than Hillary Clinton. "This country needs a big change and he's seems the man to do it."

Mr. Reagan Democrat

Mr. Reagan Democrat is a retired factory worker living in the Midwestern city where he and his long-ago bride grew up. Their three children are married and have given them eight grandchildren: their pride and joy. His oldest child works in the same factory as Dad, but, as his other children had to move far away to get decent jobs, Mr. and Mrs. RD don't get to see them much.

Their parents had revered FDR and were staunch Democrats, the party of the people, bringer of prosperity to the working man. Mr. RD first voted in 1972, for Nixon. "Sure, we were Democrats. They'd done a lot for the working man but they weren't interested in us any more. They'd become the party of flag-burners and long-haired druggy punks, coddling criminals and disrespecting this great country." Since, he has usually voted Republican, except when the GOP seems to have really screwed up (eight years of W drove him to vote for Obama the first time) or run a candidate he can't stomach.

Just like their parents, his wife attends mass every Sunday and as many days as she can with her job as a hairdresser. He attends most Sundays more to please her and feel a part of the community than to worship. And, to show he's not one of the Godless who deny Jesus and Mary: well, Jews are OK if they believe in God. The world's in a bad mess, but without God, no one would act right. Godlessness was behind the rampant sex and promiscuity, behind people's thinking it's OK to kill a little unborn baby if it suited them, behind all the lying by politicians and corporate officers.

Mr. RD likes to say "I'm a soldier in what those left-wing announcers call the culture wars. Those people in the Establishment, those liberals, those damned smarty-pants elitists say we're angry bigots. Well, I'm no bigot, but I'm mad at a country that encourages queers to marry and promiscuous sluts to have abortions and puts out shows and movies and ads that are nothing but pornography. They've not only let it happen: they've encouraged it. Why, my parents would've beaten me within an inch of my life if they'd caught me watching stuff that's on TV every night. I'm mad that stuff excites me. I'm mad we let everyone do whatever he wants, that we pay attention to all these people and all these groups just shouting 'give me, give me, give me' like I owe them a living. I hate this affirmative action, taking jobs from my kids to give them to some Negro just because. When I think about how we've lost all sense of right and wrong, I feel I'm in a rowboat in a hurricane."

When Ronald Reagan ran for President, Mr. RD thought he had voted for his last Democrat. He loved Reagan's sunny optimism: "by God, he made me feel like it really was morning in America." He had had it with liberals. The old Democrats, of FDR and his parents' youth, they stood for the working man, for unions and the American Dream. And, they had delivered. His parents had been able to leave a slum and buy a nice little home in the suburbs: their lives became a lot better from youth to age. Not his: he and his wife haven't been able to do better than his parents and in danger of ending worse.

He and his wife have always lived in what was a good, solid neighborhood. But, it's changed and not for the better: run-down, with crime and drugs on the street. Most of the old folks — including most of his friends — have died or moved and the new people aren't always ones you want to know. Even so, the money had gotten so poor that they'd almost had to sell their house and move to a lesser neighborhood. Two of his kids live worse than he does, though both husband and wife work.

All these new Democrats seem to care about is poor blacks and themselves. They certainly haven't done anything for the working man like FDR and Truman had, like Kennedy and Johnson. Instead, they look down on people like him as flag-waving, black-hating, God-fearing boobs who haven't the intelligence and sense to get with their Godless, pro-black, anti-white program. They want to give to the poor, but what about the American worker, struggling now as not in years and pretty much ignored by the Democrats. Well, the hell with them. They've forgotten this is a great country and that a man ought to be a patriot. They don't seem to think that the national defense matters. He still thinks government can help people but it's gotten too damn big and too inefficient; and it's too expensive paying for all those damned bureaucrats.

Yet, he votes for Democrats every so often. Largely because he doesn't trust the Republicans not to help the rich at the peoples' expense. His father said their generation had done well because the gap between the rich and people like them had gotten smaller. Now, it sure feels like it's gone a long way in the opposite direction.

When he's voted for Democrats, it's been because he feared for the economic future awaiting his children. One of them lost his job not long before and none of them feels any job security. He worries even more about his grandchildren. He did some Internet research and learned that their schools tested out to be pretty damn mediocre. How were those sweet, little kids going to do well? They weren't being prepared to go to good colleges or to make it in the world of technology. Two of them are real smart, but he doesn't see how they'll be able to make it big like a couple of his high school friends did. What's happened to that promise that any one with the smarts and gumption who worked his you-know-what off could make it to the top? That didn't seem possible for his grandchildren.

And then, when he has voted for a Democrat, usually the guy acted just like those other Democrats once he got in office, trying to raise his taxes when he was having a hard enough time already. Then, Mr. RD was sorry he'd been fooled again. He's afraid for his family and his country. Why can't there be candidates who would actually try to solve problems instead of posturing and feathering their nests and acting as if their staying in office was what mattered most?

He's a strong man, but he's been afraid of the future most of his life. Well, we outlasted the Commies, thanks to good old Dutch Reagan (and Nixon too). Now, he's afraid of terrorists, Arabs and the Chinese. He's afraid of all the change in the world, more it seems every month. He's afraid of what kind of immoral country we're leaving his grandchildren, for the loss of our freedoms by a bloated Government, Presidents who act as if they're above the law, a Congress that's worse. That's one reason he mostly votes Republican, because they understand his fears and seem to want to do something about them. When his economic fears jump to the top of the pile, he usually votes for the other guys.

This time the candidate talking to his economic fears was no Democrat, and so he voted for Trump. Trump seems determined to make the economy better for people like him and his family. Mr. RD told his friends, "Sure, he's a risky candidate, but we're so screwed up that we need to take the risk. This guy gets things done. Maybe he can fix this mess."

God, how he worries about his kids and grandkids. They live in soulless suburbs moving around for a new house or new job, without much of the life he'd had as a kid — and they'd had as kids — centered on the church and local town center. They seem rootless and the effect on the children does not seem good.

He sometimes thinks he should get active in politics but never does. "What's the use? It's all money and TV and I'm just a little guy who can't talk back to the box. It's my duty so I vote. There's no point in anything more."

He'd been a hopeful man in his twenties, but no longer. Maybe, he thinks, that's just what happens to people as they get old. He used to look up to leaders in government and business: now, they all seem to him a bunch of hypocrites and crooks. "Well, that's just the way it is, I guess. It was a great country; it still ought to be, but, but, but." More and more he loved the music and movies of the Forties and Fifties, soaking in how those days must have felt.

He used to do what his gut told him. He used to feel grounded but now feels unsure of himself and of how to cope with a world so changed from the one he grew up in. These days, he finds that he usually does what he thinks he's expected to do. Not what God and morality tell him is right (though he is a moral man): that would come from his insides; but more what his boss, his neighbors, other people think is right. How did that happen? He used to feel that he could take charge; now, he feels that when he tries to make things better, he doesn't make a difference. How could he make a dent in anything when all those massive companies and government agencies control everything? This isn't his world any more.

Ms. Working Mom

Like Mrs. Evangelical, Ms. Working Mom is forty or so and lives in a middle class suburb with her children, eleven and nine. Their lives are otherwise very different. She's a single mom, divorced from their father when the younger child was two. She works in the city, a long commute away, as a junior member of large company's finance department. She struggles to juggle her children and work and has little time for anything else — including meeting men.

She is devoted to her children and makes every weekend game and school event. It hurts her deeply that she rarely can get to school events on weekday afternoons. Finding and keeping good child care is difficult and she worries what's happening to her children without mother at home and with mediocre day care.

She worries greatly about money. Her ex-husband is a good father and pays adequate child support. But, the money seems to go less far than when they first divorced and his middle manager job in a big company is insecure. Two of his work friends were let go in the Great Recession and he worries the other shoe will drop on him. She feels none too secure in her job. Though she has received good reviews and has survived three downsizings, the company has disappointed Wall Street for the past several quarters. She believes another riff is coming and fears it could sweep her job away.

She worries especially about her children. How much has the divorce hurt them? She can't be there for them like her mom had been for her. She paid more for their home than she wanted to get the best schools possible, but she knows they aren't all that great. Will her kids be able to go to a good college? Are they being well-prepared for their futures? She so much wants them to do better than their parents, but how, when they are getting an indifferent education?

She sees what goes on in the office. The best and the brightest get paid very well, and everyone else trails far behind, farther behind now than when she started working. Most of the top ones came from upper middle class families and went to the best schools. How will her kids get onto the fast track coming from an OK town with so-so schools and no connections and no college degree that says "you're one of the best"? Aren't they doomed to be in the bottom two-thirds of a society of "have-a-lot's" and "don't have much's"?

She belongs to a church, to give the children a religious education. She rarely goes herself. She'd like to — she gets comfort from the old familiar prayers and the sense of God, but she's too busy with chores on Sunday morning when the kids are in Sunday school.

She feels confused about religion. She learned in her college science courses that the laws of science explain the universe. Still, she believes in God and Jesus: without fervor, but belief. When she was younger, she tried to think through how God squared with Science and the world of reason she studied in college. Though she decided it's all too deep for her, every so often she feels a nagging doubt that God can fit in that world; and, if not, what does that mean?

She's also confused about the place of religion. Though she doesn't like the feeling that everything is secular which she gets a lot from the media, she's very distressed about the intolerance of religious conservatives. She doesn't like all the proselytizing and self-righteousness and all the telling her and everyone else how to live.

She usually votes. The idea that she would participate in politics is a joke: "I don't have the time for everything I have to do just to stay afloat. And, if I had the time, what's the point? The people with money and power, the people at the networks, they call the tune."

She thinks of herself as an independent ("Those parties are just collections of self-centered politicians"), but usually votes Democratic. The intolerance and dogmatism of the Christian right is one reason. "If I want to have an abortion or my friend at work wants to marry his gay lover, that's none of their business. And, I can't stand the Republicans' 'shoot-em-up' foreign policy." She believes in racial tolerance and worries that the nation has so much bigotry against minorities, especially blacks: that's one reason she was so pleased at the election of Barack Obama.

Though it almost always gets her vote, Ms. WM is queasy about the Democratic Party. Her experience with trying to help her father with his Social Security showed her how impersonal, ineffective and anti-people government agencies can be. She knows we need to have well-run government, but we don't, and the Democrats won't even look at the problem. She sympathizes with poor people and worries about how kids in the inner city ghettoes can ever escape that horrible way of life. But, she's also unhappy that the Democrats seem to care only for the poor and have stopped caring all that much for people like her. She's very worried that the country can't seem to do something about its big problems.

She would have liked to elect a woman President, but Hillary Clinton stood for everything about Democrats she disliked. Still, she told herself, "what choice do I have" as she proverbially held her nose and voted for Hillary.

She wishes that someone other than the conservatives would speak up about the loss of values. People used to feel personal responsibility, to feel it was important to tell the truth and live by the Golden Rule.

Now, everyone's out for herself and thinks the government or her boss or somebody owes her. She sees too much corner-cutting and dishonesty at work. "I wish some politicians I like would talk about that. That's something I liked about Obama: stuff like telling fathers to be fathers." That doesn't stop her from complaining that she would have graduated college with honors if a professor hadn't given her a "C" because a paper was late.

She is torn about the sexual revolution. She enjoyed the experiences she had before she met her husband, but wonders whether the very high expectations everyone seems to have for the satisfactions of their libidos didn't contribute to the dissatisfactions the two of them felt with each other. She doesn't have time for much of that sort of thing now, but is pleased that if she did, she could do as she wants. However, she is disgusted at all the sex she sees in many of the ads and TV shows and worries what it's doing to her kids.

She wishes she could think about the needs of people other than herself and her kids, but she's just too busy to find room for anyone else. She'd expected to feel emotionally comfortable when she got to her forties, but she does not. She is often ill at ease with other people. She wants them to like her, to accept her and she tries to do what is expected, but thinks she usually falls short.

She feels alone: she doesn't get to see people much outside of work and her kids' activities and hasn't made close friends. She doesn't feel as if she knows who she is or how she ought to be fitting into this strange world so unlike what she'd expected. Her father still talks like a man who feels grounded in his values, his friends, his neighborhood.

She feels just the opposite. She feels like a tiny part in a giant machine and is quite sure that if she weren't there, the machine would adjust and no one, other than her kids and parents, would miss her. Big companies like hers and her ex-husband's, the Social Security Administration, the media companies are what count now: she's too small to matter. When she thinks about how different the world is from just a few years ago, she feels as dizzy as that awful time she got horribly drunk in college.

She doubts things will improve. Her divorce was a hard blow, and she doesn't see how she'll ever recover. She is cynical about leaders. She prays her kids will have a better world but doubts they will. Who's going to make it better? Certainly not the politicians.

Mr. Meritocrat

Mr. Meritocrat is in his late fifties. He's done well as a marketing executive ("though not as well as a lot of people I know.") He and his second wife live in an upscale apartment in the city. He has three grown children: his oldest son married with two children; the middle girl just broken up with her long-term boyfriend and his younger son in a stable gay relationship. They work for professional service firms or large companies: two in New York and one in the city where he's made his career. His children blame him for the bitter divorce from their mother when they were teens. The wounds have not healed and he is less close to them than, some days, he wishes.

Mr. M is a winner in the marketplace of modern America. Though he hasn't become mega-rich, he's earned enough over the years from high salaries and bonuses and two big stock option payoffs to be fixed for life. He knows his job could vanish overnight: even if it does, he'll be financially all right. He believes in the American dream: after all, he's living it, with a nice apartment, a big bank account and the accoutrements of having plenty of money to allow him and his wife plenty of luxuries. He has done what's expected of him since he graduated from that fine college and it has paid off.

He is a passionate believer in the triumphant economy, in the great free market which has unloosed inventors, entrepreneurs and people with the brains and work ethic to create wealth. He expects his children and grandchildren to do at least as well as him, and his sons are on the way. His daughter is drifting, unsure of what she wants to do, making a pittance. "Damn, she's leaving her talents on the table. Where's her get-up-and-go? I've worked hard to get her every advantage: living where there are great public schools, an Ivy education, connections. She's throwing her birthright away."

Mr. M is a strong Democrat. He's willing to pay more taxes for social good and believes in some regulation. He distrusts big government and over-regulation but thinks "it's bred in Democrats' bones" to think otherwise. He is passionate about racial tolerance and deplores prejudice against minorities, especially blacks. He supports affirmative action to help blacks get college spots and jobs though he's concerned some aren't accountable for their lives and think the nation owes them too much. He is contemptuous of everyone on the Right as "a bunch of stupid, thoughtless, mindless bigots". He applauded when Hillary called Trump supporters "deplorables".

He wonders whether the country can ever solve its problems and is furious at the Congressional Republicans' use of obstructive tactics to stop legislation. "Maybe this country will go the way of Rome because we just can't get done what we need to do. We used to have real leaders you could trust to try to make things better: no more." When a politically active colleague urged him to do some political work, he declined: "That's just not me. I make some contributions for ads, but the idea of actually doing that stuff is boring. Anyway, it wouldn't make a damn bit of difference."

He's very unhappy with the country's sharp move to the right. He despises the callousness, fundamentalism and militarism of the conservatives who have dominated politics since he was a kid. "They don't believe in separation of Church and State. They say they're good Christians but have no Christian charity towards people who need help." He is terribly frightened about global warming and the environment. "How can people of God despoil God's creation?"

Despite references to God, Mr. M is a modern secular atheist. He believes that what counts is life in the here and now and that God is not necessary for people to act well. He believes in the sanctity of reason's sound thinking. He's a humanitarian, taking his ethics from books he's read and from the good fellow-feeling he finds within himself. He isn't spiritual; his world is desacralized as, he thinks, it should be. America's public religiousness annoys him: he wishes public prayers and appeals to God would go away.

He's confident he knows what's right and what's wrong. He is quite concerned that standards of integrity have plummeted over his years. Especially in the workplace. When he began work, he saw people who lied and cheated and broke ethical rules, occasionally even the law. But, not nearly so many and nearly as often as he sees now. "Where are we heading? It feels as if more and more people think they can do whatever they want, and don't allow much to get in the way of their God-given right to get ahead."

Mr. M says he thrives on change. Yet, even he sometimes feels overwhelmed trying to keep up with everything new. It still galls him that, in the mid-Nineties, he lost a good job because he missed the impact of the Internet. He thinks he could have survived the mistake if he'd been more skilled at company politics. But, he's never really mastered how you navigate those bureaucratic monstrosities.

He loves the sexual freedom that began before he was a teen; and he's had, as he puts it, "plenty of great fun over the years". But, when his ex-wife had an affair while they were married and his kids started being sexually active as young teens, he was dismayed.

When recently pressed by a friend, he admitted the city isn't a community, just a collection of people in the same place. Though he said that's fine with him, he's not sure.

Though Mr. M tells everyone how contented he is with his life, at heart, he is not. The one obvious blemish is the distance from his children. And, every so often, he has feelings of unease. He wishes he felt more connected to more people. He knows he doesn't think enough about other people, except his wife, sometimes his kids and a few close friends. He feels anxious, without reason. His wife says, "Dear, that's existential anxiety. Most people I know feel that way."

When these dark moods descend, he feels like a stranger, vaguely disappointed in his life but he can't for the life of him understand why. He used to feel optimistic about the future, but not any more, especially not after the election of Donald Trump "Well, that's just how it is. In a lot of ways, things were better in the Sixties. Man, I sure wish the music were as good now. But, life goes on." Fortunately, his dark moods don't come all that often and don't last too long: a good dose of the Beatles usually cures the disease.

****

We said at the outset that modern America is ailing from the interlocking effects of the ideas, economy, culture and politics of the modern world. Each of these ideas and social forces is making a profound impact on the lives, thoughts and emotions of our four typical Americans. Though they react in different ways to secular materialism and extreme individualism and to the culture wars' clash between the old and new moralities (especially about sex), these ideas discombobulate them all. Each feels unsettled, alienated, disempowered, etc. — reactions, we shall see, both to the emptiness of secular materialism and to mass culture. Each struggles with the degree and pace of change.

Each of them is less grounded, less at home in the world, than she wants. They are (save Mr. Meritocrat) hurt by the class divide. While they have very different politics, there is much contempt for the other side. Each of them, other than the successful Mr. M, feels that the American Dream — that everyone who works hard will make a better life for himself and his children — has gone away.

None thinks much of the country's future. We now dive deeply to see why.

PART TWO: LIVING IN MODERN TIMES: WHAT'S PUSHING AND PULLING AMERICA

So, what gives? What ails us? What's wrong with the country we love? The heart of the answer is that we're living poorly with the ideas and forces of modernity. They've undermined our psyches, souls, hope and community and fostered anger, distress and paralysis.

Part Two's first section discusses the ideas at the heart of our world view: secular materialism and extreme individualism. It shows how belief in and against these ideas is causing unhappiness all around and examines how they have changed the old moral code and brought on our explosively divisive culture wars.

America in the Fifties was a religious country, secure in its disparate faiths and largely sharing a common set of mores. It still is (somewhat less) religious, but the impact of these ideas has brought big changes. Secular materialism is at odds with faith, spirituality and religion. It alienates and angers many religious Americans and puts holes in the hearts of many secularists. The first group believe, strongly, that the dominant culture demeans and undermines their faith. The second group believe, just as strongly, that these people of strong faith are determined to impose their beliefs and values on them. Contemporary individualism has evolved from Emersonian self-reliance to self-centered self-absorption which avoids personal responsibility: this, too, has divided us and wounded the country.

The second section discusses the role of economic and social forces. As recently as the early Seventies, most Americans felt reasonably secure in their jobs, their culture and their community. Not any more. Well before the Great Crash, the American economy had stopped working well for most Americans. While capitalist dynamism since the Seventies has made many people rich, it has left most Americans behind, breeding deep insecurities about the future. Most of the gains of prosperity have gone to the few at the top, creating a class society divided between the quite well-off and the everyone else for whom the great American Dream has receded.

This has happened as, and to a significant degree because, we've embraced an extreme free market ideology. This is the third enormous idea, with secular materialism and contemporary individualism, that unhealthily dominates our culture. It proclaims that the market is king, to be much more than the economic mechanism apostrophized by Adam Smith and others. Rather, it pronounces that we should instantiate market forces, self-interest and greed everywhere, to leave the market little regulated either by law or by the tenets of ethics. This enshrines economic rapacity.

Americans have struggled as the country has become a mass culture. We are unsettled and frightened by the speed and extent of change. The sense of national and local community have much eroded. It seems our foundations but "lie on the whispering wind".[9]

The last section discusses what's gone wrong with American politics. It's not news that our democracy is working poorly. A healthy democracy is based on dialogue among citizens; but active citizenship is in retreat and dialogue rare. American politics have become angrily polarized and dysfunctional. The Republican Party has been captured by the hardest edges of the conservative movement while American liberalism has self-immolated for nearly fifty years, alienating large groups of potentially sympathetic citizens. The success of conservative politicians in appealing to fear has blown smoke over the sun of intelligent political discourse. Politics has become dominated by big money, a trend which five right-wing Justices of the Supreme Court enshrined as a constitutional right. The nation has major problems. These are solvable with political will and skill, but its political system seems incapable to address them. It is at risk of failing the American people and of drifting into despotism. Perhaps, having elected Donald Trump, it's now scarily on that road.

---

[9] Led Zeppelin, "Stairway to Heaven" © 1971

SECTION ONE: "USING IDEAS AS OUR MAPS"

"Crimson flames tied through my ears rollin' high and mighty traps
Pounced with fire on flaming roads using ideas as my maps
We'll meet on edges soon said I proud 'neath heated brow
Ah, but I was so much older then, I'm younger than that now."
Bob Dylan, "My Back Pages" © 1964

Few people think about ideas. Hard stuff like money and power, not thoughts, that's what makes the world go.

That's wrong. Ideas drive the character of every time and place. Think of America without Christianity and our beliefs in democracy and human rights. The ideas central to one's time and place shape who we are, the state of our psyches and how we feel about what happens in our world.

Every era of human history has had a comprehensive conception of the world. This world-view provides the era with its perspective, makeup and spirit, its sense of how the world works. That perspective, character and spirit mold the thoughts of the age. They are as the air people breathe, though often as unnoticed as oxygen. Our dominant world-view gives our thoughts and beliefs their context — even thoughts and beliefs which dissent from the dominant point of view. You may rebel against some or all of it — many people do — but you can't escape the fact that it shapes the subject and manner of your rebellion.

The ideas of our world-view mold who each of us is. How those ideas mesh with a person's personal circumstances and beliefs has much to do with the well-being of her psyche and her soul. At the heart of our world-view are three big ideas. Each is a profound cause of our present malaise.

The first of the big ideas is "secular materialism", that the world is made up solely of matter and the idea of "spirit" a fiction. There is no purpose to life, other than to embody the laws of physics and evolutionary biology. Religion is a fiction men have invented to hide the fact that their lives have no extra-physical meaning. Secular materialism is the subject of Chapters Three and Four.

The second is the contemporary, extreme form of individualism, that what most matters is what each of us wants. Far different from the individualism at the heart of our Founding, our individualism believes that personal rights and desires trump personal responsibility and the idea of duties to community. As George Harrison's song says, "I, Me, Mine".[10] It is the subject of Chapter Five.

The third big idea is free market ideology and the marketization of society — that the market is, and should be, the arbiter of most everything. That markets ought to be left alone, unregulated, and that the market values of efficiency and making money do, and should, be the hallmarks of public and private action. That everything can be calculated by its dollar worth. It is discussed in Chapter Seven, on economic matters.

These big ideas have wounded our psyches and souls. Secular materialism is at odds with faith, spirituality and religion. Contemporary individualism makes it easy to avoid self-responsibility and communal ties and duties. The marketization of society has replaced the Golden Rule with greed, coarsening our discourse and behavior to a single-minded focus on how to get the most money. The first two ideas have alienated and angered traditional and religious Americans and have left holes in the hearts of many who are not. They have led to divisive changes in the old national moral code, the subject of Chapter Six.

These ideas affect people in different ways. While it oversimplifies to label Americans as "traditionalists" and "secularists" (most of us are

---

[10] George Harrison, "I, Me, Mine" © 1970

bits of both), they are useful labels to understand the effects these ideas have on different Americans.

These cornerstone ideas of modernity have angered and alienated traditional Americans. They rebel against much or all of the modern world-view. They feel their faith demeaned, their values rejected. They feel as if the dominant culture in America is not at all theirs, even as they've dominated our politics. That culture they see does not believe in God; tolerates but has no respect for religion; celebrates sexual promiscuity and self-centeredness; and denies the truth that each person is responsible for himself. It has created a world of Godless immoral materialism which is both terribly wrong and terribly threatening to the physical and moral well-being of their children. It threatens everything they hold holy.

While many of these rebels against materialism are evangelical Christians and political conservatives, these feelings are spread wide across the social and political spectrum.

The cornerstones of modernity have also profoundly wounded many secularists. At its heart, secular materialism is empty, teaching that life is without purpose and meaning. There is little possible meaning if existence is nothing but atoms, molecules and other physical stuff: no spirit, nothing outside of oneself other than other sets of molecules, though we are deeply attached to some of those sets. Deprived by modernity's materialism of meaning and purpose richer than to get the most they can, they lose hope and turn resigned, cynical, and pessimistic. And so, the core of the secularist world-view tears holes in their hearts.

CHAPTER THREE: "NOT MUCH IS REALLY SACRED" IN OUR SECULAR MATERIAL WORLD

"Disillusioned words like bullets bark
As human gods aim for their mark
Make everything from toy guns that spark
To flesh-colored Christs that glow in the dark
It's easy to see without looking too far
That not much is really sacred."
Bob Dylan, "It's Alright Ma, I'm Only Bleeding" © 1965

It may seem odd to begin thinking about America's malaise with secularism. After all, America is — by far — the most religious country in the West. If any nation has escaped the clutches of secularity, surely, one might think, we are it.

Not so. Secularity has a massive influence on American culture.

The Christian medieval world-view was shattered long ago. Though most (it seems) Americans are religious, our culture's dominant ethos long ago moved from spiritual to secular and material. We will see how secular materialism dominates our world, as world-views do, even as fundamentalist rebellion against it seems to have taken charge.

The medieval world-view was omnipresent Christianity. Before we turn to the very different ideas of the modern world-view, let's turn the clock back to the Middle Ages to see from whence we've come.

A. The Spiritual, Christian World of the Middle Ages

The medieval world was saturated with God, Jesus, Mary and Christianity. Medieval life centered on religion: the one true Christian religion of the Church. It was the one and only Church, catholic and universal, not having to share people's spirits with the sects of the as yet unimaginable Reformation. Medieval Europe's few non-Christians (Muslims in Spain, Jews) were sometimes tolerated but only if they kept their heathen beliefs to themselves.

The calendar revolved around the many Christian holy days: today's major holidays plus a myriad of saints' days and the like. Everyone attended mass; everyone prayed; everyone shared a common belief in the divinity of Jesus Christ and in the beliefs of the Church. Laws enshrined the morality of the Church's teachings. Even the masses of the poor gave of their scarcity to the Church, to support the clergy, to sustain the vast and rich dioceses and monasteries and to build beautiful, enormous churches to the glory of God.

People being people, there was much sin and impiety and few understood Church dogma; but they were firmly believing Christians all the same, confessing sins to their local priest to gain Heaven and avoid Hell. Everyone knew they had to show reverence for the Christianity in all they said and did. Those few Christians with heterodox views knew to hold their tongues to avoid prosecution for blasphemy, an offense often punishable by death.

The world was saturated with the supernatural. God's influence was everywhere. One prayed in part because what happened here on Earth was deeply affected, often decided, by what happened up there in Heaven, where God and His angels and saints lived. God decided whether your plans would be fulfilled, whether the harvest would be good, whether the enemy would triumph, whether one had children, whether they recovered from disease, etc., etc.

The belief that the world was controlled by the spiritual did not stop with God and his cohorts. It included not only Satan and his devils but ancient pre-Christian forces and beings, belief in which the Church had failed to exterminate. Many continued to believe the world was full of such supernatural beings as fairies and elves, demons and sprites, good and bad. They sought the influence of good fairies and elves and took steps to keep away the evil ones.

Secular rulers strained at the bit of the Church and challenged papal and ecclesiastical power. Over several centuries, they eventually undermined the Church's secular dominance. Their slow successes were one factor which eroded the medieval sacred world-view.

But, each challenge to the Church put the secular ruler at peril. Popes did not need armies (which they didn't have until late) to enforce their will. The excommunication of a ruler or powerful man could, and did, bring the recalcitrant on his knees begging for forgiveness and reinstatement in the community of God. The great image is from 1077 when the Holy Roman Emperor Henry, ex-communicated for challenging Pope Gregory's power, walked barefoot in a hair shirt across the snowy Alps to Canossa, to be kept waiting for three fasting days at the gate before the Pope would admit him and grant the beggar forgiveness.

So, while Christian Europe was by no means the city of God, it was utterly centered on and dominated by the religion of Catholic Christianity. Its symbols, speech, metaphors and points of reference were soaked in that Christianity. Though there were strong secular rulers, today, we would call such a society a theocracy.

People were rarely individuals, rather parts of society. There were no individual rights. Each was a part of her community, owing duties and succored (when there was succoring) by what others in the community offered her. Likewise, there was no such idea as economic man. People engaged in economic activity, of course, and some made their way by commerce. But, there was no sense that commerce was good in itself. Rather, it was devalued and subject to a host of religious regulations.

For the true believer, to whom his faith is the center of his world, this was the ideal society. A world that did not doubt, that barely permitted doubt, that one's faith was true, that one's God was present in all things. A world in which those who thought otherwise were condemned to the eternity of an afterlife in Hell and who, on this Earth, either kept quiet about their irreligion or suffered the earthly consequences of the denial of the true God. Not the heavenly City of God, but the city devoted to God.

B. The Modern World-View of Secular Materialism

The medieval world-view shattered long ago. It's been centuries since the Western world was suffused with God and spirituality and the dominant ethos was centered on religiosity and the teaching, presence and institution of the (or any) Church. How things have changed to our disenchanted world of secular materialism (and extreme versions of individualism and free market economics).

The world-view of our modernity has become secular and material: hence, "secular materialism".[11] European thought — starting, as such things do, with hard thinkers and percolating into society's world-view — has undergone a revolution. Two causal paths converged: successful attacks upon the dogmatism and abuses of the Church and the development of modern science.

By the late Middle Ages, many Europeans chafed under the Church's dominance. Over time, this growing band of dissenters came to regard the Church as oppressive, overly dogmatic, and entirely too controlling of individual consciences and every aspect of existence. They were fed up with its earthly abuses (sales of indulgences and the like) and had come to believe much Churchly dogma wrong.

The resulting Reformation shattered the unity of Christian Europe. The unraveling of the medieval world-view did not stop with the emergence of Protestant sects. Before long, many took the attack on Catholic privilege the large next step into an attack on religion's dominance of society, even for some to assail religion itself.

Few Enlightenment thinkers were atheists. Many were Deists, believing in God but seeing no need for organized religion. At least for themselves: some thought religion was necessary to provide solace and morals to the common people. These Enlightenment leaders were especially scornful of the Catholic Church and its, to them, dogmatic

---

[11] I use materialism not to mean the pursuit of material goods but rather the idea that there is no spirituality because the only reality is material.

tyranny over society. Their most famous rallying cry was Voltaire's "écrasez l'infâme": "crush the infamous".

That our world is no longer medievally Catholic is the most visible part of the change in world-view. It is not the most important. What has utterly transformed our world is the triumph of materialism, a reflection of Newtonian physics.

All this time, modern science was developing. Scientists and philosophers embraced the use of rational thought to learn how the world works. Two centuries after Copernicus moved the earth far from the center of the Universe, Isaac Newton developed the laws of physics, that physical phenomena could be explained, quite well, quite clearly and quite certainly, by the laws of mechanics.

Dazzled by Science's knowledge and its miraculous-seeming technologies, its belief that the world is caused and determined solely by matter swept modernity's intellectual boards. All of life — thought, feeling, mind and will, apparent manifestations of anything seemingly spiritual, everything one believes, thinks and feels — is wholly explicable in terms of physical phenomena. Everything is reducible to the particles and laws of Science, all of which are available for discovery by the application of human reason. Spirituality is a fiction, at most a manifestation of the workings of the matter of which we are made.[12]

This belief in the material nature of reality is the heart of the modern world-view. It is both the underpinning of modernity's achievements of science and technology and the basis for its de-mystifying and secularizing the world by dismissing the reality and possible truth of the spiritual and of faith.

In the disenchanted post-Newtonian universe ruled by the laws of

---

[12] This materialism was a heresy in the Middle Ages because if the world is wholly explained by material causes, there is no room for a God who created the world and whose presence explains much of reality.

science and mathematics, humans went from the crown of God's creation to bundles of a-spiritual atoms that make up living machines executing the laws of physics, chemistry and natural selection. As everything is wholly explicable in terms of physical phenomena, there is no room for the soul and God, even free will. Just the working of those brain neurons and connecting synapses. God and spirit are fictions as they are said to violate the laws of Science. An irony as Newton was a most spiritual man.

Once we have understood how the brain's neurons work and are connected, we will know why I like the Beatles and you don't, why you prefer not to eat mushrooms which your brother craves, why your neighbor took that opportunity to commit fraud while his partner didn't. We will know why she is a Buddhist and he is a Christian and you think all that religious stuff is poppycock. It's all just a matter of how each of us is wired. No free will, no soul, just the working of those neurons and synapses.[13]

The amazing successes of Science and Technology have spawned the belief, proof if you will, that the world is material. We are blessed with the ability to reason, and Science is the acme of Reason. Reason does, or some day will, unveil the material causes of everything. There are no unsolvable mysteries: only problems we have not yet reasoned, researched and experimented to solve.

Thus, it's no miracle that life exists. Life somehow emerged from a primal soup of chemicals. We don't yet know how, but we will. All life evolved from there by natural selection, so that everything about all living beings, including humans, including the most complex organs (the brain, the eye) and all aspects of human behavior, can be explained by how genes and their variations and mutations advanced the survival of the species. We are who we are because genes are

---

[13] As many (far from all!) scientists proclaim that everything has a material explanation, there is even a recent book by a leading scientist claiming that Science can provide us with laws of ethics.

selfish, driven inexorably to cause behavior which enables their survival at the expense of whatever might be in the way.

That God or any other super-sensual Entity exists or has anything to do with all of this is an impossibility, a hypothesis which violates the laws of physics, mathematics, chemistry and biology, which fully and completely describe the realities of existence.

Life has no purpose other than blindly to execute the laws of nature. Whereas spirituality posits meaning derived from a super-human reality, secular materialism posits that we are alone in a sterile, unfeeling universe. We live, die and are gone: that's that, with no meaning to our lives.

In the ancient world, before the triumph of the Christian, spiritual world-view, Reason co-existed with faith and spirituality. There was the world of Athens, of Greek thought, and the world of Jerusalem, of the spirituality of the Hebrew Bible and early Christianity. Though their explanations of the world conflicted, each thrived. Then, Jerusalem won and we had the Middle Ages. Reasoned thought became subservient to faith. Think of the neoPlatonist philosophers who built a philosophic foundation under the early Church and of Saint Thomas Aquinas' bringing Aristotle into Christianity in his *Summa Theologica*.

Now, Reason has trumped over Spirituality. Athens has triumphed (though ancient Greece was not so thoroughly materialist as are we). Materialism has become the dominant world-view of the modern world. For much of Western culture, certainly in Europe and also for many Americans, spirituality has been driven far underground. Even many religious people worship at both churches, of Reason and Science. They thus manage to keep their religious spirituality sufficiently separate from their everyday secular materialism that they don't have to choose between God and Reason. Faith for Sabbath and Church; Reason for everything else.

CHAPTER FOUR: "I STAND ALONE WITHOUT BELIEFS": SECULAR MATERIALIST LIFE

"And so you see I have come to doubt all that I once held as true
I stand alone without beliefs; the only truth I know is you."
Paul Simon, "Kathy's Song" © 1965

We are not, you and I, wholly free agents. Our minds and hearts are not blank slates. Rather, we're all shaped by our society and so by our times' dominant world-view. This deeply imprints on us what society values and what it doesn't, how it sees reality and what doesn't get from eyeballs to our reason and feelings. Since a world-view's value judgments can be as invisible as air, we aren't always aware of them. But, they are ever-present.

As our world-view, secular materialism profoundly affects all. No world-view commands universal assent, certainly not ours, especially for many spiritual people who reject the modernist ethos. But, rejected or not, the nature of a world-view is that, even in dissent and rebellion, anti-secular materialist people of faith cannot help but (unhappily) breathe the world's secular and materialist air. We each, traditionalist and secularist, in our own ways, accept, adjust to, or reject all or parts of secular materialism. This chapter examines how secular materialism affects us modern Americans.

A. Boons and Burdens of Secular Materialism

Secular materialism has been both a boon and a burden. It has freed us to think, believe and act for ourselves. It has brought us the wonders of Science and Technology, human rights, tolerance. It has also caused us moderns to feel empty, unsettled, ungrounded, often disrespected and angry and just plain out of joint.

1. Boons

Medieval Christianity had bound mind, spirit, society, morals, thought and art in a Gordian knot. These were not autonomous aspects of human life but subsets of the Church's Christianity. Medieval thinking, art and ethics could follow whatever paths people chose so long as those paths were within, or could be incorporated into, the Church's garden.

The cutting of this Gordian knot has been a great boon, liberating society and thought from the bounds of Churchly dogma. We've been freed to have our own beliefs, to use our reason without fear of displeased authority, to employ science to advance knowledge and improve lives, to live under a Bill of Rights. Etc.

Leading thinkers explained that we have basic rights, such as to believe and speak as we please. A corollary is to tolerate different ideas, values and ways of being of others. Though some of this is in the Bible and the ancient Greeks, what's new is the governing notion that man is the measure of all things.[14]

From that has flowed much to prize in social and personal life. We insist that humans have rights to personal freedoms and say we believe in pluralism and tolerance. We've abolished slavery. We believe that people ought to live in a democracy. We have done some work to liberate the oppressed, with much more to be done.

It's difficult to imagine our lives without the advances of Science and the inventions of Technology: harnessing energy, much eased transportation and communication, medical techniques and treatments which have improved health, etc., etc. Though, as the environmental bills have now come due, we no longer unreservedly admire these wonders, it would be folly to want to return to the levels of health and welfare and the nature of work and existence of 1900, let alone 1400.

---

[14] While the Sophists taught that man is the measure of all things, that never was the center of the Greek world-view as it is of ours.

2. Burdens: Skepticism and Emptiness

Skepticism and Intolerance

The modern world-view is skeptical. One of the central teachings of the great Enlightenment philosophers Hume and Kant is that there is no one Truth knowable to humans. This is because when a person thinks, she can never get wholly outside her own mind and perspectives, and these differ from the minds and perspectives of others. As Bob Dylan (no materialist) said in his "Gates of Eden", "There are no truths outside the gates of Eden."[15] Except, that in materialism's desacralized world, there is no Eden.

Skepticism underlies modernity's respectful tolerance. As I can't be sure I'm right, I have no basis to label your belief as surely wrong. Being outside the gates of Eden, if I'm honest and understand the limits of thought, I must acknowledge that there is no certain basis to choose between us, no matter how much I disagree with you. I can't be sure, much as it distresses me, that you may not be right.

Since there is no absolute truth, there are no absolute moral standards. There are as many possible codes of conduct as there are people capable of rational thought. As we will see in Chapter Six, this has been a powerful factor in eroding traditional values. Oh, yes, some beliefs are beyond the pale even if we Humean skeptics cannot satisfactorily refute them through pure reason: the genocidal ideas of the Nazis, for instance. But, most moderns agree that this is one of the rare exceptions to the duty of tolerance.

Toleration is not, however, the same as respect. Being secular, the modern world-view tolerates faith, but does not itself have faith. It tolerates people's spirituality, but it does not respect them.

And so, intolerance lies at the heart of modernity's tolerance. The secularist adherents of modernity are proudly self-assured that they're stewards of a great tradition which has made the world infinitely

---

[15] Bob Dylan, "Gates of Eden" © 1965

better. In their superiority, they disdain the faithful, especially fundamentalists and evangelicals whose faith lacks the veneers of rationalism and civility, unlike more traditional sects which have tried to make peace with modernity. Evangelicals and fundamentalists see and despise this superiority.

Anti-Spiritual Materialism and the Loss of Meaning

We saw in Chapter 3-B that, once the Enlightenment liberated thinking, ethics and social arrangements from the medieval chokehold, what happened (it happened quickly as historical changes go) is that everything became subjected to the new master of scientifically-based philosophic materialism.

Secular materialism is the belief (actually, the faith) that Science and Reason explain everything. As spirituality, religion and faith are non-material, they simply can't be true, merely residues of a prior age which survive because few people can accept that the world is mechanized and purposeless, that there's no meaning beyond the here and now. You have every right to be religious and spiritual. But the plain fact is that you're wrong.[16]

With Reason enthroned, there was no place for the spiritual. All beings were but soulless instruments of the laws of rationality. Now, "sound" thought, from morals to analyses of the behavior of people and societies, had to fit the new mechanistic paradigm. Thinkers who dissented were, well, not really sensible.

Banishing spirituality, this desolate world-view has emptied life of meaning. With no larger purpose, we might just as well not be here. It's no wonder modern secularists feel empty, unsettled and ungrounded and the faithful feel disrespected and angry.

---

[16] If man were consistent, Hume, Kant and skepticism would teach secular materialists to be skeptical of skepticism.

Secular materialism has been abetted by the immensely influential thinking of Darwin, Freud and Marx, though there are now few Freudians or Marxists. They each taught that the world operates by scientific laws (of evolution; drives and unconscious; and economics) and that motivation is a matter not of God-given souls and ethics but of the iron laws of selfish genes, desires and money. Each is thus a crucial reinforcing buttress to the bleak modernist edifice that human life is but material and selfish.

Darwin's immensely influential work has given secular materialism a powerful scientific foundation. Hobbes famously said that in the state of nature, before the formation of societies, life was a war of all against all, being "solitary, poor, nasty, brutish, and short."[17] While the life imagined by the believers in the "selfish gene" is not necessarily short or poor, it is a brutishly predatory incessant war, lonely and bereft of meaning beyond the purposeless survival of species for their own sake. What matters is to get to the top of the heap and get rid of whatever and whoever is weak and in the way. With the triumph of the idea that society is, and ought to be, little more than a series of free markets, "social Darwinism" (which Darwin would likely have decried) rules America.

Marx taught two things now embedded in the materialist air. Dovetailing nicely with the notion that we are creatures of "selfish genes", the first is that people's actions and opinions reflect their selfish, material interests. Period. Anyone who says to the contrary is either cynically prevaricating or deluded. The second Marxian teaching is that we disguise our selfish motivations with contrary words. Ethical precepts, such as the Golden Rule, are not what's real: they're mere contrivances created to disguise the dominance of those in power. What's real is having the power to get what I want.

Freud taught that these conclusions are inherent in the human psyche. What people think and feel rest on a vast reservoir of the unknown

---

[17] Thomas Hobbes, *Leviathan*, chapter 13, "Of The Natural Condition of Mankind as Concerning Their Felicity and Misery".

unconscious. That unconscious is dominated by our "drives," our animalistic wishes and needs (our "libido"). The libido is utterly selfish: the only reason we don't always act like brutes is that we've internalized society's commands in a stern superego which employs fear to suppress libido and keep behavior in check. The Freudian image of humankind is that we're self-centered, value-free machines, capable to reason but barely controlled by rules we've internalized, governed by deep and strong forces even the most devoted student of oneself will only slightly understand.

The Darwinian, Marxian and Freudian images are that man is a machine, driven by forces utterly beyond his control and with no more meaning or purpose than those chemicals in the primal soup. How different from Genesis that human beings are "the crown of creation," created by God in His image. Beings with a purpose beyond themselves, connected to a reality bigger than their lives, beings far richer than mere collections of soulless matter.

Though they often had no such intention, what the materialists did was to tear God, spirit and soul out of the universe. They redefined existence as nothing more than an insensible set of linked parts so that human consciousness is no more than a very complex instance of those physical links. They thus drained life of meaning beyond oneself.

To breathe the air of secular materialism is to be isolated in an indifferent universe: a lonely object of vast, impersonal forces. However much one learns about science and the material world, the materialist can get not one shred of comfort from her world-view for the angst of feeling alone in a de-spiritualized cosmos.

That world has been desacralized of meaning and holiness. It's the empty world painted by Bob Dylan, quoted earlier, that "it's easy to see without looking too far that not much is really sacred."

B. Secular Materialism in America

America long escaped the modernist storm. The harsh winds of secular materialism had buffeted Europe for decades when they swirled into America in the second half of the twentieth century.

America's Enlightenment was not nearly so anti-religious as in Europe. Enlightenment America had no Church against which to rebel. Though seventeenth century Puritan New England had been a theocracy, the other colonies were religiously relaxed, and by the American Revolution, the Puritan vise had loosened in New England. Indeed, by the mid-nineteenth century, the dominant religion in the old Puritan stronghold had become an almost deistic Unitarianism. Because Americans continued to be church-goers, religion provoked little disdain or rebellion from its intellectual leaders.

One consequence of the Enlightenment was a tendency to Utopian thought. The medieval world believed in a Heavenly Utopia, the afterlife with God. When modernity dethroned Heaven, some thinkers moved the possibility of Utopia to earth, that men and women could, with Reason, discern how to make the world perfect. That took the form of political radicalism, most notably Communism (and, in a way, Fascism).

Bolstered by the belief that America is a blessed nation, America escaped the seductions of this kind of Utopia. Also, having no titled aristocracy and free of the class distinctions which bedeviled Europe, it lacked the targets of political radicalism which enraptured millions of Europeans.[18]

So, it is no surprise that America had little of Europe's modernist tumults until the eruptions of the Sixties. Until then, Americans were little inclined to question the old verities or to ponder the conflict

---

[18] America's non-revolutionary Utopian faith that it's a sacred, uniquely blessed nation has driven its oft-messianic foreign policy to use American power to bring peace, prosperity and freedom across the globe, by force if necessary. This policy strongly opposes Communism and Fascism.

between a materialistic universe and personal faith. Then, the dam holding back the corrosive effects of modernity broke. Perhaps it was the stresses of the Cold War. Perhaps it was that having leapt to the vanguard of modern Science, Americans could no longer ignore the a-spiritual materialism at its heart. Perhaps it was the turmoils of the Sixties. Whatever the causes, the emptiness of modernity suddenly hit America very hard. One day life was a comfortable well-stuffed sofa, like the popular sense of the Fifties. The next day, a raging wind had shred the seams and whipped the stuffing away.

The Sixties were a most turbulent time. The fight for civil rights and the ensuing racial turmoil, a long, destructive and unsuccessful war and the youthful rebellion against core values and mores all divided the country sharply and angrily. Millions of one-time progressives in "middle America" turned away from liberal politics, from voting their pocketbooks to voting on the basis of the conservative "social agenda". Threatened by dissent against the Vietnam War, they embraced aggressive patriotism. Afraid of the counter-culture's assault on their old values, they embraced law and order, "family values" and a war on crime. Some voted their racial antagonisms.

When the dam broke, the corrosive effects of secular materialism flooded the land. Traditionalists now felt its assault upon their faith. It hit them that the underlying ethos of the powers that be was that faith was passé, that believers were tolerated but disdained. Shocked and battered by modernity, many of them became evangelical fundamentalists.

Secularists who were not at all or especially religious began to feel secular materialism's isolated desolation. Their hearts became emptier, their psyches diminished by resignation, cynicism and the loss of idealism.

C. The Unsettling Effects of Secular Materialism

Let's examine the negative effects of the dominance of secular materialism — the downside of Science, free thought, tolerance and our humanitarian ethos. By transforming God's world of connected spiritual beings into a fragmented world of meaningless atoms, secular materialism laid waste the heart of human existence. It devalued spirituality, desacralized the world and assaulted religious sensibilities. It eroded the foundations of organic culture and social cohesion. Not incidentally, by deconsecrating the natural world and enthroning material progress above other values, it spawned, or perhaps it's better to say propelled, our present ecological crisis.

The emptiness of secular materialism has, in one way or the other, shaken most of us Americans. It has devalued the faith at the core of millions of peoples' identities and sown the seeds of despair and pessimism. It has bred passivity, resignation and cynicism. It has deeply unsettled the feeling that our society rested on a solid foundation. No wonder we Americans feel out of sort.

1. Holes in Secularist Hearts

One of the basic human needs, it seems, is to feel grounded, to have roots in belief as in place and community. Until modern materialism, the humanity we know from history was grounded in religions which for a long time have mostly been spiritually-based belief systems. By excising spirituality from the modern world-view, secular materialism has deprived its adherents of their solid ground.

The millions of secularists who abjure spirituality have no firm source of meaning on which to root their lives. Some feel the emptiness keenly; others are free of its pain because, in Pink Floyd's words, they "have become comfortably numb".[19] One reads that many people in their late teens and early twenties have no interior life at all, which ought not to surprise in light of a world-view that we have nothing meaningful and non-material inside.

Many secularists feel free-floating anxiety even when things are going well. Like an annoying low-grade fever, it's a feeling of background distress that's just there, making one feel at sea, anxious without

---

[19] Pink Floyd, "Comfortably Numb" © 1980

apparent cause. It isn't always conscious and when the sufferer thinks about it, he's likely to look for psychic causes ("is this from childhood?") or attribute it to natural stress, which only sometimes it is. In fact, it's a symptom of his secular materialistic emptiness (and, noted later, of the stress of coping with the rapid pace of contemporary change).

Many secularists are deeply pessimistic. They have lost hope and traded their youthful ideals for cynicism and resignation to a distressing world. This pessimism is new to American history.

Secular materialism took hold in the Enlightenment, and progress is an Enlightenment ideal. Before then, history had been almost universally regarded over the eons as either cyclical or as declining from a Golden Age in the misty past. It simply had not occurred to people to believe that life on this Earth actually was fated to get better and better. The heady optimism of the overthrow of Churchly dogmatism and the enthronement of the wonders of Reason and Science changed that. In place of belief in Heavenly perfection, mankind came to believe that it could think and act its way if not to perfection, then to an ever improving future.

America was created during and of the Enlightenment, conceived in liberty, to build a free, prosperous and expanding nation. Americans drank deeply from the bottle of faith in progress. American history seemed proof that, if our nation kept the right principles and its people continued to work hard, our future would get ever better.

Until recently, most Americans believed progress to be inevitable. We would leave our children a better world, as our parents had done for us and as our children would do for their children. Progress was ingrained in our world, because, having harnessed Reason and Science, we were on the upward escalator with no end in sight to its happy climb. As Martin Luther King said of social ethics, "The moral arc of the universe bends at the elbow of justice."

That belief is much harder to find today. Now, a distressing pessimism dominates: that tomorrow will not be better, that we will not leave our children a better world than we inherited, that they will not have better lives than ours. That life is getting worse.

Why? One explanation is the difficulty of recent history. The last several decades have been economically and socially unkind to "middle America". The record of the last century — World Wars, genocides, terror, etc. — has taught that Reason, Science and the materialist view have not birthed a kinder, gentler world. Nor does human nature seem to be improving: we moderns seem to have as much greed, selfishness, dishonesty and brutality as our forbears.

A full explanation is deeper. The belief in inevitable progress was born of the early, heady days of the Enlightenment before materialism had excised spirituality from the modern world-view. Back in the days of Deists and Founding Fathers, the Enlightenment brought Christianity's faith in spiritual salvation into the secular world. So long as spirituality co-existed in the newly modernized mind with the faith in Reason, there seemed to be no incongruity between progress and the early form of secular materialism.

As secular materialism has evolved, there is such an incongruity today. One need not believe that life is a straight line ever upward to believe in progress: it can zig and zag, it can spiral: up now, down then, one step back for every two steps forward. If one has a ground for hope, then reversals — the Holocaust, terrorist murders, some bad years of this or that — need not scuttle one's faith in progress. Provided she has a ground for that faith.

Belief in the certainty of progress depends upon having hope for improvement. Sustainable hope needs a spiritual foundation: that life has a more than this-worldly, call it "cosmic", connection. A reason to believe in a deeper meaning than naked hope itself. This, stark materialism cannot provide. Pure Reason alone can rarely persuade us that, in the face of horrible events, we're on the path to a better future. Without faith in something beyond the here and now, hope will be dashed when events disappoint, leaving nothing but materialist emptiness.

Loss of faith in the inevitability of progress is not, itself, a bad thing. The conviction that history can be harnessed to drive in one's preferred direction enabled totalitarian regimes of left and right. More to the American point, if progress is inevitable, why put one's shoulder to the wheel. What devastates is to lose hope because hope provides the energy necessary to seek improvement. Unfortunately, many Americans have lost faith in hope.

The consequences of losing hope are severe, for hope is the antidote to resignation and cynicism. Confronted with materialism and dehumanizing, disempowering mass culture (see Chapter Eight), it's natural to believe that what one does has neither purpose nor lasting effect, without a believable guide to a better future. As Dylan said, "Although the masters make the rules for the wise men and the fools, I got nothing, Ma, to live up to."[20] If she's but a tiny cog in an immense, meaningless world, why care about anything outside the narrow confines of her life. Resignation breeds apathy.

These beliefs lead to cynicism about people who claim to act for broader purposes. In this unprincipled world, everyone does what she can to get what she wants. There being no real ideals, people who speak of principles are just cynically using mellifluous words to advance themselves. And so, deprived of hope, meaning and purpose, she becomes resigned to a world she does not like, cynical and passive about anything outside her constricted personal range.

She also is likely to be excessively anxious. When secular materialism melted the solid foundation of meaning and values like butter in the heat, it deprived secularists of the spiritual beliefs that once grounded psyches (and caused traditionalists to fear that their grounding ideas may not survive the assaults of modernity).[21]

---

[20] "It's Alright Ma, I'm Only Bleeding" Bob Dylan © 1965

[21] Increased American anxiety is also caused by economic distress, by the accelerated rate of change and by the loss of community, all discussed below

She may become gripped with nostalgia for aspects of the past which warm her heart. It must have been better then: life seems to have meant more, people were more connected, there was meaning there. The image of that particular past to which she clings is irretrievable — the past always is. But nostalgia is a fantasy incapable of giving empty "meaning" to a present life. Rarely seen until recently, it's a symptom of the malaise of modernity.

She feels empty usually without knowing why. Her ignorance is not stupidity or lack of reflection. It's rather that the reasons for her malaise are difficult to see: so pervasive, so ingrained, so much a part of the air she breathes, that they are hard to discern. She may be unable to articulate that modernity is empty of meaning, but she feels it in every atom of her mind and body.

2. Trying to Compromise with Secular Materialism

Many secularists have turned from materialism to spirituality, embracing religion (traditional, fundamentalist, Eastern), being "spiritual but not religious", or adopting religious-like "New Age" beliefs. Many seek solace in the humanitarian ideals of the Enlightenment or of spiritually and religiously-based ethics. While spiritually based humanitarianism can dispel emptiness, we've seen that it can't escape groundlessness if it rests solely on materialism.

Some of us are mixtures of secularist and traditionalist, accepting modernity's ethos while believing in God, religion, and spirituality. They live with secular materialism in one of three ways. They may be blissfully unaware of the contradiction between their spirituality and materialism. They may repress the contradiction, as we are wont to do with conflicts which defy resolution. Or, they may put the two perspectives into impermeable compartments: faith, God and spirituality for church, synagogue or mosque and the Sabbath; Reason and Science for the everyday world.

None of these is a real solution to the contradiction between spirituality and materialism. That is because none excise the germs of secular materialism within. Though she may be unaware of, repress or compartmentalize the contradiction, it is there. Perhaps to erupt one day unannounced; or, remaining hidden, to fester, not quite conscious but causing perplexing dismay.

3. Traditionalists and Evangelical Fundamentalism

America has had many religious revivals, and in every age many Americans have belonged to fundamentalist Protestant sects. Since the Sixties or Seventies, there has been an historically strong surge in the extent and fervor of evangelical fundamentalism.

The emptiness of secular materialism is a major reason. Evangelicals and fundamentalists yearn for a stronger, deeper, more emotionally and spiritually satisfying faith than available from traditional churches, which have often diluted their spirituality in trying to adapt to the ideas of modernity. Evangelicals and fundamentalists feel the emptiness of compromising with emptiness.

Where secular materialism sees everything as matter without spirit, fundamentalist faith enthrones spirit and soul. Where secular materialism is without meaning, fundamentalist faith is suffused with meaning derived from God and, for Christians, Jesus Christ, Who offer eternal salvation. Where secular materialism sees people as unconnected sets of atoms, fundamentalist faith makes a connected community of the church.

Evangelicals are people who have found meaning. Americans who are not evangelical Christians are troubled that fundamentalist faith tends to be self-righteous and intolerant. This is the way it usually is when a new form of faith takes hold. True believers tend to be self-righteous and intolerant of those who have not seen the light they are blessed to have found. And, especially intolerant of secular materialists who don't even get the centrality of God to human existence. This helps explain why much evangelical and fundamentalist religion is harsh and politicized, a major part of the hard Right which has long dominated American politics.[22]

The harsh political beliefs of the Christian Right are hard to square with Christian ethics. Christianity teaches men and women to love their fellow man. Adherents of the Christian Right often despise opponents with vicious vehemence; show little empathy for the poor and disadvantaged; clamor to starve social services and undo the (modest) American safety net; so oppose Government that they support massive tax cuts which primarily benefit the very wealthy; are enraged at government actions to improve education and health care; and (at a 2011 Presidential debate) cheer the idea that a man without insurance be left to die at the door of the emergency room.

Christianity teaches brotherhood and peace, but the Christian Right has a strong strain of anti-Muslim prejudice, hates (not too strong a word) liberals and supports the most muscular and aggressive military policies. Christianity teaches that we are stewards of God's Earth but the political face of evangelical fundamentalism refuses to take seriously the notion that man's actions are changing the earth's climate in devastating ways. Rather, it condones, even encourages, environmental degradation.

Many evangelical fundamentalists are intolerant because of the strength of what their faith must oppose to make its way. They challenge the world-view which has long dominated the West at its materialist core. The lesson of modernity's triumph over medieval Christianity and of the Church's victory over Antiquity is that such challenges must be fierce and persistent to succeed.

Evangelicals see their opponents as entrenched and all-powerful. To liberals, the immense political clout of the Right makes this seem a delusion. But, evangelicals feel under the sway of powerful hostile beliefs and ethics, that their opponents control culture, ubiquitous in the media and in politics and dismissive of their core beliefs. The

---

[22] It is important to note that many evangelicals and fundamentalists do not believe that the divine messages of their faith lead to right-wing politics.

government looks like an intrusive behemoth administering liberal policies. The country is in the grip of modernity's Godless forces which have trampled the moral verities and stability of the Fifties.

We have seen that the modern world-view disdains people who don't get that faith is false. Religious people sense this disdain and hear scorn in the tone and voice of secular voices in the media, politics and community. Evangelicals know that, however polite the words, secular materialism's cultural leaders disrespect them and their beliefs. They return the compliment.

There is another reason for this vehemence. For a time after World War II, if you were white, straight and prospering, America felt like a land of milk and honey, especially if you were a man. Then the disruptions of Vietnam, the culture wars and economic stagnation exploded the feeling of living the beautiful myth. A natural reaction of deeply religious people to great disappointment is to turn to apocalyptic visions and extreme, intolerant, messianic views.[23]

Tocqueville offers a further reason: that Americans (including many evangelicals) are imbued with money materialism. Too much of that causes "a sort of fanatical spiritualism... [because]...The taste for what is infinite and the love of what is immortal...is fixed in human nature".[24]

Let's not forget the crucial fact: Fundamentalists and evangelicals feel that modernity has diverted Americans from the satisfaction of their spiritual needs. Their forms of Christianity satisfy them.

---

[23] See Michael Walzer, *Exodus and Revolution*, (Basic Books 1985), pp. 135-36.

[24] Alexis de Tocqueville, *Democracy in America*, (Henry Reeve text, per Phillips Bradley, Alfred Knopf 1945) vol. 2, pp. 134-35. If these needs of the soul are not satisfied, people often turn to pleasure so that then the soul "grows weary, restless, and disquieted amid the enjoyments of sense."

D. The Future of Secular Materialism

No world-view is a stable, permanent thing. Medieval spiritual Christianity eroded over several centuries as secular materialism emerged. There are signs that the strength of modernity's world-view peaked in the middle of the twentieth century, that we are living is a time of transition. Faith and spirituality (thought by some, not that long ago, to be on the road to extinction in the West) are on the march in much of the world; secularity is on the defensive.

Science claims the capacity to explain everything about the universe, and the materialist's world seems to make sense as a matter of the theorems of Newtonian science. And yet. There are seemingly solvable questions to which scientists' efforts have so far found no answer: big questions such as how life began; where consciousness came from; how natural selection can account for the vast changes in living organisms (think of the brain and the eye) over the available time. Science believes it will eventually find answers. Perhaps, but perhaps these are mysteries unsolvable by the materialist paradigm.[25] Perhaps, they are loose threads in that paradigm from which thinkers employing a new perspective will unravel the edifice of philosophic materialism.[26]

Though we cannot know to what we are transitioning, it's likely that the new world will be more spiritual than ours, less devoted to pure Reason. It would not surprise if that new world-view incorporates quantum physics and field theory to believe that existence is not a mere mechanistic collision of tiny particles, but rather that all things are deeply connected, even that there is a scientific basis for spirit.

---

[25] See Thomas Nagel, *Mind and Cosmos: Why the Materialist Neo-Darwinian Conception of Nature Is Almost Certainly False* (Oxford University Press 2012)

[26] See Thomas Kuhn, *The Structure of Scientific Revolutions* (University of Chicago Press 1962)

Whatever is on its way, whatever vanguards of a new era have already arrived, secular materialism still holds the boards.

CHAPTER FIVE: "I, ME, MINE": INDIVIDUALISM AND THE PURSUIT OF SELF-INTEREST

"All I can hear: I me mine, I me mine, I me mine.
Even those tears: I me mine, I me mine, I me mine.
No one's frightened of playing it, everyone's saying it,
Flowing more freely than wine, all through the day: I me mine."
George Harrison, "I, Me, Mine" © 1970

Individualism is modernity's second cornerstone idea. It's long done much good, underwriting the human rights, opportunities and personal freedoms indispensable to our sense of good lives. Until, that is, it took an extreme, rabid turn to become a major cause of our malaise. How can it be that this great Enlightenment cornerstone of America's founding has evolved to make us ill?

A. The Emergence of American Individualism

Individualism is a modern phenomenon. Until it emerged, every human being in every society of which we have knowledge was, first and foremost, a member of that society. Of course, there were powerful individuals who gained great fame and honor: think of Pericles, Julius Caesar, Saint Thomas Aquinas. But even these strong individuals took their identities primarily from their communities.

The ancient Greeks prized honor, and many Greeks were commanding, famous people. And yet, each of them was, in his mind and the mind of his contemporaries, first and foremost, a member of his polis. However unique an individual, however much he strived for honor, he felt his identity to be social, as a citizen of his polis. One of the worst fates which could befall an Athenian was to be ostracized, exiled as a threat to the community.

The contemporary version of individualism is very different. Though part of society, his identity is primarily that he is himself, not an American or a Frenchman. Being French or American is but one part of who he is. Rather, what he thinks defines him is the sum of his beliefs, memberships and interests. It's a modern homily that the "right" answer to the question "explain who you are with three words or phrases" is "I, Tom Lemberg, child of God". No pre-modern would have considered such an individualist answer.

Individualism rooted in the Renaissance and blossomed in the Enlightenment. With the community of believers no longer central, the crown of life's purpose passed to the individual, now able to be himself because liberated from conformist medieval chains.

The individual gained rights: to happiness, liberty and property; to speak and believe freely; to be free from arbitrary state power. As before, the individual had social duties, now not of obedience to Church and social hierarchy, but the duties of a good citizen.

Individualism is logically connected to secular materialism. Where medieval man saw things in wholes, because materialism sees things as the sum of small parts, modern man naturally focuses on the individual before the collective community.

The Enlightenment had a strain, begun by Rousseau, that freedom meant freedom to be a part of, and bound by the needs of, the community. This was a paradox: not the right to act freely but rather the right to do one's duty to satisfy the needs of the liberating state (the "general will"). It led through Robespierre to the Terror and through Marx and others to totalitarianism.

That strain did not take in America. What took hold was, as the Declaration said, that we have "inalienable rights" to "life, liberty and happiness". That we have the freedom to live as we wish with minimal restrictions. Leavened for a long time by the obligations of active citizenship, our sense of social duty has recently weakened. Now, many Americans regard the central legacy of the Founding as: "Don't tread on me." "Give me liberty or give me death."

B. Contemporary American Individualism

Like their Enlightenment peers, America's founders believed that individuals had liberty within community, where duties to the common weal were as important as rights. That has changed, so that individualism has eclipsed community, material success has become all-important, and rights have trumped duties. It has become all about "me".

1. Self-Absorption

Modern thinking teaches that we are selfish beings. Following Marx, Freud and the Darwinist apostles of the selfish gene, the dominant strain of modern thought is that we are mere bundles of desires constantly seeking to satisfy our wants, ever out to gain personal advantage. We are taught that it must be thus and that this is good because the road to improvement is paved with egoism: ride those selfish genes or fail as a species.

This lesson has taught us the virtues of self-absorption. The contrast with the past is not that we once thought only selfless thoughts: being human, of course not. All people expend a lot of thought, energy and action "looking out for number one". What is different is the degree and proportion of self-focused behavior, that self-centered thoughts so dominate our "me" culture.

Contemporary Americans find it harder than our forebears to consider other perspectives. We're less inclined to put aside what seems best for me (usually calculated in the shortest of runs) for what's best for the overall community or for others. We are less considerate of the feelings, needs and wishes of others, usually too into ourselves to have compassion for strangers.

2. Self-Reliance and Personal Responsibility

Americans had always greatly prized self-reliance and personal responsibility. Until recently, Americans lived by the belief that you're responsible for what you do and who you become. Now, self-absorption has undermined self-reliance and accountability.

Consider Emerson's celebrated essay, *Self-Reliance*. "A man is relieved and gay when he has put his heart into his work and done his best; but what he has said or done otherwise shall give him no peace." As he concluded, "Nothing can bring you peace but yourself. Nothing can bring you peace but the triumph of principles."

What made the essay famous was not that it said something new. It was that it expressed so well beliefs central to American culture. Work hard, do your best, look inside yourself for strength and motivation. You are responsible for what you do and who you become. You are what you make yourself.

That is how Americans mostly felt from the landing of the Pilgrims through the "Greatest Generation". The general response to hardship was to take responsibility for oneself, to overcome the difficulties in the way of one's goals, to get on with the business of one's life stoically and with little complaint.

Some time after World War II, self-gratification displaced self-reliance for many Americans. Individuality became all about me, and as it did, "I" felt much less accountable and responsible for my life and deeds than had my parents. Many people have now come to consider themselves playthings and victims of vast forces out of their control. It's become society's job or school's job or one's employer's job to put her in position to get what she wants. People have come to feel entitled. For the first time, many Americans feel they have the right to paternalistic care.

Now, many Americans, rich, middle and poor, religious and not, no longer feel much personal responsibility for their actions. For instance, one is obese, her children are obese, because they eat the wrong foods. Not because they can't afford better (sometimes they can't) but because they feel no self-responsibility to live healthily.

When we fall short, too few of us feel accountable. It's everyone else's fault, certainly not mine, if I didn't get that job or failed at something or committed some dastardly deed. Why, had society or someone not put me down and held me back and treated me unfairly, I'd have done just fine. My failure is someone else's responsibility. As comedian Flip Wilson had his Sixties' character Geraldine say, "The devil made me do it." Like Geraldine, many of us excuse what was, not so long ago, inexcusable behavior in ourselves and in others. Accountability for one's mistakes is rarer and rarer.

Consider reactions to crime. Not long ago, a person who committed a crime was, correctly, judged by society to have acted destructively, both to his victim and to the community. Punishment was due and appropriate, and the perpetrator was expected to feel deep remorse. Unless he was a psychopath, generally he did. That is still how most Americans feel today.

But not all. For a large part of society, it came to pass that, if the perpetrator was a black ghetto resident or otherwise was born, bred and lived in disadvantageous circumstances, many liberals blamed not him but the society which had treated him so poorly. The harm he had done to society and to his victim receded before the demand to be just to a disadvantaged perpetrator driven to crime because society had given him a raw deal. Quite a few criminals also bought into the excuse, to feel less remorseful than aggrieved.

Though well-intentioned, this compassion for the perpetrator wounded community ethics when it set aside personal responsibility and accountability. Since the rest of the country continues to believe that robbers and murderers should be held accountable, this has, as we will see, deeply undermined respect for liberal thinking.

3. A Culture of Entitlement

Contrary to our Founding, we've come to have a culture of entitlement, where everyone has rights but not much in the way of duties. The Founders intended our Constitutional rights to be inextricably entwined with the duties of citizenship. As George Washington said, "It may be laid down as a primary position, and the basis of our system, that every citizen who enjoys the protection of a free government owes not only a proportion of his property, but even of his personal services to the defense of it."

The "rights" of the culture of entitlement are considerably broader than those protected by the Constitution. For many, they now include the right to be taken care of. More and more of us think that, having been blessed to live in the USA, someone, some institution, somebody somehow ought to provide my needs and wants (not just basic social services and a safety net), to "take care of me". Feeling a victim, they are passive. Understandably, people who believe in personal responsibility hold them in contempt.

The individual's right to do just what he wants often trumps morals and law. Many of us, secularists and traditionalists alike, have come to think that the "rights" of the "me" culture include the right, as an American privileged to live in the land of the free, to do as he pleases unbound by duties and many laws. The definition of the acceptable has moved, for too many of us, far away from the direction of fair play and obligation to one's fellows.

Oh, sure, there are laws to be obeyed. But, too often the real worry these days is not that it's wrong to break the law or act dishonorably, but that one might get caught. If it's more profitable to sell adulterated food, ignore one's mines' safety or cook the books, then why not do it, unless the risks of detection are too great? If one can win the game by cheating, why not, so long as the likelihood of discovery is low or the cost of getting caught is small?

Anyone who would impede these free Americans kills freedom just as surely as if he were a despot. There's no place in his idea of a free society for Washington's belief that citizens have public duties to offer service and pay taxes or that sometimes we must sacrifice for the common good. Instead, the contemporary individualist wants a society in which government neither regulates his behavior nor taxes his resources for much beyond police and security protection.

C. Costs of Our Contemporary Individualism

1. Constricted Self-hoods

The paradox is that by putting individuality first and foremost, contemporary individualism has constricted our self-hoods. We take our identities from within and without. Descartes' "I think, therefore I am" centered meaning on what I think, what's in me.

But, that's only the half of it. Like our primate ancestors and relatives, we are social animals who must live in communities to survive, evolve and thrive. We need connection to community and our fellows. We need to carry not only me within myself, but also others, our world. We couldn't have evolved, developed, learned language, gotten past being brutes except in society.

Extreme, contemporary individualism would deny this reality. It finds identity only within. I am who I am; you, community, society, everything else are only adjuncts to me. But, this has shriveled the social part necessary to make our selves whole and well. No wonder we feel discontented, unfulfilled, dissatisfied and malaised. No wonder so many of us feel it's OK to depart from the moral rules we learned as children not to lie, cheat, act wantonly and cruelly.

2. The Effect Upon the Common Weal

A successful democratic society requires citizens with a sense of union. Our Founders believed their new government required a citizenry committed to preserve and nurture it with their time, energy and loyalty. The intense political disagreements of their time didn't frighten them. They believed their Great Experiment would succeed so long as Americans, regardless of differences, remained connected as committed citizens.

Until recently, Americans shared a common responsibility for the common good. We felt, for all our disagreements, that we were in the same boat. Most of us felt actionable empathy for the unfortunate. We wanted to get on with solving big problems. We understood that that often called for political compromise. We were willing, when the need was important, to engage in mutual self-sacrifice.

In recent years, extreme individualism has weakened our emotional ties as citizens and our shared civic and moral commitments. It's as if America no longer is the joint country of us all. With less personal accountability, we feel less shared responsibility. We feel little stake in social problems that don't directly and immediately affect us personally. What's best for me trumps the common weal — almost always. Being self-absorbed, we've less time and energy for, and interest in, communal needs. Feeling entitled, we find quaint President Kennedy's stirring words to "Ask not what your country can do for you, but what you can do for your country."

As we'll see, greed and the power of money have taken over our politics. We care less about the plight of the unfortunate. We insist we care deeply for the world we'll leave our descendants, but we don't walk the talk. Problems linger with no political solution possible. Compromise has become, for millions, a dirty word. Too many of us insist on getting my way, all the way, all the time.

Politics has become all about individualism and little about society. David Brooks recently said: "For a generation no matter who was in power, the prevailing winds have been blowing in the direction of autonomy, individualism and personal freedom, not in the direction of society, social obligations, and communal bonds."[27] Liberals have extolled individualism in morals, conservatives individualism in the freedom of the untrammeled market.

---

[27] *The Social Animal*, (Random House 2011) p. 315

We consider below both how this loss of commonality is greatly endangering our democracy and why its is at odds with a healthy human nature.

CHAPTER SIX: "ANYTHING GOES": ERODED VALUES

"In olden days a glimpse of stocking
Was looked on as something shocking,
But now, God knows, anything goes."
Cole Porter, "Anything Goes" © 1935

A. Modernity's Impact on Values

Modernity has been very tough on our old moral code. Each of us now seems to have his own moral ideas, which lots of other people often think, well, to lack morality.

Secular materialism and extreme individualism have undermined the spiritual and religious foundation of the values we more-or-less used to share. Free market ideology, a subject of the next chapter, has dismissed values from the calculus of what is good. Not surprisingly, this has disoriented our national moral compass.

Most people took their ethics from religion, learning how God tells us to live. We learned traditional morality at home and in Sunday School. As religion lost its importance, that was bound to change for secularists. It's also changed for many traditionalists, whose moral compasses have, to one degree or another, been moved by the ideational forces of the age.

In the Middle Ages, Christianity was the only source of truth; and ethical rules came straight from the Church's interpretation of the sacred texts. When modernity de-spiritualized the world, it took away God's sanction for the old morality. By exploding the idea that there's only one truthful doctrine, It birthed moral relativism, the conviction that there's no objective truth.

Relativism is central to the secular materialist, individualist worldview. The notion that no beliefs can be proven to embody "Truth" dispelled the authority of the old teaching of what's morally required.

No beliefs being certain, all beliefs are possible. There is no absolute morality but many possible ethical answers to the question, "how shall we live?" Just as I can't assuredly claim my beliefs about spirituality and religion are correct while yours are not, I can't be certain about my notions of right and wrong. If you believe it permissible to do things I abhor, with some limits at the extremes, that's just a difference of opinion. Even many believers have, in some aspects of living, become ethical relativists.[28]

We've seen that some secularists moved to atheism. Some atheists followed the absence of God to the logical extreme that without supernatural sanction there are no values at all. The great literary example is Dostoevsky's Ivan Karamazov who said, "If God doesn't exist, everything is permitted". While few atheists follow Ivan's logic to banish ethical values (Ivan inconsistently didn't), the thought is in the air. The specter that any behavior whatsoever is considered permitted frightens believers.

And so, the moral verities of my youth in the Fifties have lost their power. It's not that the country has become utterly amoral: the impulse to (some) goodness seems innate in the human condition. We do not easily rob and murder. But, the turn to relativism and the weakening of religious sanction has deprived ethical values of the force of authority. (As we see, this is not all to the bad.) We first consider the explosive issue of values related to sexual behavior.

B. The Erosion of Traditional Values

1. Sexual Mores and the Social Fabric

We've been roiled since the Sixties by stormy disagreements about sexual mores. Until then, there was plenty of sex outside the supposedly permitted bounds: premarital and adulterous sex (see the

---

[28] Influential modern thinkers validate moral relativism. See, *e.g.*, Ludwig Wittgenstein claiming it's meaningless even to make ethical pronouncements; and Freud's and Marx's avowals that beliefs are but disguises for psychic or economic interest.

Kinsey Report); homosexuality though it seemed much rarer than it apparently was; and some abortions. But, since all this violated the moral code, it was mostly hidden.

The Sixties changed all of that, radically. It began with the young. Much of a generation became very rebellious. They dissented loudly from national politics, especially over civil rights and the war in Vietnam. They grew their hair long and dressed messily. And they celebrated "sex, drugs and rock and roll".

Their music was cacophonous to parental ears. They took drugs, from marijuana (illegal if mostly benign) to cocaine, LSD, even heroin. They dressed provocatively. And, they engaged in promiscuous, frequent, certainly pre-marital sex, proclaiming loudly and proudly their liberation from their parents' strait jackets.

They drove shocked conventional Americans into a furious frenzy. How dare these punks flout decency? Where do they get their nerve to flout God's will that people restrain their sexual desires? What would the world become if sex didn't mean family, if everyone indulged himself (even worse, herself) as she pleased. The sexual moral code was an essential part of the country's foundations: unravel the threads of morality and their world, the good American world, would fall apart.

The unraveling of the threads of the old sexual morality quickly moved from the visible, noisy young to much of the rest. Pre-marital sex became common across the land. Teenagers were reported to be rampantly into casual and frequent sex. Divorce became common and so, increasingly, did adulterous sex.

Research showed that many people are naturally homosexual, one implication being that before gay liberation they had to live a painful life untrue to themselves. When the times removed homosexuality's stigma, gay people came out of the closet to live openly with same-sex lovers, or even more provocatively, as promiscuous gays.

The weakening of the moral verities of the Fifties has done much good. By unhinging excessive repression, the sea change in "life-style" morality freed millions to live lives which suit their sexual identities — a great boon even though gay marriage and abortion have torn harshly at the social fabric. Pendulums tend to swing quite far in the opposite direction. This pendulum has swung wide enough that there are large "buts" which need mention alongside these blessings.

Graphic public sex, forbidden in my youth, is omnipresent in the media and ads. Of course: sex sells. Though many of us don't like it (I don't and am hardly a prude), we can't escape that everywhere, we (and our children) see and hear sex — and drugs and profanity.

The media readily display sex, and not always merely suggestively. Scenes of lovemaking are now common. Advertisements had long used sex appeal to sell. What differs is how blatant the use of sex and skin has become. How quaint Cole Porter's "Anything Goes" from 1935 that "in olden days, a glimpse of stocking was looked on as something shocking. But now, Heaven knows, anything goes." The "anything" that shocked Cole Porter is much, much tamer than the daily fare in today's America.

Many people, and not only liberals, successfully urged legislatures to relax laws limiting divorce and to promote sex education in the schools. Abortion became common, especially after the Supreme Court struck down anti-abortion laws in 1973 in *Roe v. Wade*.

Americans of traditional morality fought back. Abortion became the flash point issue. By removing the cost of pregnancy from "illicit" sex (which had become easy to avoid with contraceptive pills), it was said to encourage promiscuity. But, that wasn't what made the issue explosive. Since abortion removes a fetus, it raises the question of whether that fetus had been a living person, so that its removal would be a killing.

The Court didn't help matters by trying to draw a judicial line as to when life began, before which, it held, abortion is lawful. Opponents of abortion were not, predictably, persuaded that a living fetus did not become alive until such time as decided by a group of judges.[29] Abortion's ("pro-life") opponents have battled its ("pro-choice") supporters ever since. The most extreme pro-lifers have, paradoxically, resorted to violence and murder.

Abortion was the first wedge issue, driving a chasm between people who accepted (much of) the new sexual morality and opponents who wanted to legislate against as much of it as possible. Sex education in the schools, easy divorce and the marriage of gay people joined abortion as issues which divided liberals and many centrists from millions of other centrist and conservative Americans who wanted traditional sexual morality enforced by government. Traditionalists adopted the appealing slogan of "family values" as their battle cry.

This, even as many traditionalists drifted into the newly opened sexual world: if not abortion, then non-marital sex, divorce and even living openly as gay. This though some leaders of the "family values" Right were closeted gays and others provoked titillation and outrage when caught in sexual misbehaviors against which they had thundered from pulpit and rostrum.

Traditionalists were outraged by the country's new public face. Even if one was dipping his toes in the newly-discovered ocean of acceptable pleasure, all the focus on sex was unnerving. It infuriated that so many people were flouting the rules of a good life, rules that kept society together through a moral code. And, though many teenagers abstained, when it came to one's children, the sexual revolution struck home fiercely. The anger, the fear that one's own children were doing all those things even as teens: fear of disease and pregnancy, and even

---

[29] The distinguished scholar, now Judge, Guido Calabresi, argued that the Court would have better served the nation if, instead of deciding the matter on the "science" of when life begins, it had acknowledged that it was deciding a great clash of fundamental values. Rather than feeling the Court had brushed aside their deepest beliefs with what seemed pseudo-science, pro-lifers would've seen that the Court at least valued their beliefs, though not as much as they do. Guido Calabresi, *Ideals, Beliefs, Attitudes and the Law: Private Law Perspectives on a Public Law Problem* (Syracuse University Press 1985), in the chapter "When Ideals Clash", pp. 87-114

more fear that they were losing the holy part of themselves in hedonistic pleasure. It was as if Revelation's Great Whore of Babylon had taken up residence in the good old USA.

As the sexual revolution unraveled the fabric of the old moral code, so has the widespread use of drugs and frequent public profanity. Though using recreational drugs other than alcohol and tobacco is mostly illegal (a few states have now legalized marijuana), everyone knows it's widespread. Much American crime is the result of hard drugs like heroin and cocaine: users stealing (and sometimes killing) to get money for habits, and fights and murders among providers.

Americans see the drug culture everywhere: on streets, in the media and in their children's schools, even in their neighborhoods. All too often, in their own children. It's maddening to see the addiction and crime bred in the ghettos and among strangers. It's very scary when it's in one's own community, threatening children, the children of your friends, even, terror of terrors, your own children.

Public profanity has soared since the Sixties. Consider Cole Porter again: "Good authors too who once knew better words, now only use four letter words writing prose. Anything goes." Porter was speaking of James Joyce's masterpiece *Ulysses*. What would Porter say about hearing, constantly, language one's parents forbade?

What was forbidden not long ago is now not just permitted: it is everywhere. Though many Americans don't like it, they cannot escape. Everywhere they turn, they find sex, drugs and profanity.

2. Integrity and Personal Responsibility

While the sexual revolution's been boisterously public, the decline of integrity has crept in on little cat's feet. Quietly, little noticed, it's infected the land. Not blatant like public sex, not shrieked from movie and television screens, the change in the extent of honesty is harder to see. But, ominously, it's become a blight on our society.

The belief in, and practice of, integrity has plummeted. This is no naive statement about the purity of the past. Of course, there's always been lying, cheating and breaking of laws and morals to get ahead, plenty of people happy to sell their wares, honesty and dangers to health and safety be damned. But, as many of us who have lived a while observe, it's much worse today than in our youth.

Allow me to begin personally. I saw a big change in the level of honesty in my profession (law) from when I began in 1969. Over time, I saw, and I read and heard about, a surge in legal briefs which grossly misstated the law and the facts, in lawyers' lying to judges, in party's lying in negotiations to get an edge. Though most lawyers acted honestly, the number of liars rose substantially. To them, only success mattered: to win, to get more clients and make more money. It's become a game in which truth-telling is optional, and certainly not to get in the way of gaining an advantage. The problem grew, as Gresham's Law (that bad money drives out good) ensnared the practice of law. The problem is not confined to the bar.

More and more, one comes across dishonest behavior. Cutting corners, misrepresenting facts, cheating on taxes, violating laws because the chances of detection are small: whatever it takes to get ahead. Private lying and public lying. Prosecutors withholding and distorting evidence to get a conviction: the win being more important than justice. Presidents lying to go to war.

The moral costs of dishonesty to society are immense. To take one very big example, we have painfully learned that moral dereliction in finance is ruinously expensive. Finance offers a particularly strong temptation to cheat: rewards are enormous and detection difficult. The crime is bloodless, the victims not smashed bloodily at one's feet in an alley, just impersonal numbers on a spreadsheet. Yet, for decades after the Great Depression there were no systemic scandals on Wall Street until the insider trading and market manipulation misconduct of the Eighties. This was the first of a slew of scandals. The biggest was the widespread dishonesty and recklessness which brought on the Great Crash and the Great Recession.

Financial firms earn vast profits because they supply the money which lubricates the economy. The quid pro quo is to owe duties to the public of integrity and care. Instead, as the morals of integrity loosened, many of these firms acted recklessly and often dishonestly to make themselves unprecedented great wealth.[30] When their house of cards collapsed, they crashed the economy. Millions of people around the world lost their jobs, savings and homes. Practically everyone was hurt, except the now uber-rich, many of them the Crash's perpetrators. Bailed out to prevent another depression, they kept their not-so-well-gotten fortunes and, then, saved and enriched by government bailouts, paid themselves more obscene bonuses. Perhaps this would've come to pass before "looking out for number one" replaced felt duties to the common weal. Perhaps.[31]

A growing number of people don't even bother to hide what used to be reprehensible behavior. One hardly ever heard in the "old days" — even from the habitually dishonest — that such actions were acceptable. That has changed. In an era in which money is prized as a supreme value, it is not just Gordon Gecko in the movie *Wall Street* who proclaims that "greed is good". Now many people believe this to be a truism justifying rapacious behavior wisely denounced in Sunday School. After all, they falsely say, everybody does it.

---

[30] One example: They bought and sold immensely risky securities (some they privately called "crap") as if they were as secure as U.S. bonds. To do so, they borrowed immense sums, heedless that a small downturn in the value of that "crap" could bankrupt their firms and flush the economy down the drain.

[31] Greed without responsibility is not confined to Wall Street. For instance, some public employee unions bankrupted cities by successfully demanding pay and retirement packages far beyond the cities' means. California's powerful prison guard union got the state to enact draconian laws vastly increasing the prisoner population (jail for minor offenders, lifetime sentences for three time petty criminals) just because more people in jail means more and better paid guards.

The fall in the level of integrity is one consequence of the diminution of personal responsibility. Modern individualism encourages each of us to do what's best for me, without much concern for how it affects others. As we soon see, America is ensnared by the idea that the market is king and that what's right and good is to maximize economic efficiency and profit. Like heavy cloud cover hiding the sun, this glorification of self-seeking greed puts integrity out of sight so that too often now, profit maximization bereft of ethical behavior prevails in the marketplace.

The weakening of America's social bonds has exacerbated the tendency to greed. One is more likely to break the rules to gain an advantage if she feels little shared social connection to others, if the other she injures is not a person she confronts but a faceless, invisible thing.[32]

The coarsening of values in the market bleeds over to coarsen values everywhere else, including the public square. How could it not? Few of us are good at moral compartmentalization, able to act poorly at work and well in the community and at home. Years of experience breed habit. The habits of not valuing integrity, not caring about the consequences of what one does at work and distrusting others often infect other parts of one's life.

C. The Effects of Moral Erosion

1. Damage to Contemporary Society

To repeat an important thought, the erosion of the old morality has plusses and minuses. Before getting nostalgic for the good old days, remember what was quite bad. Gay people had to live unnaturally in the closet. Women had to get abortions in back alleys at risk to their lives. People had either to abide by sexual mores in which they didn't believe, hide their behavior or stand condemned for acting, as they felt,

---

[32] It may be that working in an abstract thing called a corporation makes it easier to forget ethics. As if what one does for an intangible entity somehow has fewer ethical consequences than if he did that same act in his own name.

naturally. Mismatched unhappy couples had to stick out a lifetime of misery in loveless marriage. The benefits have been great. So have the costs.

By taking away the stability and security of our old moral foundation, our moral decay has frayed the social bonds connecting us emotionally. We've come to see others more like foreigners and less like neighbors.

Our economic and social divisions softened much from the Great Depression to the Sixties. Though conservatives and liberals fought hard, the fights were much more within bounds than these days — as if tacitly understood rules maintained civility and mutual respect. Those frayed social bonds are a big reason this has changed.

To many traditionalists, you're a moral person or you're not. If you live a modern "lifestyle" — abortion, non-marital sex, divorce, as gay, then you are, by definition not moral. It's not a matter of difference: Americans have become tolerant of all kinds of diversity — but much less so with moral diversity. That cuts too close to the bone of what makes us good, of what gives life meaning.[33]

Because the loss of a common ethics threatens traditionalists' basic beliefs, it fosters anger. Anger that so many people are violating God's commandments — and flaunting their immorality. An angry determination to punish the culprits, breeding a yearning for Old Testament prophets to set us straight, for leaders who'll stop this immorality whatever it takes. Or, as with Donald Trump, even for someone who bears no resemblance to any admired religious figure but promises somehow to right the listing ship.

The celebrants of the new freedoms feel similarly disaffected from traditionalists. What a breath of fresh air to be myself, that others too can be free. How fortunate that miserable couples can divorce, that there's no more strait jacket on bodily pleasure, that a woman can get an abortion from a doctor instead of an untrained butcher. Those who

---

[33] At last, the anti-gay stigma is rapidly eroding among traditional Americans.

want to live their own lives in the old way are free to do so. When they try to impose their repressions on the rest of us, why, the hell with them. They're just a bunch of ignorant Puritans.

Secularists fear America's politically active traditionalism. As political philosopher Judith Shklar wrote, "a society of believers who choose never to resort to use of the agencies of government to further their particular faith is imaginable, though not usual."[34]

There's good reason to fear loss of liberty. As traditionalists work tirelessly to enact their "family values" agenda, they push hard to have governments make their beliefs official. The Texas Republican Party's 2004 platform would cut Jews like me out of America: "The Republican Party of Texas affirms that the United States of America is a Christian nation, and the public acknowledgement of God is undeniable in our history." Sarah Palin (remember her?) says that American law should be based on the law of the Bible. Religious symbols such as crosses have been erected on prominent government spaces. Textbooks in states such as Texas have been scrubbed to tell the (false) tale of Christian conservative America.

Moral erosion has greatly damaged us economically. Start with the how diminished integrity has destabilized markets and brought on to the Great Crash. It's also probably contributed to the concentration of wealth and income, discussed in the next chapter.

2. Damage to Contemporary Minds and Souls

The erosion of the old morality has damaged our minds and souls. Humans want to know their world is secure. We want stability, a solid foundation beneath our feet. We feel comforted when the rule of old verities gives us a foundation to support our lives and walls of belief on which to lean when life goes badly. Belief in God and in the old moral code provided that foundation and those walls for most

---

[34] "The Liberalism of Fear" in Judith Shklar, *Political Thought and Political Thinkers*, (University of Chicago Press 1998) p. 7.

Americans. Their loss has magnified the damage secular materialism has wrought on faith and spiritually.

Most of us, including traditionalists, have rejected chunks of the old moral code. Our era is morally confusing, even for many ardent old moralists. Perhaps they've taken a walk on the wild side of adultery or pornography. Perhaps their business ethics have fallen. Or, embracing free market "values", they've hardened, now less caring, empathetic and tolerant than their parents. They say they prize the Golden Rule, but are uncomfortable they don't live it so much.

Most people aren't cynical when they bemoan the loss of morality. Instead, they've slipped unawares into selectively accepting moral nihilism (that there are no true values). Many Americans, traditionalists as well as secularists, have taken to an a la carte morality: strict on this, loose on that, moralistic here and indulgent there. Having one foot in and one foot out of the old code is confusing: what's right and what's wrong; why is it OK to do this, wrong when I was young, while I still condemn that?

Moral nihilism has led to widespread hedonism (that the focus of life is to get pleasure) among all sorts of Americans. Unaware that "man does not live by bread alone", hedonism unbalances the self and empties the heart. Most hedonists can no more catch the satisfaction they crave than the race dog can catch the mechanical rabbit. People become bitter, not only at what's become of the old moral code but when their pursuit of pleasure proves empty.

Moral erosion is behind our outbreak of cruelty. "Nice" mothers posing as peers to post vicious Facebook entries about daughters' cheerleader rivals; wide-scale bullying — not the old fashioned meany bully kind but by "normal" kids; cheers at Republican debates that a man be left to die at the door to the emergency room because he lacks insurance; mass murders by, and of, students. Cruelty in our nasty political rhetoric of screaming epithets. And so it goes, much of it by "upstanding" people.

Many of these people feel justified. Because one's child was treated unfairly, retaliation is in order. Or, a raft of kids bully a teenager because they don't like her dress or demeanor. Other kids let it go, though intervention might save a classmate's ego, or her life. And, yet, these are people who neighbors say are good people, good kids. It's as if moral screws have come loose around the country.

Moral erosion has bred an endless spate of misdeeds by political, religious and business leaders and institutions. These, in turn, have begat corrosive cynicism about leaders and institutions which undermine community and polity. Think of Johnson's and Nixon's deceptions about Vietnam, of the criminal Watergate White House, of Bill Clinton's affair with a young intern (in the Oval Office!) and then his lying about it under oath, of George W. Bush's lying the nation into war in Iraq. And now, a President (Donald Trump) who seems incapable of saying the truth. No wonder we Americans have become cynical about political leaders.

And, then there is the hypocrisy of leaders caught in deeds they roundly condemn in others. Fundamentalist pastors having sex with prostitutes, male and female. "Family values" Congressmen having affairs and seducing young male pages. Politicians taking bribes. Corporations paying bribes, adulterating products and defrauding customers. It's all invited the unhealthy notion that leaders and major institutions can't be trusted because don't mean what they say. That we're run by a bunch of amoral hypocrites.

Losing our moral compass is not a good thing.

SECTION TWO: ECONOMIC AND SOCIAL FORCES: "SOMEONE'S IN MY HEAD BUT IT'S NOT ME"

"The lunatic is in my head; the lunatic is in my head
You raise the blade, you make the change
You re-arrange me 'till I'm sane
You lock the door and throw away the key
There's someone in my head but it's not me.
And if the cloud bursts, thunder in your ear
You shout and no one seems to hear
And if the band you're in starts playing different tunes
I'll see you on the dark side of the moon"
Roger Waters, Pink Floyd, "Brain Damage" © 1971

We've spent several chapters seeing how, pace the Marxists, ideas matter big time in how people think and feel. We now turn to the obvious fact that our economy, culture and communities have their own immense effect on how we live and how we feel about our lives. As we now see, the modern American economy, culture and communities and the ways they've changed are major causes of the unease and distress we Americans feel today.

Chapter Seven considers our economy: how free market ideology and changes in the economy over the last more than forty years have unsettled us and eroded the American Dream. Chapter Eight turns to the nature and effects of contemporary mass culture, which include how the speed and extent of the change and the rapid pace of modern life unsettle us all. Chapter Nine considers the toxic effects of the erosion of the sense of a national community and the concomitant weakening of local communities.

CHAPTER SEVEN: "DID YOU THINK THAT MONEY WAS HEAVEN SENT?": OUR ECONOMY AND THE AMERICAN DREAM

"Lady Madonna, children at your feet
Wonder how you manage to make ends meet.
Who finds the money when you pay the rent?
Did you think that money was heaven sent?"
John Lennon and Paul McCartney, "Lady Madonna" © 1968

We Americans have long celebrated our economy, often with good reason. It has been the greatest force for prosperity, opportunity and freedom in the history of the world. The free American market has unleashed the entrepreneurial spirit of a vibrant people to make use of our vast human and natural resources. It's created immense wealth and, until recently, provided good jobs for most people wanting work. It's been the engine of the American Dream, delivering to the diligent and resourceful the material blessings promised by the Founding. But, in recent times, though entrepreneurs are still unleashed and much wealth is still created, trouble has come to paradise.

From World War II until the early 1970s, the American economy soared and middle America prospered. The rising tide swept aside the deprivations, fears and insecurities of the Depression (though the memory took long to fade). Incomes rose broadly and millions of "working Americans" entered the economic middle class. They had good jobs, many in factories, with good pay, job security and decent retirement plans. They were able to move into new suburbs with nice homes and good schools. They had every reason to expect life to get ever better for their children.

The post-war cornucopia ended in the Seventies. It was not a good decade for the economy. Sparked by a sudden surge in the price of oil, the economy drifted into "stagflation", a combination of high inflation and low growth thought to be impossible. Though by the sharp recession of the early Eighties, people were shaken that the economy mightn't recover, it did, with a large bang.

The problem was that the benefits of growth no longer were broadly shared as they had been from the post-Depression recovery until the stagnation of the Seventies. The distribution of income and wealth, which had markedly narrowed, began to widen sharply. The ladder up became less accessible if you weren't blessed with well-off parents or the best education.

This big change hit "working Americans" harder than any group except the poor. Their incomes stopped rising, many of their jobs were lost, their sense of employment security vanished and their retirement plans no longer were, or seemed, secure. Where they had prospered and felt secure, now they found themselves struggling and deeply worried, with good reason, that things would only get worse.

Well before the Great Crash of 2008-09, the American economy had stopped working nearly as well as its celebrants trumpeted. While it continued to generate growth in the Gross Domestic Product ("GDP", the measure of the economy's size), a great deal of wealth and much splendid innovation, it also produced a society of ever-widening disparities in income and wealth. It has destroyed, and poorly replaced, many good jobs to the great hardship of the unemployed and not-so-well-employed and to the great anxiety of millions of others.[35]

We are increasingly divided by economic class. As many of us thrive, many others stagnate or descend through no fault of their own, despite their best efforts. For them and their children, the American Dream is receding. That's one major reason for the disquiet and malaise abroad in the land.

---

[35] The problem has not been that economic change destroyed particular jobs; it's that this growth did not provide ample good replacements for working Americans.

A. The Seeming Triumph of Unbridled Capitalism

1. The American Economy

The size of the American economy boggles the mind. In 2017, our GDP is the hard-to-get-one's-arms-around total of more than $18,000,000,000,000. That's eighteen trillion dollars: $56,000 for every one of our 320 million: adult and child, working and not. For a family of four, that's almost $225,000 per year, a princely sum to fund most comfortable and prosperous lives if, impossibly and undesirably, it was divided equally.

Americans make, buy and sell whatever goods and services people want. If people fancy something new, American ingenuity is likely to invent it — and other products theretofore unimagined. Capital is plentiful and readily obtainable at reasonable prices for people with good businesses and good ideas. Natural resources are plentiful. Americans have a rich fund of talent, skill and resourcefulness and are known for having the strongest work ethic in the West.

We've been especially innovative and entrepreneurial. We've led the development of the "information economy" based on the power of integrated circuits ("chips"), computing, telecommunications and the Internet. We're at the forefront of exciting developments in the life sciences and in "green" energy, though our position is threatened by public parsimony and the Right's opposition to crucial aspects of biological research. Open, innovative capital markets have provided the enabling money, and it's easier to start a new business in America than anywhere else in the world.

"Freedom" is a hallmark of this economic colossus. Capital and goods move utterly freely across the country; and the American government has long, until the "nationalist" Administration of Donald Trump, led the push for open international trade. Because Americans are less rooted to their birthplaces than Europeans, we are mobile, giving the economy much openness and flexibility.

We have regulation, most of it to make workplaces and products such as food, drugs and transportation vehicles safe; to protect buyers, especially of financial instruments, from deceitful sellers; and to limit the extent of pollution. But, since Ronald Reagan, "regulation" has become a dirty word. Rather than have government protect markets, the idea has taken hold that markets naturally police themselves. Because of the resulting "de-regulation" allowing businesses to do as they please, America has come to have less regulation than other advanced economies. Donald Trump and the Republican Congress have promised, and are doing their best to deliver, a great reduction in that modest level of regulation.

2. A Record of Great Success

The American economy has a long record of great success. In the depths of the Great Depression, the GDP was $600 million. At the end of the highly stimulating World War II, it was $222 billion. In 1970, one trillion dollars. Today, it is that 18 trillion dollars.

Capital has thrived. The Dow Jones Industrial Average measures the value of the stocks of a set of major companies. It was just above 40 in the depths of the Depression. By the end of World War II, it had risen over 200. In 1970, it was 630, down from a peak of nearly 1000 two years before. It was 3000 in 1990. Today, having recovered smartly from the Crash and zoomed to new record heights, it is well over 20,000.

The unemployment rate shot up in the Great Recession to ten percent; a terribly high rate[36], but has fallen back to normal levels above four percent. Ominously, while average pay, adjusted for inflation, soared from earlier in the 20th century, it has stagnated since the Seventies.

Despite these employment and wage bumps, this is a record of spectacular dynamism. There has (or had) been great flexibility for the

---

[36] Which is substantially understated as it excludes part-time workers who want to work full-time and people who have, in despair, stopped looking for work.

cream to rise to the top, for the children of the slums and factory workers and immigrants to succeed very well. The promise of America has always been to provide a better life than the alternatives.

The land of opportunity, the American Dream: to live where hard work and initiative pay off; to do well, better than one's parents; your children to do better than you. For a long time, America fulfilled that Dream for most of its people.

****

And, yet, the economy's performance is causing Americans' great angst. The surprising onset, depth of, and slow recovery for working people from the Great Recession worsened our economic fears. These have not vanished with what finally became a strong recovery. We worry, "Have we reached our peak? Are we falling into decline?"

There are three long-term sources of our economic difficulties. First, we have bought into an extreme free market ideology which harms all but the wealthiest. Our love affair with the free market has obscured its imperfections. Confusing market freedom with an absence of sensible regulation, we demand policies which substantially sub-optimize both economic performance and the quality and cost of goods and services. For instance, over-the-top de-regulation of the financial industry led to the Great Crash.

Second, the benefits of prosperity have gone largely to the well-to-do. Though most Americans didn't benefit from the growth that preceded the Great Crash, they've borne most of the costs of capitalism's "boom and bust" and of the "creative destruction" which drives capitalistic growth.

Third, much of the economy's dynamism comes from what has been labeled the new "knowledge economy". Though this produces much of our growth and opportunity, too few Americans are being educated to participate in that economy.

B. Free Market Imperfections and Regulation

Americans have always had a love affair with the free market as the source of prosperity. Never more than now when the belief has taken hold that if we just free the market of regulation's intrusive interference, the market will naturally bless us with wealth.

The facts tell a different story. From the early nineteenth century, America has had a mixed economy, in which government has been an essential actor, guiding and regulating the economy. As this mixed system continued into the early Seventies, the country prospered both through growth measured by GDP and by bringing many millions of Americans into relative prosperity. Wide disparities of income and wealth substantially narrowed. Most Americans were able to live, and feel that their children might well live, the American Dream. But, then, starting in the Seventies, that dramatically changed for most Americans. Today, despite decades of growth, most Americans are no more, or less, well-off and far more financially insecure than their parents and grandparents were in 1971.

One very substantial cause of the deterioration of the economic circumstances of most Americans is the long reign of free market ideology. That belief is that economy and society are best served if the market is unhampered. Markets should be maximally freed from regulatory restraints and governmental intrusions and as much of society as possible ought to be marketized. The less "mixed" the economy, the better.

Let's first look at a little history and then examine free market ideology.

1. The Triumph of Laissez Fare and Marketization

Public economic policy began early with "internal improvements" (roads, canals and the like), protective tariffs for infant industry, a national financial system created by Alexander Hamilton and the distribution of western lands. Public education soon followed in the mid-nineteenth century. When the nation abandoned Hamilton's (regulated) banking system in the 1830s, it suffered a series of severe depressions.

As America industrialized and the economy became more complex, the state took on a larger role. Beginning with the Interstate Commerce Act of 1887, America built a strong edifice of federal and state laws and agencies to regulate the new industrial economy where the market was thought incapable of self-control. These laws guarded against unsafe transportation, adulterated food and drugs, excessive concentration in industry, overpricing by firms with great market power and other unsafe, unethical and abusive practices the quest for gain unleashes in some of its pursuers.

The Great Depression led to the New Deal's reforms, designed to save capitalism from itself by taming its natural excesses with regulatory rules. The New Deal established rules of the road for the financial system, empowered labor unions as a counterweight to management, sought to tame inherent weaknesses in agricultural markets and assumed responsibility for macroeconomic management of the economy. Unlike socialism, popular in Europe, it was utterly capitalistic, the state protecting capitalism from failing again, always a danger unless government checks excessive risk-taking and dishonesty in the financial system.[37]

By the Seventies, free market ideology came to dominate thinking about regulation. Just as individualism was taking its extreme turn, economic thinking was seized by the "I, me, mine" of laissez faire, that each person is, and ought to be, free to do just what he wants. This new economic mainstream led social scientists, politicians and the public to embrace free market ideology. As once "there came a Pharaoh who knew Joseph not"[38], they forgot the lessons of the Depression, that markets are never even close to perfectly free and that

---

[37] Hyman Minsky's landmark *Stabilizing an Unstable Economy* (McGraw Hill 1986), explains why unregulated financial systems are naturally unstable.

[38] *Exodus* 1:8

without regulation of the right sorts in the right places, suboptimal results, mischief and needless calamity will occur.

2. The Ideology of the Free Market

Free market ideology, the third ideational cornerstone of contemporary America, now rules the day. The market is king. Here, there and everywhere, market forces have overcome counterweights restraining the market's inherent excesses. America, never tempted by Marxist allures, has always been devoted to enterprise, always a "capitalist" country. This radical ideology is different.

This "free market" ideology abjures government interference in the economy, measures the wisdom of policy solely by market-based analysis and puts more and more of the institutions and arrangements of society into the market where cash is king. This has ravaged people not at the top of the economic heap and corroded and coarsened how we think about and live our lives.

This ideology believes that, left alone, the market will reach the best possible outcome. This is because the choices made there are, as it were, an ever-exercised ballot of impersonal, rational choices by countless buyers and sellers. Markets naturally get to the best possible result — the "Pareto optimal" point (named for the economist Wilfredo Pareto). Pareto optimal points represent, in economic jargon, the "maximum possible utility". By contrast, governments can only sub-optimize, being creatures of imperfect human beings and subject to the distortions of political power.

Free market ideology is a close cousin to secular materialism and contemporary individualism. It is the outcome of a blend of utilitarian philosophy and free market economics with a large portion of Darwinian survival of the fittest thrown in.

The premise of Utilitarianism, created by Jeremy Bentham, is that what motivates people is to gain pleasure and avoid pain. From which it concludes that goodness is to maximize pleasure and minimize pain across the community. To find the "greater good" requires that "pleasures" and "pains" be quantified, which means to put everything in money terms. Because this only works for what is quantifiable and monetizable, utilitarian thought has difficulty making room for such "soft" things as values, beliefs and emotions.

In Bentham's day and for long after, there were no economic tools for calculating comparative utilities in any but the most simple cases. The dominant economic school of the last several decades has supplied, through computers and sophisticated math, the tools to enable complex calculations of utility and efficiency heretofore unavailable. Economists can now employ intricate equations and powerful computers to determine what really is utilitarian-ally optimal, dollar-wise. And so to decide how to organize the economy and calculate the best ways to attack the issues of the day.

This marriage of free market economics and utilitarianism birthed modern free market ideology. Since the Seventies, that ideology has dominated American thought about economics and public policy.

The result is something like the celebration of the selfish gene. There, the necessities of Nature are said to devalue any obstacle to the selfish climb to the top of the genetic heap. Here, the need to extract maximum value from the market casts aside ethical values and sees no worth in people who stand in the way of achieving the "best" result. As one Darwinist wrote, "natural selection is chronic competition untrammeled by moral rules. Heedless selfishness and wanton predation are traits likely to endure. If these thing are sins, then the roots of sin lie at the origin — not just of humankind but of life."[39] As in genetics, so in our "free" market.

The line is straight and short from this point of view to the contemporary definition of "success" as making the most money possible: to maximize profits and the return on capital above other people, the environment, ethics and anything else. What matters, what ought to be done, is what the free market says has the highest dollar

---

[39] Robert Wright, "Science and Original Sin", Time, October 28, 1996; quoted in Marilynne Robinson, *The Death of Adam*, "Darwinism" p. 52.

result which, by definition, is most efficient, and likewise by definition, the best outcome.

Like all successful ideologies, it has strong appeal. It is expert, preached by learned economists whose ideas are supported by sophisticated models worked out on high-powered computers. It is, at its core, easy to explain. It impersonally tames the messy complexities of human irrationality with a device of pure reason. It is comforting to learn that the market's Invisible Hand brings order to life's disarray. It offers the contentment of having the means to find how to make our society the best of all possible worlds.

It seems to be ethical because based on a major moral system, Utilitarianism. It comforts that it leads both to the most efficient economic outcomes and to outcomes which reach the most morally desirable result. It's a natural handmaiden of contemporary individualism, consoling to learn that acting just as one wants, selfishly and greedily fulfilling his desires, is to do his part to make society the best it can be. It's the perfect moral and economic doctrine for conservative politics.

However, upon analysis, matters are not so happy. The doctrine has serious ethical and economic problems.

Utilitarianism makes no room for values (though some of its adherents have unsuccessfully tried). If the overall utility of society would increase if all Jews were killed because the increased utility of many Jew-haters from being rid of despised neighbors outweighs the utility of the few victims' continuing to live, the doctrine lacks a counterweight of ethical values to condemn the murders. Similarly, because the utility to be maximized is that of the whole society, the doctrine has no room for individuals, if their needs and desires lose out in the calculus of what's best for the aggregate group. It's easy to see how problems arise when "maximizing social utility" is the benchmark for public policy. Should the economic models show that GDP is highest when 20% of the society lives in poverty and 5% are starving, free market dogma dictates that to be the best, most ethical, policy because it creates the greatest overall "happiness".

Since the market measures everything in money terms, it transforms most things into commodities. One's time, energy and actions are valued by how they contribute to what he does in the market. As family, love, generosity and goodness have no money value, they don't count in the calculus of how maximally to get on.

The second problem with free market Utilitarian thought is that it fails economically. The problem is that its nostrums and complex calculations assume that actual markets are ideal, perfectly free markets. Which they are not.

3. The Ideal Free Market

Free market ideology is based on the ideal of the perfectly free market. But, no actual market is close to that ideal. Markets are marvelous means which can, in the right circumstances, deliver efficiency, prosperity and economic freedom. But, left alone, as our ideology prescribes, they often wreak havoc and leave undone essential social tasks beyond their ken.

The ideal market is a beautiful mechanism. Adam Smith's *The Wealth of Nations* is the classic explanation of how the selfish efforts of the many will produce great boons for all:

> "Every individual... neither intends to promote the public interest, nor knows how much he is promoting it... he intends only his own security; and by directing that industry in such a manner as its produce may be of the greatest value, he intends only his own gain, and he is in this, as in many other cases, led by an invisible hand to promote an end which was no part of his intention."

Such a market produces bounty because it matches sellers of goods and services with buyers to pay for them. Prices are set naturally, by what "the market will bear", the equilibrium price determined by the aggregate willingness of a myriad of buyers and sellers to transact on particular terms: anonymous bundles of offerings and desires connected through the freedom of equilibrium pricing.

The Wealth of Nations has become American Gospel. Smith celebrated the free market not for its own sake but because he correctly believed it could bring great benefits. However, and this is where free market ideology goes astray, no market is close to ideally free and even free markets are unable to accomplish many things which a well-governed people want. Adam Smith understood this (of which more below). To our cost, our dominant ideology does not.[40]

4. Imperfections of Actual Markets

The "invisible hand" of a free market works because, blessed with perfect competition, no one has enough market power to distort it. It's free of the power of monopoly or oligopoly (market control by a few participants) by which prices, terms of sale and the nature and quality of products are not freely set, but reflect the desires of those who have market power. A free market has no, or very low, barriers to entry: a participant who accrues significant market power will then be challenged by newcomers pouncing on the opportunity he creates if he limits production or raises prices. It is obvious that very few, if any, markets have ever had anything like perfect competition: certainly not the concentrated markets of today.

In the ideal free market, all consumers have perfect information: everyone knows the facts necessary to make as informed a market choice as the other fellow. But, this condition is (almost) never met. Consumers usually don't know as much as producers and small buyers and sellers rarely know nearly as much as large ones (a problem exacerbated in concentrated markets). Moreover, information flows are often distorted by fraud or insider dealing.

---

[40] See Robert Kuttner, *Everything for Sale: The Virtues and Limits of Markets* (University of Chicago Press 1999), a fine analysis of the market's limitations.

Two other characteristics of the ideal free market are that sellers, buyers and money (capital) can readily move if they don't like what a market offers and that transaction costs are low. But, neither is rarely true. Take the example of distance: a grocery store twenty miles away may have lower prices, but it's too expensive in time and money to drive that far to shop there. Or, consider someone whose employer has reduced her pay: she cannot take a better paying job far away if moving is impossible or highly disruptive to her family.

A free market also does not have "externalities". Externalities are costs or benefits which the market price for a good or service does not reflect. The pollution caused by burning coal to generate electricity or the harms to health of smoking tobacco are examples of major social externalities which are not reflected in the price of power and cigarettes. Externalities can also be social goods which market prices do not capture, such as the benefits of clean water, good universal public education and vaccination programs.

The ideal of the free market also assumes that people behave in ways which, being human, they don't behave. Free market theory rests on assumptions that people are always rational and always seek to maximize their economic preferences.

The briefest glance at human nature demonstrates that these assumptions are not so. It hardly needs saying that people do not always behave rationally. Consider decisions about whether to buy this or that object or to buy a watch or instead keep the money in the bank: sometimes "rational", often not at all.

Moreover, how many of us really want to spend much of our time gathering and digesting all the information necessary to thrive in ever-evolving markets? How many of us want to be devoted to being profit-maximizing thinking machines? How many of us want to be at the mercy of free markets, perpetually afraid that market forces may ruin us in an instant?

Nor are people always deciding what to do solely, or often at all, on value-free economic grounds. They act on values which are headwinds to the gale of market forces. They choose to give money to charity, devote their time to good works, work in other than the highest paying job because they find more psychic satisfaction, etc.

Furthermore, people regularly support all manner of limitations on the application of market forces: laws which prohibit child labor and the sale of body parts; laws which limit pollution and require standards of safety and honesty, etc. They do not want every aspect of life to be decided in the marketplace. For instance, though they participate, they bemoan commercialization of Christmas.

Mancur Olson explains another imperfection, that markets become distorted as rigidities develop over time.[41] At their outset, institutions and group arrangements, being new, can take whatever shape seems most efficient. They're created to enter a race and win it. But, that flexibility naturally corrodes over time as people and institutions become invested in these structures. They develop habits and self-interest in the current ways and means. They build incentives into institutions to help them, and protections to insulate them, from losing the benefits and comforts they've come to enjoy.

As this occurs, the raison d'etre of structures and institutions slowly shifts from offense — being as effective as possible in a competitive market — to defense, protecting the advantages they've gained. "Let's do as well as we can, so long as we don't jeopardize what we have." Caution and fear replace innovation and adventure; dynamism becomes turgidity. If/when newcomers enter the arena (often from other countries), being as yet unburdened by the rigidities of time, they often leap-frog earlier movers.

Rigidities have, naturally, entered the American economy. Many important American businesses are large, slow-moving institutions now paying the price of resisting adaptations to changes in the

---

[41] Mancur Olson, *The Rise and Decline of Nations: Economic Growth, Stagflation, and Social Rigidities* (Yale University Press (1982).

marketplace.[42] Many American markets have become highly concentrated oligopolies, which naturally tend to reduce innovation, fix and/or increase prices and impose barriers to entry as the companies become large, sluggish bureaucracies.[43]

The American labor movement is another victim of the sclerosis of success. For years after the National Labor Relations Act of 1935 allowed unions to flourish, many were vibrant institutions, achieving needed reforms of employer-employee relationships. But, over time, they've often come to stand for entrenched privilege: too often now defenders of work rules and other barriers to workplace flexibility.

The free market is also distorted when government sponsors industries. One form is to provide large tax breaks and subsidies, such as those long granted to companies in oil and other energy industries. Another is the "military-industrial complex" of arms and other defense companies sustained by military spending kept very high by the complex's political power.

5. Deregulation in Contemporary America

Let's understand better deregulation in America. When it began in the Seventies, regulation of the rates of, and entry into, the power, transportation and telecommunication industries was ripe for reform. The regulatory rationale was that because these industries had "natural monopolies" in rail tracks, power lines and scarce broadcast spectrum, it was impossible to have competitive markets.

The deregulators had the vision that these industries could be opened to competition by unbundling combined services; isolating the natural monopoly to its part of those markets; requiring the owners of

---

[42] Thus, the Big Three American auto companies went from world leaders to clumsy behemoths threatened with extinction by foreign competitors. Finally, their existence threatened, they're now unlimbering their joints.

[43] It's not clear whether it's possible to use antitrust or other means as remedies or whether this concentration is made inevitable by economies of scale.

monopolist-inducing essential facilities such as power lines to deal on fair terms with competitors; and removing many restrictions on new firms' entering markets. For the most part, this successfully unleashed market forces: thus, the telecommunications boom after the breakup of the telephone monopoly.

There was a second sensible string to this deregulatory bow: to have regulators use the market to achieve regulatory goals. Rather than ordering regulated firms to do things in a particular prescribed way, tell them to achieve prescribed goals and free them to figure out how best to achieve them. Where this happened,[44] it has unleashed innovation and enhanced efficiency and freedom.

Deregulation took a sharp turn with the Presidency of Ronald Reagan. It became a major theme of the new conservative ascendancy to free the market from the intrusion of government regulation. This went far beyond dismantling the over-regulation just described to dismantling as much regulation as possible. The dominant political rhetoric became, and remains, harshly anti-government, as in Reagan's famous battle cry "Government is not the solution to our problems; government is the problem."

Lawmakers relaxed or repealed laws and regulations designed to protect consumers and markets from unwise, dishonest and unethical behavior. In the rush to shrink government, they rejected the notion that regulation is often necessary to keep people safe from dishonest, unhealthy and unsafe business practices and from the financial industry's attraction to extreme risk.

Deregulation was particularly prominent in the financial services industry. Beginning in the 1990s, the Clinton and George W. Bush Administrations, Congress and the pertinent regulatory agencies reduced substantially the limits on and requirements of financial firms. As markets became more complex and as new kinds of financial firms emerged (such as hedge funds), they were left unregulated in the name

---

[44] It hasn't happened nearly often enough.

of economic freedom. De-regulation was to unleash creativity to benefit everyone by making the economy wealthier. We now know that while creativity did make great fortunes on Wall Street, deregulated creativity engendered the reckless behavior which caused the Great Crash.[45]

6. The Economics of American Deregulation

Free market ideology promised that if we just let the market alone, all would be as good as good could be. One branch, the "rational expectations hypothesis" became the dominant school of economic thought. It held that finance needed little regulation because market participants will act with rational good sense to avoid crises, since avoiding crises is in their interest. One of the school's predictions was that something like the Great Crash could not occur in a billion years. Just our bad luck it happened so soon.

The deregulatory promise could never be kept since actual markets are imperfectly free and even ideal markets will not, by themselves, curb reckless and unethical behavior. Unlike free market ideologues, Adam Smith understood that regulation is sometimes necessary to protect the weak from the strong: "When the regulation, therefore, is in support of the workman, it is always just and equitable; but it is sometimes otherwise when in favour of the masters."[46] Abraham Lincoln put the point with his usual acuity: "We all declare for liberty; but in using the same word we do not all mean the same thing.... The shepherd drives the wolf from the sheep's throat, for which the sheep thanks the

---

[45] The largest financial firms demonstrated their power over the American government when, after Lehman Brothers collapsed in 2008, they refused to limit their pay for a time as the price of the massive cash bailout which they and the economy desperately needed. Rather let the world economy collapse than accept any brake on their gargantuan incomes. They got the cash anyway.

[46] http://economistsview.typepad.com/2006/09/the_many_faces_.html

shepherd as a liberator, while the wolf denounces him for the same act as the destroyer of liberty."[47]

Smith understood that unregulated markets are dangerous:
> "Such regulations [relating to banks' issuance of securities] may, no doubt, be considered as in some respects a violation of natural liberty. *But those exertions of the natural liberty of a few individuals, which might endanger the security of the whole society, are, and ought to be, restrained by the laws of all governments*; of the most free, as well as of the most despotical. The obligation of building party walls, in order to prevent the communication of fire, is a violation of natural liberty, exactly of the same kind with the regulations of the banking trade which are here proposed."[48]

Free market ideology has served America poorly. It fuels hatred of regulation, government and taxes. It caused the Great Crash and is a major factor driving immense economic inequality. It enables the wealthy to persuade the non-rich to despise government in favor of a market stacked against them. It's the ideational engine behind Ryan and Trump budgets to undo a century of policies protecting ordinary people from the depredations of untrammeled markets.

It has contributed to the erosion of integrity, compassion and trust as "non-market" values have little place in the profit-maximizing, efficiency-creating marketplace. Now, little eclipses the pursuit of wealth. Where we once prized businesses for acting to benefit community, workers, customers and the public interest, even if that dented profits, now the reigning ethos is that their one and only sacred duty is to maximize shareholder returns.

Yet, anti-regulatory rhetoric still rules the day. When markets fail, the reason, we are assured, is that government has any economic role at

---

[47] Address at a Sanitary Fair, Baltimore, April 18, 1864

[48] adamsmithlostlegacy.blogspot.com/2008/05/adam-smiths-advice-on-banking.html (emphasis supplied.)

all: all would be well except for too much regulation, too many taxes, too much interference in the market.

****

Free market ideology has not only changed public policy: it's why we're marketizing more and more aspects of our society.

We're putting a great deal up for sale. People pay someone else to stand in lines or buy a speedy pass through airport security. Parents pay children to do well at school. People pay to kill endangered animals. We can buy securities which bet on whether an insured human being will die sooner than the actuarial tables predict, giving us a rooting interest in his early death. We allow companies to buy naming rights for all manner of public facilities. Major League Baseball sold an insurance company the right to have its logo flash on the television screen when a runner slides safely into home while the announcer said, "Safe at home. Safe and secure. New York Life safe."

Michael Sandel sets forth many such examples in his important book, *What Money Can't Buy: The Moral Limits of Markets*.[49] Sandel demonstrates that what happens when such things are marketized is both unfair and corrupting. Unfair because it allows people with more resources to buy things which used not to be for sale and which people with limited means cannot afford. And, corrupting because it reduces something with meaning and value to nothing more than another cash commodity.

Mass marketization not only corrupts the institution or thing being corrupted. It corrupts society. It enthrones the notion that money trumps values, even in areas historically removed from the marketplace. It coarsens social discourse to be largely about self-advantage and dollars. It pushes considerations of values and morals out of the public square and public discourse. It dehumanizes people from fellow souls to market participants, transforming them from what

---

[49] Farrar, Straus and Giroux 2012.

Martin Buber famously called "Thous" to impersonal "Its". As Sandel observes, "The era of market triumphalism has coincided with a time when public discourse has been largely empty of moral and spiritual substance." (id. at p. 202).

C. Inequality: Economics and Ordinary Americans

America has become a class society. The well-off get richer and everyone else stagnates. Now, most growth in good times goes to the people at the top. Most of the costs when things go wrong are borne by everyone else. While the American Dream isn't dead for "everyone else", it's badly ailing. It long was the proverbial elephant in the room: the great fact no one would talk about it. Now we do.

1. The Costs of Capitalism

Consider how we bear capitalism's costs.

Capitalism naturally runs with dynamic friction. Stoked by innovation and new competitors, markets are always changing. Today's success must adapt to thrive, even survive. Yesterday's choices and opportunities are replaced by something very different: think of our information-technology fueled knowledge economy.

Joseph Schumpeter celebrated capitalism's "creative destruction": akin to biological natural selection by wiping out what's become weak and outmoded to make way for the new and better. This dynamism produces wealth and opportunity: better products and services, better jobs, higher pay, more job satisfaction. But, most of that "better" is available only if one is able to take advantage.

Capitalism is naturally cyclical. For decades after the Great Depression, economists and political leaders succeeded in ameliorating the harshness of the business cycle. Recessions were fewer, shorter and less intense. But, beginning in the early Eighties, as free market ideology triumphed, fierce recessions returned, culminating in the devastation inflicted by the Great Crash.

The costs of recessions and capitalistic change have largely been borne by people below the top, They generally live in economic fear, often only a few missed paychecks from financial disaster.

Creative destruction means that companies die and jobs exported to lower cost locales. When the economy doesn't do well, more jobs are lost and pay stagnates. While some lost jobs are in upper management, the bulk of down-sizing is borne by people down the corporate food chain. When people at the top lose jobs, they're usually well cushioned: savings and severance to weather the storm and education, connections and mobility to find something robust. The rest lack the new skills and cushions to thrive in the new world.

The need to succeed against competition creates never-ending pressure to restrain and reduce costs. The easiest costs to control are generally the number, pay and benefits of employees. As costs for such benefits as health care rise, employers pass more and more on to employees. Automation is good in many ways but it does eliminate jobs. As a company reduces its workforce, those still employed are stretched ever thinner, required to work harder. Though Americans already work many more hours than their Western counterparts, they now put in more hours for no more, often less, (inflation-adjusted) pay than not so long ago.

They also have much less job security. Many jobs have vanished or moved offshore where costs seem lower. That pension, if not wiped out, is insecure. The new jobs need new skills, which the factory worker doesn't have and has no reasonable way to get. He lacks the education to slip into a software, Internet, biotech or green energy firm. If he did, he'd probably have to uproot his family, if he can.

Dreadfully unlike the post-War years, the fortunes of many, many Americans are stagnating or declining. Their present is fair-to-poor, their future prospects frightening. They feel radical insecurity and fear worse for their children. The contemporary economy is one big force eroding the solidity of the ground beneath their feet.

2. The Emergence of a Class Society

Let's look at some data. Don't be numbed by all the numbers, for we need data to grasp the immensity of the problem. From 1973 until 2010, the American economy grew by 266%. That means that in 2010, after the onset of the Great Recession, America had, in inflation-adjusted terms, two and two-thirds times more income than thirty-seven years before. America has become much richer.[50]

During the post-World War II prosperity, incomes of people in the middle and bottom rose faster than average: hence, the decline in inequality. Had the gains since 1973 been broadly shared, real incomes of those not at the top would have risen approximately as much as the growth of the economy. But, the facts are otherwise. The lion's share of over forty years of immense growth have gone to the best-off among us. That's why the gap between the richest and everyone else has shot through the roof.

From World War II until the Seventies, the distribution of income and wealth among Americans narrowed. One measure is the share of total income earned by the top ten percent. Having risen in the Twenties to 45%, it quickly narrowed so that from the early Forties until the mid-Seventies, the top 10% earned 32-33% of income; the remaining 90% shared the balance. In the Sixties, the top 0.1% (one in one thousand) earned some 2% of national income.

Beginning in the Seventies, the gap began its long, persistent widening. We are now more than four decades into a great U-turn in which inequality has returned to the levels of the Twenties. Look at the distribution of income by quintiles, that is by the top 20%, the bottom 20% and the three sets of 20% in between. From 1947 through 1973, the growth in real family income was shared nearly evenly, except that the bottom 20% saw their income grow by 116% while the top 20%

---

[50] I always state income in "real" terms, that is, adjusted for inflation.

gained 84%. During the post-war boom, the middle three quintiles gained between 97 and 103%.[51]

Matters have changed greatly since. From 1979 through 2003, the lowest quintile gained 1% in real household income; the next two quintiles gained 7 and 9%; the quintile between 60 and 80% gained 20% and the top quintile gained 49%. The top ten percent, who had earned 32-33% in the Sixties took home 38% of national income in 1987 and 45% in 2007 (the pre-Depression level).

Slice the data further and we see that the vast proportion of gains for the top 20% have accrued to the few at the very top of our ever steeper economic pyramid. In 1976, the richest 1% of Americans took home 9% of total national pay. By 2010, that number had soared to 24%. From 1980 to 2005, more than four-fifths of the total increase in American incomes went to the richest 1 percent.

As well as the top 1% have done, the data show that even these gains have gone disproportionately to the very wealthiest among them. In the Sixties, the wealthiest 0.1% took home one in every fifty dollars. Now, this group — one in one thousand of us — takes approximately one of every eight dollars earned in America.[52]

Let this sink in. Since the election of Ronald Reagan, over 80% of all our enormous growth went to the least needy 1%. That left less than twenty cents of growth for the 99%. 12% of all income has enriched the richest 0.1%: that is, the richest person of each one thousand

---

[51] Much data here is taken from the presentation made by Barry Bluestone (noted economist and founding dean of Northeastern University's school of public policy and urban affairs) on Oct. 5, 2011 at the university's Open Classroom (available at the Open Classroom website). Some data is found in Nicholas Kristoff, "America's Primal Scream", *New York Times*, Oct. 15, 2011.

[52] In the Clinton boom (1995-2000), income of the top 10% increased 40.5%, the top 5% by 50.5%; and 75.6%. the top 0.1%: 117.8%. The incomes of the richest .001% (one in every ten thousand) rose 156.0%(!).

Americans. So much for the conservative nostrum, to justify policies which favor the rich, that "a rising tide lifts all boats".

The data on wealth is, unsurprisingly, even more skewed. In 2004, the top 1% owned 42.2% of the financial assets owned by American individuals. The next 9% owned 38.7% of the financial wealth. The other 90% owned 19.1%. The 400 wealthiest Americans own more wealth than the bottom 150 million Americans. As one business publication put it, "It's official: America is now a banana republic".[53]

There are many possible explanations for this U-turn to mega-inequality, some matters of policy and some not. The Bush tax cuts much reduced taxes on the rich. De-regulation unrestrained markets and shifted national wealth to the finance industry. Other government policies contributed: free trade without retraining for displaced workers; immense defense spending at the expense of social needs, etc. The knowledge economy puts a premium on education just as educational quality has fallen for much of the country. Pay for CEOs and other senior officers has soared in proportion to the pay of untitled workers. High tech companies have created vast wealth for founders and senior managers.

Whatever the reasons, the facts are plain and socially unhealthy. As before the Depression, most of the money, opportunity and fruits of American bounty go to a wealthy elite.

For the rest of the country, the American Dream is vanishing. That elephant is standing on the table. Politicians still mouth the rhetoric of the Dream and most people still hope for it. But, for millions, it's become too distant, too unlikely, too hard to visualize happening to oneself and her children. The wide gulf between America's promise and their reality makes them understandably angry, bitter, cynical and depressed. And prone to demagoguery.

---

[53] Henry Blodget, "It's Official America Is Now A Banana Republic," *The Business Insider*, Nov. 7, 2010. www.businessinsider.com

One reason the Dream has not up and died is that Americans are bedazzled by the success and wealth of the very rich. This bedazzlement is not healthy. As Adam Smith explained,

> "The disposition to admire, and almost to worship, the rich and the powerful and to despise or at least to neglect persons of poor and mean conditions...is the great and most universal cause of the corruption of our moral sentiments."[54]

3. The Consequences of Large Inequalities

Today's large inequalities breed tomorrows'. Money gives power. The more unequal the distribution of wealth and income the more unequal the range of opportunities and distribution of education, health care and other services. As Adam Smith said in the *The Wealth of Nations,* excessive inequality erodes the social fabric:

> "What improves the circumstances of the greater part can never be regarded as an inconvenience to the whole. No society can surely be flourishing and happy, of which the far greater part of the members are poor and miserable."

Thomas Piketty's magnum opus *Capital in the Twenty-First Century* is one of the most widely read and influential books on economics of the last several decades.[55] Piketty shows that it is inherent in the structure of capitalism for returns on capital to exceed the rate of economic growth. The consequence is that, without the intervention of strong countervailing public policies, our economy will naturally produce ever more extreme inequalities, as capital's earnings (substantially) out-pace the rate of growth and the growth of the income accruing to labor.

Piketty's lesson is that unless government acts vigorously to reduce inequalities, the class divide, the diminishment of the American middle

---

[54] Adam Smith, *The Theory of Moral Sentiments*, ch. III.

[55] Thomas Piketty, *Capital in the Twenty-First Century* (trans. by Arthur Goldhammer) (Belknap Press of Harvard University Press 2014)

class, will only increase. We will more and more resemble the highly unequal, class-based societies of most of world history. It's already begun that the few ever-richer American "haves" economically lord it over the great mass of everyone else. This is a terrible outcome. We begin by considering the social costs of our current levels of inequality on all of us, rich and not.

The costs of wide social inequalities are enormous, not just to the less advantaged but to the wealthy. In *The Spirit Level* Richard Wilkinson and Kate Pickett report that study after study reach the same conclusion about well-off societies.[56] Those with lower levels of inequality are healthier, have better social relations and greater human capital than wealthy societies with high inequality. Indeed, the best-off in highly unequal societies do less well on multiple measures of health and welfare than the best-off in more equal societies, even when those societies are less rich.

Of the twenty-three richest market economies, the United States is the second most unequal. Measured by calculating the income of each fifth of the population, the top 20% of Americans earn 8.5 times the bottom 20%. The ratios in some other countries are 3.4 for Japan, 4.8 for Austria and (on the high side) 6.1 for Ireland.[57]

Thus, what counts for well-being is not the extent of national wealth (once a decent level is reached), but the extent of inequality. Pause for a moment to consider that on measure after measure, America is less healthy and has lower well-being than much less rich countries such as Austria, Japan, Ireland, Spain, etc. whose people have lower (often much lower) income per person.

These studies have measured a wide array of indicia of social and personal health: all correlate well-being with relatively low income inequality. On each indicia, America scores poorly compared with

---

[56] Bloomsbury Press, 2010. In England, a "spirit level" is a carpenter's level.

[57] As we saw a few pages ago, the disparities would be much, much greater if the focus were on the top 1%'s share of the pie.

other market economies. Its scores on such measures of health as infant mortality, drug and alcohol abuse, life expectancy, mental illness and obesity are distressing. So are its rankings on such measures of human capital as child well-being, rates of high school dropouts, measures of math and literacy skills, teenage births and levels of social mobility. As are American scores on indicia of social relations: violence and homicide, imprisonment, conflicts among children, social skills and trust (a must for society to function well).

Americans pride ourselves on our mobility, on careers open to talents, on the ability of anyone to rise with hard work and pluck. But, it's no longer true. The level of intergenerational mobility in America is one-third that of Denmark, well less than half in Canada, Finland and Norway and two-thirds of Germany's and Sweden's.[58]

High inequality countries have weaker social affiliations, their children carry more stress beginning in the womb, they (rich and poor) feel more superiority and inferiority and so more status insecurity, their people worry more about how they are seen and judged. They are more susceptible to having low self-esteem.

From World War II into the early Seventies, America was less unequal, healthier and more contented than now. Wilkinson and Pickett demonstrate that this is no coincidence but cause and effect.

The political costs of our gushing levels of inequality are also immense. Begin with this: As discussed below (Chapters Eight and Eleven), it takes a great deal of money to be elected to federal and major state and local offices. So that, the more unequal we are, the more power is taken by people with the money to write large checks to office holders, office seekers and arch-conservative causes. The result is that the rich can, and do, bend elections and public policy in directions that preserve their privileges and beat back efforts to adopt policies that would reduce inequalities.[59]

---

[58] See also Barry Bluestone, slides from October 5, 2011, above.

[59] Some of the wealthy do contribute to progressive candidates and causes.

Great inequality strikes at the heart of our constitutional system. Ganesh Sitaraman has shown in his *The Crisis of the Middle-Class Constitution* that what made our Constitution possible, and the foundation on which it rests, is the then-historically unprecedented level of equality in America at the time of our Founding.[60]

Until the American Founding, thinkers about government from Aristotle on had assumed that constitutions had to be designed to manage class conflict. The central goal of principled government was to seek to assure that the inevitable clashes between rich and poor did not erupt into class warfare that would destroy the republic. Which is what happened to the Roman republic.

Late eighteenth century America offered the opportunity to devise a different, much better form of government because it was by far the most equal developed society in recorded history. This allowed the Founders to design a system of government in which there was no need to assume classes and their inevitable conflict.

Rather, they could base the Constitution on what Madison famously called "factions".[61] Factions are shifting interest groups in which, where society is not based on class divisions, in which (1) no interest group is dominant and (2) most people belong to several "factions". In these circumstances, those of America of the Founding, factions form ever-changing coalitions to compromise and reach agreements to get the business of the country done. As no one "faction" dominates (as does an upper class in a society with large inequalities), coalitions of factions can form, un-form and change depending on the issues and needs of the moment. This relative level of equality defangs the prospect of class conflict, so that a system based on the ability to make compromises is possible.

Of course, America then had plenty of inequality, as societies always will. But, the range and extent of that inequality was (slavery aside)

---

[60] *The Crisis of the Middle-Class Constitution* (Alfred A. Knopf 2017).

[61] Most directly in *The Federalist Papers* #10.

limited so that the Founders could devise a Constitution resting on the prerequisite of a strong middle class. Unlike the Founders' historical examples of "republics" (classical Athens, the Roman Republic and contemporary England), America could for the first time in history adopt a "middle class" Constitution.

Now that rising inequality is eroding the American middle class, our Constitution cannot provide the free, open, what we call "democratic", government promised by our Founding. As Piketty shows of rising inequality, the problem is self-perpetuating. We see in Chapter 11 below that the more inequality, the more power to the powerful, the less government benefits average citizens, the more inequality. And so, on and on it goes.[62]

4. The Mostly Black and Rural Underclass

There are huge swathes of deep poverty in the richest country in history. America has an immense underclass of, in Adam Smith's phrase, the "poor and miserable". Many live in mostly black urban ghettoes. Many others live in rural pockets of poverty such as Appalachia which progress has passed by.[63]

It hardly needs saying that this is a disaster for those Americans. In a land of plenty, they cannot live decently. Their housing is poor, their food innutritious and the social services they receive generally well below par: education, infrastructure and health care in the poorest neighborhoods are most often terrible. They live in failed places: in locales like Detroit, in failed cities.

---

[62] The turn to class division is probably one reason the Republican Party has become more extreme and deeply averse to compromise. As explained by political savants Thomas Mann and Norman Ornstein (Ornstein is a Republican), our system cannot function if one party is ideological and extremist. Thomas Mann and Norman Ornstein, *It's Even Worse Than It Looks* (Basic Books 2012).

[63] In the Sixties, one American in nine still lived in poverty. Since 1980, poverty has risen to between 13 and 15% so that in our rich nation, in which billionaires bloom like azaleas in April, one American in seven lives in poverty.

Worse than the economic deprivation, the poor live in a culture which perpetuates their poverty. The criminal justice system is the most pervasive social institution because their world is ridden with crime, drug addiction and violence. The rule of law is little respected. Hopelessness and despair are common. The quality of education is low and the benefits of learning as a way up and out, even were education better, are not widely appreciated.

People see no way to get to the ladder of upward mobility climbed by poor Americans in times past. They live in poverty. Their parents lived in poverty. Their children are highly likely to live in poverty. They are engulfed in a bleak miasma of perpetual privation. So far as they can tell, should the thought occur, there is no way out.

The cost of our permanent underclass, in terms of crime, drugs and social services, is great. America jails far more of its people than other advanced countries, and the costs of the criminal justice apparatus are immense.

The culture of poverty nourishes racism. The black underclass is increasingly divorced from the rest of the country (except when we see its athletes and performers). When we see the ugliness of ghetto life, the images do not, in many people, breed tolerance and understanding.

Poorly educated and trapped in the culture of poverty, forty million Americans, citizens, people who could be adding to the store of national wealth if they had good education and gainful employment, are largely unproductive. All these people prevented or severely handicapped from making what they can of themselves could be contributing to our stock of innovation and constructive work. This is a loss not only for them but for the country.

There's a great moral and morale cost to knowing that in our land of plenty, children are hungry and homeless and millions live in wretchedness. How often we blame them: if only they weren't shiftless and shared our values, they'd do fine. But, one senses that not all that many of us really believe that's the heart of the matter, that deep-down most of us know this is our problem too. It breeds the nagging, subconscious worry: is this yet another symptom something is quite wrong in America?

D. Advancement in the Contemporary Economy

1. The Globalized Knowledge Economy

As the economy boomed during and after World War II, America's working men prospered.[64] Thanks to strong unions and strong demand for skilled labor, the pay of factory workers, and so their standard of living, rose smartly. At the same time, there were many new "white collar" jobs, which needed the skills and developed intelligence of a good education.

Just then, American education blossomed and opened to merit. Millions of Americans could now get a good education and use it to climb the economic ladder. The sons and daughters and grandchildren of impoverished immigrants and indigent tenant farmers could achieve beyond their forebears' wildest dreams. The American middle class exploded in size, opportunity and success.

Today, that gate to opportunity has been closing if your family hasn't already made it. We're developing an aristocracy of the already well-off and well-educated, whose children get most of the best opportunities. Two reasons are the shift from an industrial to the "knowledge economy" and our problems of education.

Until recently, rich country economies were "industrial": dominated by the industries and processes of production begun in England at the outset of the Industrial Revolution. Since the Eighties, that has changed. The dynamism of today's American economy now comes from the production, use and transmission of information.

The knowledge economy is results from, and is made possible by, the interplay of explosions in telecommunications and computing power. For decades, "Moore's Law", named for one of Intel's founders, has

---

[64] Except for during the war's labor shortages, they were then mostly men.

held that the amount of computing power that can be put on an integrated circuit doubles every eighteen months. The availability of telecommunication band-width for transmitting information has grown even faster. The personal computer; open, really free, telecommunications capacity; and the Internet have changed the way the world works. As a result, much of the new value of economic activity comes from the creation, manipulation, storage and transmission of the information these new technologies make possible (including information from explosions in knowledge about biology and energy fueling biotech and green energy).

The information revolution has enabled the globalization of much work. A great many jobs can be done anywhere the best people can be found at the lowest salary: all that's needed is a connection to the Internet. People can collaborate who live in different continents. If you can't work well in the knowledge economy, your job, or the job you wanted, will be taken by someone in Bangalore or Lagos.[65]

The knowledge economy is the present and the future; and America has led the way. Most of the most innovative firms have been hatched in America and the most profitable markets are dominated by American companies. Many Americans have been greatly enriched, many others have found good, well-paying jobs, as entrepreneurs, employees and investors in the knowledge economy. This new economy is the fuel of much growth and prosperity.

That's splendid for those Americans able to participate. But, many of us are ill-equipped to join in.

2. Education

The globalized knowledge economy puts the highest premium ever on education. Growth comes from new products and services and better ways of doing business. Innovation is crucial to prosperity. Many economists believe sustained innovation is essential for average income to grow.

---

[65] Especially when it can be well done there more cheaply.

The connection between education and innovation is strong, for two reasons: acquiring knowledge and learning how to think and communicate. Science and technology have become so complex that a practitioner often needs deep learning and a strong background in math and science to succeed. Likewise, innovators need to have minds trained to think logically and creatively, to know how to question what others say, to be mentally flexible and open-minded and to communicate well in writing and with spoken speech. Few people can gain these without a good education.

Unfortunately, the quality of American education has fallen badly just as the information age has emerged. Statistics measuring educational performance across the world show a shocking decline in the ratings of our schools.

For many/most Americans, education was better in the postwar industrial economy when education mattered, but less than today. Now, when a good education is crucial to get into, and do well in, the knowledge economy, the overall quality of education has declined.

The data on American educational performance are averages, and the averages disguise great discrepancies. Education levels are said to remain quite high in the neighborhoods of the highly educated, already quite successful upper middle class. By contrast, schools in poor neighborhoods are usually atrocious, and schools in the not-upper-middle-class neighborhoods are generally mediocre. That's one reason economic inequality has widened substantially.

Education at the best American universities remains the envy of the world, and the best suburban and private pre-college schools are much admired. Yet, even in the gilded suburbs and the major universities, there are deep concerns about educational quality.

Americans in all kinds of schools take less math and science than peers elsewhere. There is a tendency to expect students to memorize facts, rather than to learn how to think and write. Even in the best high schools, students tend to be assigned poster and audio-visual projects rather than papers whose preparation would teach them how to analyze and express complex thoughts for themselves. They are taught much less about their country's history and culture than their parents and grandparents.

Standards have fallen. Even in the most elite colleges, professors reportedly expect less of students than in the past. Not long ago, an educated person was expected to have some understanding of the wellsprings of her culture and the basic forces animating human life and the life in his society. Not now.

Despite the emphasis on memorization, students of recent years know much less than their parents. The level of knowledge of the basic facts of American history is appalling. Even successful students with good grades from good schools are often abysmally ignorant of the chronology of America's past or of the key issues, forces and people responsible for having shaped the past, and so the present. They frequently know little about how the nation's institutions work. Even many graduates of the best universities know very little of the great literature, art, music and thought of the western world. Matters are a good deal worse in average and sub-par American schools.

The anecdotal information sadly makes the data look as if it understates just how bad American education has become. Educators, employers and other observers say, over and over, that today's students don't know how to amass facts and principles to make a convincing argument; don't think rigorously; can't write clearly; have sub-standard vocabularies; and are abysmally ignorant of basic facts of history and geography.[66] They can't reason and can't write up to the level of good employees whose jobs call for the use of the mind or to the level of good citizens able to formulate and understand positions on issues of the day. This is said to be true even for some graduates from the most admired universities.

---

[66] See, *e.g.*, a representative of an earlier generation, Donald Trump. When I first wrote, it was unimaginable we would elect someone so (cheerfully) uninformed.

Too many students and graduates are said happily to wallow in their ignorance. One student disputed a poor grade on a research paper which cited no authorities, by informing her professor that she knew better than he that a research paper simply meant she should tell how she felt about the matter. If only students like her were rare. There's a strong strain in today's youth, coming from extreme individualism, that one is entitled to think what she wants, without having to become aware of pertinent, sometimes inconvenient, facts or to consider other opinions. It is cool to be anti-intellectual.

It's scary to think that these are the people to take America into the future, to spur our economic competitiveness and growth and to be the good citizens our democracy needs.

3. The Class Divide in Education

As education has come to matter more than ever, access to the best education has become narrowly constricted by class. This is a major source of our growing economic inequality.

Before World War II, the elite universities were largely attended by the children of the economic elite. They were fine schools but not nearly as good as they soon became, nor nearly so important. The state universities were still relatively modest in size. After the war, "Ivy League" schools both became world-class and opened up to the children of the unprivileged (like me). State universities expanded, many to join the ranks of the best. The timing was perfect, just when the booming economy needed many well educated graduates.

Postwar America became a meritocracy. Prosperity enriched many who had been poor or near-poor. They moved to good neighborhoods and fine new suburbs. Their children went to good local schools and the most accomplished of them attended the best colleges. The best and the brightest got plum jobs in the burgeoning economy. They lived in the best neighborhoods, assured that those neighborhoods had the best schools.

There's an underlying conflict of principle between elite education and democratic belief that opportunity should be equal for all. We've smoothed over the conflict believing that elite education is open to all, that the best and the brightest can get into any of these schools if they apply themselves. It was reasonably true during my time in the Sixties. It is much less true today. As schools not in the best neighborhoods have slipped in quality, it has become harder to get into those colleges if you're not from one of those privileged neighborhoods with the finest schools.

The Ivy colleges have become far more ethnically, but not so economically, diverse. In one professor's words:

> "Elite schools pride themselves on their diversity, but that diversity is almost entirely a matter of ethnicity and race. With respect to class, these schools are largely — indeed increasingly — homogeneous. Visit any elite campus in our great nation and you can thrill to the heartwarming spectacle of the children of white businesspeople and professionals studying and playing alongside the children of black, Asian, and Latino businesspeople and professionals."[67]

Their experience of college is different than at less prestigious schools. They are academically coddled. Everyone gets decent grades and as many extensions of time to complete assignments as he wants. Life in the workplace is not like that. Nor is life in other colleges where many students work long hours because they need the money. William Deresiewicz cites the woman working her way through Cleveland State as a waitress who was given a "D" for turning a paper in an hour late because she had just got off her shift as a waitress. This is very unlikely to happen at Yale or Duke.

The best schools are turning out a new class of aristocrats. Many of their graduates come to believe that they are superior to the hoi polloi who haven't had their privilege. Like gentry from time immemorial,

---

[67] William Deresiewicz, "The Disadvantages of an Elite Education," *American Scholar*, Summer 2008.

they think themselves a better sort: smarter, more qualified for the best jobs, more suited to lead the country, entitled to the benefits which their education will facilitate because they have gone to Harvard, Berkeley or Princeton. Walled off in their fine neighborhoods and behind ivied walls, they learn how to talk to and empathize with each other but not so well to people less fortunate.

This makes a self-perpetuating, self-entitled elite, an aristocracy of education and level of employment. It is un-conducive to healthy democracy. Ironically, their arrogance and isolation from the rest of America makes them ill-suited for political leadership.

****

The Great Recession sparked fears that America is in decline. As our economy tumbled, China, India and others continued to rise. Of course, other nations can prosper without America's becoming poor, as we thrived after Europe and Japan emerged from the ashes of world war. The problem is the sense we've lost our way. Though the economy has rebounded, that feeling remains.

There have been times of national worry before. One was after the Soviet Union launched Sputnik and seemed to have gained the edge in the Cold War. Another was in the Eighties when Japan seemed poised to become the world's dominant economy (just before it fell into a long recession). Many thoughtful Americans worry that this time is different, that we've been living too long off the accumulated capital of past success.

There are thoughtful observers who are optimistic about the prospects of the American economy. One hopes they are right: the economy is the fuel of the American Dream. What is also required is somehow, someway to move the nation away from being a banana republic of deep inequality. To move to the way we were until the Seventies, where the divide between rich and poor had diminished and where most of us could reasonably aspire to climb the ladder of success with intelligence, skill, pluck and hard work.

CHAPTER EIGHT: LONELY LIFE IN MODERN SOCIETY

"All the lonely people, where do they all come from?
All the lonely people, where do they all belong?"
John Lennon and Paul McCartney, "Eleanor Rigby" © 1966

A. Contemporary America

1. A Mass Society

Alexis de Tocqueville was much taken with the America he found in the 1830s. At its heart were a slew of "public associations" — groups of all kinds, interests and characters. Most people in that land of joiners belonged to more than one.

Most non-slaves worked for themselves on farms, as artisans, in small shops. Except for a few factories of the nascent Industrial Revolution, most non-slave people who had a boss worked in small enterprises. Public associations gave each (free) American opportunity to chart his life's course outside of work, to get out and about and participate in community and politics.

He could not, of course, control the weather and harvest, the economy and disease. But, other than such vicissitudes, he was free. He felt, and was, autonomous. He was what was later called "inner directed", living by his own internal compass which pointed both to his individual and his social selves. He had the freedom the Founders envisioned to be a good citizen of his republic.

Most of the 13 million Americans lived on farms, in rural communities and small towns. They learned what they knew about state and national politics and the outside world from the many newspapers, to which they were passionately devoted, and itinerant merchants. They had strong opinions about the issues of the day.

Much has changed since the 1830s. Industrialization, population growth and the winds of modernity have made America far different from the society Tocqueville admired. Now, we more than 320 million Americans mostly live in (often vast) cities or their suburbs. Our lives center on very large organizations with which and for whom we work, with which we deal as consumers, which deliver our entertainment, which govern us. Though modern transportation and communication have brought us closer together, we usually know our communities much less well than in Tocqueville's day.

Driven by technology, America has morphed from that "civil society" into a "mass society". Better transportation and communication have shrunk the world. The Industrial Revolution's mass production, and modern salesmanship created the consumer society. Mass production and bigness have homogenized differences. The scale of size permitted, often required, by modern technology birthed and nurtured the development of very large bureaucratic organizations. So that as we moderns, like Gulliver in the land of the Brobdingnagians, are overwhelmed by vast, impersonal structures and forces, we've lost our Tocquevillian autonomy.

2. Dominated by Large, Impersonal Bureaucracies

Consider America on the eve of the Civil War. The country had grown to 27 million free residents (plus 4 million slaves). Most of them still lived on farms, in small towns and small cities, usually working for themselves or for small organizations. Though the North was beginning to industrialize, most businesses were small and there were few large factories. Outside the largest cotton and tobacco plantations in the South, most farms were family farms. Only nine cities had as many as 100,000 inhabitants; New York was much the largest with 800,000. Governments were small. The standing military was small. Though the country was changing rapidly, its institutions were still human-sized.

Jump forward to 1940. The population had quintupled to 132 million, much from the great wave of immigration of 1880 to 1920. Five cities had more than one million people: New York had over seven million. Half of the country lived in urban areas (defined as anything as large as a town of 2,500); the rest lived on farms or in small rural communities. A great part of the economy was not yet under the the dominion of the many large companies, factories and unions. Government had grown; but, even after the reforms of the two Roosevelts and Woodrow Wilson, it remained modest in size.

In both eras, while people were mobile, few moved far from home. Thus, in 1940, most people still were regularly connected mostly to people they'd known all their lives.

America in 2017 is quite much larger, over 320 million people. It's much more urban (home to three-quarters of us). In 1940 most urban Americans lived in cities; now most live in the suburbs. We drive our cars everywhere, often with long commutes. It's common to work either for large corporations or government or for employers which depend on the business of these.

Markets are generally huge and global. A hiccup in China or Germany, a strategic mistake by the expensive suits in corporate headquarters can have immense consequences for one's employer's health — and her level of pay and job security. She has little or no acquaintance with people whose decisions shape her work life.

Everywhere she turns, she is enmeshed in, or much affected by, institutions and structures of superhuman scale: companies, her megachurch, national groups, government. Unless she rises to a position of leadership in one of these institutions, she's but one of many seemingly interchangeable human parts in a vast machine. She has no connection with most people she sees in public.

These huge bureaucracies are uncomfortable homes for homo sapiens. Their size requires complex structures and rules. Each organization has its own set of expected and unwanted behaviors which are difficult to master. Like medieval theologians proficient in the intricacies of scholastic philosophy, it much helps the modern denizen of bureaucracy to master his company's abstruse system so that she can advance up the organization. But, she must learn it all anew when she joins, or has to deal with, a different organization.

Decisions are made impersonally on grounds of efficiency, not human needs. Employees are "assets" (or, worse, when layoffs are coming, liabilities). The human relations department's job is less to humanize relations between employees and management than to enforce management's will. Bureaucratic structures value people as instruments to get the work done: other than to be sure they're motivated, their humanity is frequently beside the point.

Bureaucracies are not nimble or efficient. They move slowly and inconsistently, with the plodding, powerful inertia of great mass. There is too much going on, too many different interests within the giant structure, too many forces pulling in different directions keeping the giant engine from striving together in a desired direction. More likely, one set of shoulders pushes here, another pushes there and a third pushes against the first. It should not surprise that outcomes are often quite different from those for which action was planned.

These baffling, inefficient, demanding, dominant structures live and die in markets. The market's natural anonymity and impersonality reinforce the dehumanized experience of our work and much of our lives. At least one's giant employer knows who you are. When she steps outside her company, she is likely to be utterly unknown.

The market can take her job, even if she is performing well. It can tell her she must do some new kind of work, whether she likes it or not, or that her job has moved a thousand miles away. When the goods she buys are shoddy or unsafe, she can rarely get redress from the companies which produced and sold them. When the economy collapses because a bunch of strangers took wild risks, she suffers the consequences. Since she isn't wealthy, political action is only effective if she joins with millions of others. Naturally, she feels disempowered, far from the free, self-reliant citizen she was raised to expect, as an American, to be.

3. Contemporary Mass American Culture

In the civil society of Tocqueville's day, there were no authoritative, dominant institutions, no oligopoly of views. "Common" people could make themselves heard. But not in a mass society like ours where mass media control the public expression of opinion. For us, only the few with access to the media can have any kind of public voice.

Today, we mostly seek entertainment passively, watching sports more than doing; watching television and movies more than reading and discussion. Our role is to decide to watch, to become in the marketeers' terms "eyeballs" to whom they can sell goods and services. We share the same passion for the local sports team as our neighbors, but our common fandom is often all that connects us.

We watch a very great deal: on average four hours of television a day. This leaves little time after work, chores and parenting for much else — and too little for good parenting. Being christened a nation of "couch potatoes" is not a compliment.

The media we watch are highly concentrated. Television is dominated by four networks. Thanks to cable and to the Internet, though the array of choices is immense, the most watched shows and events are what those four networks choose to show.[68] One of them, Fox, is dedicated to advancing the causes and views of the hard right-wing. The quality of the entertainment they offer rarely raises the level of culture, enlightenment or discourse.

There are plenty of useful and entertaining things to do besides passively watch television four hours a day. But, we humans are creatures of habit, accustomed to following cultural paths of least resistance. We crave connection. So, most of us take the default option by tuning in like most everyone else, able to share the conversation with friends and in the office over lunch and coffee.

---

[68] Popular music is the exception to concentration, having fragmented into many varieties with little crossover among them. No present artist is remotely as popular as were Sinatra, Elvis or the Beatles.

Tocqueville's America had all those associations to knit people together. They were the connecting tissue of a society of free autonomous beings. Such connecting groups are much less important today. We mostly interact with mass culture passively, alone or in small company. Facebook and other social media to the contrary notwithstanding (connecting while alone at the computer), the social networks which once linked us have been enfeebled. We've largely lost the pleasures and comforts of intricate webs of social association.

Michael Sandel has observed:

> "Democracy does not require perfect equality, but it does require that citizens share in a common life. What matters is that people of different backgrounds and social positions encounter one another, and bump up against one another, in the course of everyday life. For this is how we learn to negotiate and abide our differences, and how we come to care for the common good."[69]

There is little of this in today's America.

Mass society is like a hub: each person her own spoke, not much differentiated from the other spokes nor connected to them. As if she's a lonely atom orbiting a distant sun through the void of space.

B. Mass Culture and Politics in Modern America

1. The Experience of Modern Government

Modern American government is a set of vast bureaucracies even more rule-bound, inflexible and maddening than the largest corporation. Though active government is unavoidable in mass society, its inevitable bureaucratic mass saps Lincoln's notion that government be "of the people, by the people and for the people".

---

[69] *What Money Can't Buy, ibid.*, p. 203

"Of the people" presumes that the electorate has ultimate authority over government action. Which it manifestly does not.

"For the people" means that government's purpose is to benefit the public. But, we see too little that serves the public interest and too much that advances personal agendas and "special interests".

"By the people" means that people have a role in their government. But, as government has become so big and so remote, individuals' roles rarely go beyond voting (not enough do) and paying taxes.

Though large organizations are essential to deal with the size and complexities of modern life, they endanger liberty. Listen to Tocqueville worry about the "compromise between administrative despotism and the sovereignty of the people":

> "The nature of despotic power in democratic ages is not to be fierce or cruel, but minute and meddling. Despotism of this kind, though it does not trample on humanity, is directly opposed to the genius of commerce and the pursuits of industry. "The will of man is not shattered, but softened, bent, and guided: men are seldom forced by it to act, but they are constantly restrained from acting: such a power does not destroy, but it prevents existence; it does not tyrannize, but it compresses, enervates, extinguishes, and stupefies a people, till each nation is reduced to be nothing better than a flock of timid and industrious animals, of which the government is the shepherd."[70]

Many Americans have come to despise their government's size, bureaucracy and cost. Though one reason is the Reaganesque dogma that government can't help, that's not the all of it. Government seems remote — until one encounters an agency: then often to find ineffective, impersonal and intrusive officials.

---

[70] *Democracy in America*, vol. 2, pp. 140, 319

We Americans are angry because government has become spectacularly ineffective. We've come — and the intensity is new — to widely distrust and disrespect our public officials. We need big solutions to big problems, but little gets done. There is much meanness, venality, hatred and bombast, but little statesmanship. When we see so much parochialism, pork and greed, passionately delivered hokum and policies to benefit the wealthy and powerful at the expense of everyone else, we feel disgust, contempt and cynicism. We reasonably conclude that self-interested elites with little interest in, or sympathy with, us run government.

2. Mass Politics in Television America

As television's dominance has transformed the public square, our mass culture has become inhospitable to democracy.[71]

Television is a "hot" medium, appealing to emotions and not naturally igniting thought. It thrives on controversy and the extreme and on the drama of combat and harsh rhetoric.

Since American politics became a television game, plays on emotion (always part of politics) have drowned out appeals to thinking. Sound bites and ads of thirty or less (ill-suited to, and not used for, dialogue) replace what reasoned discourse we once had. Political messages tend to appeal to fear, because it's the strongest emotion.

Every political event is immediately "spun" by the "spinmeisters". Candidates schedule events and statements solely to get the right sound bite. Ads are crafted like commercials to buy cars and drugs to overcome erectile dysfunction. Their purpose is to sell by emotionally appealing to the lowest common denominator — certainly not to convey any semblance of the truth.

Dialogue is in retreat. You can't talk back to the television. Dialogue requires personal contact, which is rare because then, political leaders lose control. Better to have dueling sound bites and marketing

---

[71] See, e.g., Al Gore, *The Assault on Reason* (Penguin Books 2007)

messages than an actual exchange of views. Our Presidential debates offer little opportunity to exchange ideas and probe each other's views with facts and logic, as the candidates mostly "answer" questions with unresponsive speeches.

Reading newspapers and books has greatly declined. Most of us get our information — or its illusion — from a handful of networks or from websites (often extremist) which appeal to our biases. A handful of people at the networks determine what is "news" to be aired — that is, which events people who watch the networks will know happened. Even when these deciders of what is news are honest and non-partisan, they only have so much time on the air, and their decisions must be mindful of the need to sell ads.

Television is more likely to dwell on a storm, personal tragedy or crime than on events and facts relating to the quality of education in Appalachia, Detroit's collapse or the effect on health care costs of the concentration of health care insurers. Contrast the days of non-stop coverage of the O.J. Simpson murder case in the mid-1990s with this: Few Americans know that we've greatly expanded our military presence around the world since the end of the Cold War.

This is not to over-glorify olden times, which had, of course, plenty of emotional appeals and dishonest messaging. Nor is it to say that everyone got unbiased news: in Tocqueville's day, newspapers were usually highly partisan. The point is a matter of degree, and television has moved that degree far away from reasoned discourse.

It's not that our past politics was mostly like the *Federalist Papers* or the Lincoln-Douglas debates. It's that these discourses happened and were instrumental in resolving major issues. It's hard to imagine anything like the Lincoln-Douglas debates today or more than a small minority of contemporary Americans' reading something like the *Federalist Papers* on any issue.

A large number of Jacksonian Americans belonged to groups which deeply influenced the politics of the day. Today, the public expression of opinion is largely in what makes it to television. Without coverage, civic expressions make the sound of a tree falling in an empty forest. Groups can have little effect on public opinion without media access, but few have the money to buy time or get the coverage bestowed on what is "media hot". When coverage happens, as the media bestowed on a few small, angry demonstrations of the new Tea Party in 2009, they can have a vastly disproportionate effect on public discourse.

The power of money is crucial. Television is very expensive. As television ads have become the centerpiece of campaigning, the cost of running for office has soared, requiring vast sums to be a competitive candidate. Though money can be raised in small doses from ordinary citizens, the power of money mostly means the power of those who have a lot of it to give.

Money's dominance of politics has never been greater than in the last forty-five years of burgeoning inequality. As the rich have gotten richer, politics costs more money, which the wealthy are happy to provide. Since the majority of them are conservative, most of the money swamping our politics supports conservative candidates and policies. Abetted by the Supreme Court's disastrous removal of restrictions on corporate political spending in Citizens United, the public square has become a marketplace, up for sale as if elections were so many cars and cases of beer. The home of the free has become a plutocracy of wealthy oligarchs, un-conducive to reason, in which average citizens are ever more disempowered. Chapter Eleven will discuss this more deeply.

C. The Social Psychology of Mass Culture

Living in a mass culture has exacerbated the dispiriting, dis-ease and distress we suffer because we can't well digest modernity's big ideas.

1. Disappointed and Disempowered

The Declaration of Independence pledged Americans the blessings of "life, liberty and the pursuit of happiness". We've always considered "liberty" to mean I'm in charge of my life. A big part of that has ever been the freedom to reach for the American Dream. But, now that mass culture and our economy are frustrating that hope and defeating that opportunity, we feel deeply disappointed and newly (how un-American) disempowered to take charge of our lives.

In my youth, the great promise of the Dream was alive and well; and we felt deeply empowered. The children of the vast middle correctly believed they could climb higher than their parents, perhaps very high. Grandsons and daughters of immigrants, factory workers, small farmers and shopkeepers had opportunity and the good education to grab it. We mostly made more prosperous lives than our parents, and some joined the elite. But, now, as we've seen, it's much rarer for "middle Americans" to have a realistic shot at that beautiful Dream and we're likely to feel less able to take control of our lives.

The promise of American democracy is that each person will be, roughly, an equal citizen. While some will always have more influence, our covenant was that everyone's voice could be heard. But, that's no longer possible in our culture of grossly unequal citizenship dominated by television and money.

Freedom wasn't supposed to be like this. Rather than having a grip on their destinies, modern men and women feel swamped by immense forces, reduced to tiny pieces of a vast indifferent whole, like particles in the cold, impersonal world of materialistic science.

Modern man is one of many employees of a large company, one of millions of viewers of some show, one of his Congressman's 700,000 constituents (twenty times more than in the nineteenth century). He's little more than a statistic, a small piece of immense machines, consumer of what vast entities sell. What difference can his thoughts, hopes and actions make to how the machines function, to how society works, to what officials and managers do?

Materialism's emptiness fosters not only resignation and cynicism, but disappointment and disempowerment. These feelings are magnified by the cognitive dissonance between the individualistic expectation that I can do as I please and get what I want and our actual circumstances.

It's no wonder we feel cynical about politics, resigned to our disappointments and deflated from seizing the day.

Powerless, disconnected people feel anonymous. Modern mass men are, and often feel, faceless.

2. Alienated and Other-Directed

Alienation is an anxious, depressed feeling one is estranged from society. Somehow he doesn't belong. His sense of identity is weak, almost as if he were a thing not a person. Mass culture induces alienation.

One cause of our alienation is that secular materialism empties our spirits. The other is that impersonal mass culture offers too few genuinely human connections.

Look at connectedness through the lens provided by Martin Buber, that people relate to each other either as "I-Thou" or as "I-It". "I-Thou" is the relationship of two human beings treating each other as subjects rather than objects. Who she is and how she thinks and feels matters to me, not just because she might do what I want, but because I relate to her as a person, as she so relates to me. She may be my parent, child, lover or friend. Or, only someone I casually meet. What matters is that, even if our connection is superficial, I treat her as a person, more than just a means to my ends.

We are "I-Its" when we relate to someone solely as an object to serve a purpose, to help me accomplish something or as an obstacle in my path. She'll sell me what I want; help or retard me in achieving my goal. As "I-Its", we have no interest in each other as real people, only as instruments of our wishes. The relationship would work as well if she were a robot. The less we deal with other people as "Thous", the more we feel like robotic "Its".

We need human connections, which are more difficult to find in mass culture. We seem to relate to others more often than before as connection-emptying "Its". But, without "Thou"-like connections, we feel as empty husks inside. When we think of others as "Thous", we feel compassion for their difficulties; and our common humanity is more likely to influence our actions and opinions.

The process is a circle, virtuous with many "Thous", vicious with mostly "Its". The more I treat others as "Its", the more I feel like one myself. And, the more likely others are to reciprocate, which induces me even more to treat others as instrumental means rather than ends in themselves. The more I treat others as "Thous", the more humane I act; the more humanely others treat me, the better I feel about myself and the better I act. And so on.

Our hedonism furthers the vicious circle. One's focus on getting pleasure trumps his thoughts about the humanity of others; they are but means to pleasure. Take pornography, watching sex not caring who the performers are as people: it wouldn't matter if they were androids so long as they looked the part.

Social media abets the drift to alienation. People need real connections — like meeting face to face and talking. Texting is a way of communicating impersonally, even with the people to whom one feels close. As an adjunct to real personal connections, it has its value. As the principal way two people relate, it is empty at its core.

One of the most influential books of the Fifties was David Riesman's *The Lonely Crowd*. Riesman made the case that while most Americans had formerly been "inner-directed" (defining oneself by his internal compass), they had adapted to the newly emerged mass culture by becoming "other-directed" (self-definition now based on what others want and expect so that she can act to best fit in). The other-directed person is full of free-floating anxiety that he won't fit in well, that as Riesman said, he "wants to be loved rather than esteemed", to know he is emotionally in tune with others.

To conform as much as possible, we make ourselves the pliable employees and consumers our world wants. We repress our souls and cede our inner selves to get on as well as we can in a world of organizations, institutions and forces which want us to behave their way. And so, we make ourselves Buberian "Its".

Determined to be good instruments, we look outside, as our insides atrophy. We become superficial, able to offer the appearance, but not the reality, of intimacy. Ungrounded, we may seem at ease, but we're not. We're like Dylan's protagonist, "On your own, with no direction home, like a complete unknown, like a rolling stone."[72] To become like what Leonard Cohen sang, "I couldn't feel, so I learned to touch."[73]

3. Disrespected Elites

Mass society generates distrust of quality and contempt for elites. As Jose Ortega y Gassett said in his great and influential book: "The mass crushes beneath it everything that is different, everything that is excellent, individual, qualified, and select."[74]

This is not wholly new in America, wary since the Revolution of elites. Thus, the Federalist Party died in the early 1800s because citizens believed its leaders thought themselves an aristocracy; and the Jacksonian democracy which followed was the triumph of the common man. What's new is the strength of the feeling and its ripening into contempt, not only for elites but also for quality. The Right especially blames the "Establishment" for disappointed expectations, disempowerment and alienation.[75]

Today's elites tend to be the most successful meritocrats, often educated at the best colleges, facile at climbing organizational ladders, articulate, full of ideas and inclined to speak as if theirs is the only rational answer. Proud of their intelligences and accomplishments, they exude an air of being the better sort, naturally successful, the right

---

[72] "Like A Rolling Stone" Bob Dylan © 1965

[73] "Hallelujah" Leonard Cohen © 1984

[74] Jose Ortega y Gassett, *Revolt of the Masses*, (W.W. Norton 1957) p. 18

[75] Human psychology being complex and contradictory, people who berate elites often admire them for their success.

people to lead. "Ordinary" Americans can't stand this arrogance, intellectualism and superiority. Their feelings were a major factor in the election of Donald Trump.

The mutual contempt of "the people" and elites divides us and undermines our sense of community. It reduces standards to the lowest common denominator. The association of rationalism with Ivy League smarty pants fosters anti-intellectualism, disbelief in the virtue of reasoned thought and rational dialogue which stokes the politics of raw emotion. Emotional policy-making tends to be produce outcomes generally thought to be undesirable. Consider policies about incarceration and guns, which increase violent crime.

Understandably angry at crime, we imprison, at great expense, many more people than any other developed nation. We impose longer sentences and jail people for petty crimes rarely imprisonable in those countries (e.g., possession of a bit of an illegal drug). We not only waste money but breed ever more violent crime because American prisons are poor at rehabilitation but superb schools of crime. We refuse to spend modestly to educate prisoners and keep them safe, so that our prison culture is as violently criminal as the most crime-infested streets. Convicts are at great risk of rape and assault and left unprepared for productive life upon discharge.

Americans love guns. We admire old West gunslingers and military heroes. Our guns make us feel protected from criminals. Many politicians would commit political suicide by supporting bans on assault rifles (whose only purpose is to kill lots of people quickly), registration of revolvers (the only purpose is to shoot humans) or keeping guns away from people with criminal records or psychic illness. The result is that America has, by far, more gun-based crime and more deaths from gunfire than any other advanced country.

4. Uniformity Squelches Creativity

Societies can only thrive if their people frequently infuse them with creativity.[76] The principal cause of economic and social improvement and prosperity is the innovation which develops new, better ways of getting things done. The ingenious spirit and entrepreneurship of Americans has fueled the dynamism of high technology, biotech and a raft of inventive, resourceful ways of doing business and so have driven growth.

Uniformity is a natural product of mass culture — and it's the enemy of creativity. Enthralled to concentrated media, watchers are inclined to think about the same things. Herded into mass groups which naturally squeeze our thoughts and opinions into like channels, we tend, for all our divisions, to develop a commonality of taste. Though we remain innovative, might more years of sameness of culture lead to a deadening sameness of thought?

D. The Speed of Change and the Pace of Life

Change is endemic to the human condition. Every aspect of life is constantly changing. As we grow from infancy to adulthood, learning new skills and information, our cells turn over constantly as the body matures, then atrophies. We retain our personal identities, but are quite different in mind, body and spirit now than at times before.

I change moment to moment and so does everything else. The world never stays the slightest bit still. As Heraclitus said twenty-five hundred years ago, "Everything flows and nothing stands still" so that "No man ever steps in the same river twice, for it is not the same river and he is not the same man".

Each of us is also an agent of change. Just by living, he makes his world new and different. Actions have unintended consequences, so that what I do often causes effects I neither expect nor want.

We've always had change. The prehistoric world, the times of ancient and medieval human history may look static now, but they were constantly being transformed. They seem slow-moving to us because

---

[76] Creativity is, of course, not limited to art.

the pace of change then was much slower than now. One imagines that our pace would stun Heraclitus. Sped by technology, the rate of change is rapidly accelerating. Propelled by the law of momentum, change feeds on itself, apparently getting ever swifter.

Change is disconcerting. Most people crave stability, wanting to feel our roots reaching deep in the ground beneath our feet. Even when we embrace change, we want to launch from a firm base, one we choose. After all, change may be tolerable if we can manage it. Which, especially when it's rapid, we cannot. We can rarely anticipate the directions of change. Most of us don't pretend we can, but go with the flow, trying to adapt when surprised by something new.

The pace of contemporary change is fast and getting faster. It's exciting but immensely disconcerting. Change comes so quickly and from so many directions that the ground keeps shifting beneath us, at breakneck speed. Marx said of 1848's modernity that "all that is solid melts into air". The rate of change since has accelerated greatly, frustrating and unsettling us moderns.

The world has become, and quickly, so different from what one knew. The feeling that life is out of control generates fear. What's happening? Why don't I understand the forces pushing and pulling my life? I thought I'd finally gotten some grasp a while ago. Now, with all this new change, I realize I have no grip at all. I'd felt at home in the world: now I feel estranged and alienated.

The world moves at a pace and intensity heretofore unknown to mankind. Everything has to be done quickly, faster today than yesterday. It will be faster tomorrow. Instant communication through the likes of cell phones are a most mixed blessing. Now, one is connected, as they say, 24/7, with very little downtime to put aside cares and responsibilities for a brief respite. Modern computing and telecommunications makes available an immensity of information, so that our minds are on sensory and data overload, struggling to separate not only the wheat from the chaff but to digest all that wheat, to keep her internal balance against the waves of images and "facts" bombarding her psyche and mind.

The speed of change and the pace of life magnify feeling an important cog in a giant machine. Just when I thought I had a decent plan, boom!, the foundations shift, and I have to start all over from a different place. How can I make things better when I don't understand what's happening? Since I don't have the time or the processing power to make sense of it all, I feel no choice but to turn off when I can and let the masters make the rules and tell me what it all means.

All this rapidity fosters anxiety. It exacerbates the widespread angst: feeling ill at ease, worried and tense, even when nothing particular ought to provoke angst. Many people find it almost unbearable. The job one did well yesterday may be gone tomorrow; he's not trained to do the ones now available. The need always to be "on" carries the concomitant worry that I'll miss something or act unwisely on little sleep, putting my work and career at risk. By putting a premium on adaptability in the workplace, the speed of change exacerbates the unfortunate effects of the decline in American education.

The unease of rapid change and pace is leaving strong marks on American politics. The craving for stability engenders emotional politics: anxious voters are particularly susceptible to appeals to fear. Their anxiety makes them what to hold on to the old and familiar and fearful of what is new, and perhaps, better.

The classical scholar Christian Meier wrote about the ancient Greeks: "Accelerated change can cloud a society's senses. But, it also tends to be liberating if new forces drive that change and succeed in directing it towards a new form of human existence and a new understanding of the world. This may very well have been the case with the Greeks."[77] Our experience so far has been less happy. Might we come, like the Greeks, somehow to grasp change to make it liberating?

---

[77] *A Culture of Freedom* (Oxford University Press 2012), p.104

CHAPTER NINE: EMPTY AND ACHING FOR LOST COMMUNITY

" 'Kathy, I'm lost,' I said, though I knew she was sleeping
I'm empty and aching and I don't know why
Counting the cars on the New Jersey Turnpike
They've all gone to look for America
All gone to look for America
All gone to look for America"
Paul Simon, "America" © 1966

Community has ever been an American mainstay. One reason we've been a strong, healthy nation is because we've had sturdy local communities and a strong emotional bond of national citizenship. The Founders counted on these ties of community to make possible their great experiment. But, local communities have weakened and our shared national feeling has waned. Our loss is large: feelings of being disconnected and ill at ease and the weakening of democracy.

A. Atomistic Thinking and Individualism

Secular materialism encourages atomistic thought. Being based on a material view of the universe, it sees things as does classical physics in which particles are the basis of everything. Where medieval man saw a connected world imbued with spirit, modern men naturally see things as purely material individual bundles of atoms. In consequence, we think of wholes as collections of individual parts.

Thus, when we analyze a thing, our natural tendency is to see its constituent parts before, often instead of, seeing the whole. We're more likely to think of an object or living thing as something self-contained than we are to envision its context. To see the tree well and not fully grasp that it lives in a forest. The opposite of atomistic perspective is holistic thinking. Holistic thinking starts with the forest and looks for big pictures and patterns. It naturally wants to know how all these separate parts fit together, into a whole.

Our atomistic perspective naturally views people as separate and autonomous and society as a collection of disconnected beings. To the medieval mind, the community was itself an organism of connected people united in their humanity and shared sacred spirit. To the modern mind, community tends to seem but a loose mental construct of aggregated individuals who happen to have some things (like geographic proximity and language) in common.

Under the spell of contemporary individualism, the modern mind naturally gravitates to individual rights at the expense of communal obligations.[78] To think it more important to pay few taxes than to contribute to the costs of community, more important to tend one's own garden than participate actively in civic affairs. Atomistic thinking obscures the truth that life, prosperity and happiness are embedded in the health of the biological whole. Among other things, it makes it difficult for contemporary man to appreciate how much we need a healthy planet and healthy ecosystems or think the damage being done to the environment is not so important as perpetuation of one's "lifestyle".

Though atomistic thinking is often attributed to progressives, it's hardly just a liberal idea. That greatly influential modern traditionalist Margaret Thatcher said, "There is no such thing as Society. There are individual men and women, and there are families."

B. Loss of Local Community

I'm guessing Mrs. Thatcher wouldn't have spoken thus before World War II. Then, most people lived in the same neighborhoods and towns as their parents. People knew each other's families, histories, characteristics and peculiarities. They knew the local policemen and the proprietors and employees of the local shops and often participated in community politics. Their community was a collective home, not just where they slept and their children went to school.

---

[78] Both are essential. Problems arise when one is so accentuated as to smother the other.

That began to change after World War II. America became an automobile-driven society. Some people moved from cities to new suburbs while others left small towns for jobs in cities. Few of them had friends or even acquaintances in their new homes. When they got enough money, the new urbanites too moved to the suburbs.

Few suburbs had the center and coherence of an old-fashioned small town or urban neighborhood. The father (few mothers then worked) spent hours commuting. Being where breadwinners slept and relaxed on weekends, they were dubbed "bedroom suburbs": home but missing the webbed network of associations of childhood.

People in towns and urban neighborhoods walked. They saw their neighbors, stopped on the street to visit, knew who lived where. In the suburbs everyone drives, usually to shopping malls. There one sees mostly strangers with whom there's no opportunity to make acquaintance. One runs into and out of the store, much less likely than a parent to talk to anyone there because they're strangers.

Many people lived in extended families. Children grew up with three or four generations of grandparents, aunts, uncles and cousins a regular part of life. Now families usually live apart.

The post-war economic boom created a host of new jobs. People moved to unfamiliar places far away from family and the friends and acquaintances of a lifetime. As they did, the family became nuclear: mother, father and children. Grandparents and the rest were mostly consigned to telephone calls and occasional visits.

Before World War II, local communities had been a major pillar of stability. Not so for today's suburbanites, driving around bedroom suburbs far from where they grew up, frequently moving every few years to a different part of the country or to a new and better house in a different suburb.[79] Pillars of stability need roots, and we moderns have many fewer than our forbears. An ancient Greek needed his

---

[79] Many companies require up-and-comers to take a new, usually distant, job every few years, a practice destructive of local community.

community to live a good and full life. It was a terrible fate to be ostracized and forced to live as an exile.

Mothers naturally put down roots through their children. As women entered the work force, the number and quality of these roots diminished. Now, Mom races off to work, getting home late, stressed and tired like Dad. After working, commuting, shopping and such, all they can do is take some care of the children and watch them play sports on weekends. They've little time and energy left to make a community life outside the lives of their children. The connections they do make usually are fewer and weaker than they used to be.

Millions of Americans now have little opportunity and time to put down communal roots, and so are far less connected than any Americans in our history. Without a web of communal connections, they often feel alone, alienated and fearful. They have many fewer "Thous" to enrich their lives. They don't have the support systems of extended family and community to help them pull through hard times.

Lost community contributes to decaying civility. One is less likely to be rude to an acquaintance than a stranger. It's much easier to cut off a car if you don't know the driver, speak sharply to a sales-person you've never seen and shout at someone on the phone when she's a disembodied voice rather than members of one's community.

The loss of local community is a major cause of the loss of civic responsibility. Former Speaker of the House Tip O'Neill famously said, "All politics is local." O'Neill was from urban Cambridge, when politics was a central part of city and neighborhood life. He would probably have said the same thing had he lived in Tocqueville's day.

Now, most suburbs have little local politics. The suburban "town" is often just a post office address with little or no government of its own. Even when it has government, it seems unimportant. Citizen participation is low. Local governments were Americans' school of democracy. Now, most of those schools have closed.

Loss of community has hit the poorest areas especially hard. The waves of immigrants who came to America through 1920 settled in neighborhoods that were, despite intense poverty, poor housing and other deprivations, strong communities based on the values the immigrant group brought to the New World. They were poor in money, but rich in the connections and values of community. And so, their children were able to assimilate into American society by grafting American values to those of their communal cultures.

Most of today's American poor are communally impoverished. Their urban neighborhoods are largely bereft of the values and connections which ground people to strive to escape poverty. They live not in the old immigrant blend of the Old and the New Worlds, but in a culture of disconnected hopelessness. A professor reports that people in Camden's terribly poor black ghetto no longer look to neighbors for help and support. Instead, they see them (all of them, not just the violent and criminal) as strangers more likely to cause harm than do good. The message they give their children is "don't connect; don't talk about anything that matters; just stay apart".

Margaret Thatcher said there is no society, only individuals and families. To the extent that's true, it's something new and awful in human life. The loss of local community is unhealthy for people who need society and it's unhealthy for the prospects of democracy which depends on citizens imbued with civic responsibility.

C. The National Community

Our national community is also weakening. Americans have always disagreed about issues, having differing visions and beliefs as to what problems ought to be solved and how best to solve them. Such is human nature.

Yet, for most of our history, we've been more united by common citizenship than divided by difference. We've usually felt like the close of Lincoln's First Inaugural:

> "We are not enemies, but friends. We must not be enemies. Though passion may have strained it must not break our bonds of affection. The mystic chords of memory, stretching from every battlefield and patriot grave to every living heart and hearthstone all over this broad land, will yet swell the chorus of the Union, when again touched, as surely they will be, by the better angels of our nature."

Of course, as Lincoln spoke, the "bonds of affection" had broken and Civil War soon began. Slavery had so divided the nation that it could not continue as it was. For the rest of our history until recently, the "mystic chords of memory" have held. However strong our differences, we've felt as citizens of one great, beloved country. Until now when connected citizenship has faded in three ways.

First, our sense of civic responsibility has decayed. The Founders believed national self-government required people to be active citizens, participating in politics and sacrificing when needed for the national good. Until struck by modernity, Americans fit the bill. But now, as we've seen, modern ideas and forces have undermined the idea of social duty and sacrifice for the common good.

The second way in which our citizenship has faded is loss of trust in leaders and institutions. Trust is essential to collaboration, compromise, mutual sacrifice and taking chances. But, having been been often burned by lying leaders, we've learned to distrust leaders and institutions.[80] As we see below, our harshly divided politics has shredded our trust in the bona fides of the "other side".

The third way in which our citizenship has eroded is our lost sense of a common weal. Democracy requires dialogue, respect for contrary opinions, readiness to compromise and toleration of results one opposes — which we've lost. We're more divided than since just

---

[80] For instance, LBJ about Vietnam, Nixon and Watergate, misbehaving financial leaders causing the Great Crash and now a serially lying President.

before the Civil War. As then, our divisions are over the preservation of ways of life, which are the most explosive disagreements. Public life was so virulent then because each side felt the other's position on slavery would destroy its way of life. The Southern slave society believed it would only survive if slavery expanded. The North believed that expansion would destroy its world of free labor.

Nietzsche thought national strength required a genuine community sharing a sense of the right way to live. Not agreement on everything, of course, so long as most people shared a core set of moral beliefs that inform life's basics. That was true of America until some time before the Civil War. It was true of America from the Civil War's end until the 1960s or soon after. It has not been true since.

Traditionalists and secularists, conservatives and progressives fear the other would make the good life impossible. Traditionalists fear a faith-free society destroying religion and morals. Secularists fear an intolerant theocracy enforcing absolutist morality. Conservatives fear the destruction caused by high tax big government. Liberals fear destruction from inattention to urgent problems.

Thus, many Americans are more loyal to their side of the divide than to the common whole, a proud "red stater" or "blue stater", conservative or progressive. The other side is stupid, ill-informed, thoughtless and immoral: people who don't have the best interests of the nation at heart, who aren't joined with us in good will and common devotion to America's well-being. We'll soon see that this divide is very dangerous for the future of our democracy.

Patriotism is the only tie which seems to bind. But, celebrating our military and shouting, "USA! USA!" for being the biggest and toughest kid on the world playground is not active citizenship.[81] As David Brooks (a conservative) says:

> "Hamilton, Lincoln and [Theodore] Roosevelt had been able to assume a level of social and moral capital. They took it for

---

[81] Soldiers' military service shows their good citizenship, not anyone else's.

granted that citizens lived in tight communities defined by well-understood norms, a moral consensus and restrictive customs. Today's leaders could not make that assumption. The moral and social capital present during those years ha[s] eroded, and it need[s] to be rebuilt."[82]

These final words from Tocqueville pertinent to our politics:

> "There is, indeed, a most dangerous passage in the history of a democratic people.... *In their intense and exclusive anxiety to make a fortune, they lose sight of the close connection which exists between the private fortune of each of them and the prosperity of all. It is not necessary to do violence to such a people in order to strip them of the rights they enjoy; they themselves willingly loosen their hold. The discharge of political duties appears to them to be a troublesome annoyance, which diverts them from their occupations and business.*"

> "A nation that asks nothing of its government but the maintenance of order is already a slave at heart, the slave of its own well-being, awaiting only the hand that will bind it.... *When the bulk of the community is engrossed by private concerns, the smallest parties need not despair of getting the upper hand in public affairs.*"[83]

---

[82] *The Social Animal*, p. 334. I disagree with the phrase "restrictive customs" which evokes repressive restriction (as in the Norman town of *Madame Bovary*).

[83] *Democracy in America*, vol. 2, pp. 140-41; 141-42 (emphasis supplied).

SECTION THREE: OUR POLITICAL WORLD

"We live in a political world where love don't have any place
We're living in times where men commit crimes and crime don't have a face...
"We live in a political world where mercy walks the plank
Life is in mirrors, death disappears up the steps into the nearest bank...
"We live in a political world, the one we can see and feel
But there's no one to check, it's all a stacked deck
We all know for sure that it's real."
Bob Dylan, "Political World" © 1989

We turn to politics. The forces of modern life we've surveyed have crippled our politics and government. They've unleashed anger, fear and intolerance which infect the moods, votes and actions of citizens, parties and politicians. We've been unable to address our deeply daunting problems, certainly not with the necessary speed or with skill, justice or compassion. So far, we've seen no way out.

Chapter Ten discusses the capture of the Republican Party by hard right-wing conservatism and the (unhappy) politics of American liberalism. Chapter Eleven explores our corrosive political life. Chapter Twelve discusses the dangers that American democracy will so fail that we fall into despotism.

CHAPTER TEN: OUR POLITICAL SCENE: REPUBLICANS AND DEMOCRATS, CONSERVATIVES AND LIBERALS

"I love the country but I can't stand the scene.
And I'm neither left or right
I'm just staying home tonight,
getting lost in that hopeless little screen."
Leonard Cohen, "Democracy" © 1992

Let's begin by asking what President was a superb environmentalist, proposed a health care bill to the left of Obamacare, presided over the most intrusive regulation of the economy in our history and opened a long-closed dialogue with our pariah enemy? Yes, that President was Richard Nixon, the liberals' bane, the (correctly) disgraced partisan rightist (as he then was). Let's follow his party to its very different incarnation today.

A. The Republican Move to the Right

The Republican Party has been the more conservative party for most of its life. Born to eradicate slavery and foster development of an industrial nation, the party of Lincoln and Radical Reconstruction had morphed by the 1880s into the party of big business. Theodore Roosevelt, an accidental President after McKinley's assassination, briefly pushed the party in a progressive direction, an anomaly of his charismatic person. His distant cousin Franklin identified the Democrats with liberalism, and so it's been ever since.

Conservatism is a broad term. In his day Dwight Eisenhower was a (moderate) conservative. Today, his views would place him well outside the continuum of views which make up the Republican Party. What has been dubbed the Reagan Revolution is the movement of the GOP far to the right, away not just from Teddy Roosevelt but from the party's Eastern Establishment wing which secured Eisenhower's nomination. Now, the GOP has moved well to the right of Reagan.

1. From Richard Nixon to the Ever-Farther Right

Let's begin with Richard M. Nixon, the liberals' bête-noire. A poor, socially-awkward boy, Nixon was most certainly not part of the Eastern Establishment. He made his name as a virulent anti-Communist, the man of dirty tricks, his zeal to do in his opponents unrestrained by law and principle. Proudly conservative, his Presidency seemed a triumph of the Right. He is remembered unfondly by most Americans, especially liberals.

Nixon was indeed a harsh partisan. He and his Vice President Spiro Agnew, forced to resign for taking bribes, cheerfully polarized the country. He ran on his "Southern strategy" appealing to racism to dislodge the "solid South", angry at JFK's and LBJ's civil rights policies, from the Democrats. Nixon ranted at anti-war protesters as anti-American and used every means his fertile mind could imagine to label Democrats as unpatriotic, pro-crime and pro-black.

He abused the power of his office. He was forced to resign, inter alia, because he personally led a cover-up of his staff's burgling the Democratic National Committee. Contemptuous of civil liberties, he utterly disregarded the legal limits on the power of his office. Well beyond Watergate, he believed the Constitution did not apply to him, that "If the President does it, that means it's not illegal." He had an "enemies list" on whom he sought to sic the Internal Revenue Service and other agencies. His Administration had more than its share of financial corruption, and the secret fundraising by The Committee to Re-Elect the President (known, how nicely, as "CREEP") from large companies and wealthy donors was considered a scandal.

True to his Red-baiting past, Nixon continued the Vietnam War with virulence. Although he'd promised voters he had a "secret plan" for peace, he did not. His policy to "preserve American honor" achieved nothing beyond perpetuating American involvement in the war for four uselessly bloody years and, in the bargain, destabilizing neutral Cambodia so that it fell to especially brutal Communists. Advertised as manifesting the folly of resisting American power, his massive 1972

"Christmas bombing" killed and destroyed for no purpose: he withdrew the last American troops shortly after, and the Communists took over South Vietnam two years later.

Shades of George W. Bush. But, Nixon's Presidency was very far to the left of W's, and Nixon's Asian policy is the pivot to examine how. That is because Richard Nixon, the country's foremost hater and baiter of "Red China", flew to Beijing to end twenty years of American refusal to have anything to do with Communist China: a policy which no one had done more to foster — than Richard Nixon.

Nixon's domestic policies were no paragon of conservative orthodoxy. He proposed a health care bill more "liberal" and with greater government intervention than "Obamacare". It even included the mandate, hated by all current Republicans, that every American buy insurance. To combat increasing inflation and a declining balance of payments, Nixon intervened deeply in the economy, imposing wage and price controls, limiting currency movements to other countries and taking us off the gold standard. No President, even FDR, ever intervened thus in American economic life.

Nixon was a superb environmental President. He created the Environmental Protection Agency and proposed or supported a raft of major environmental legislation: the National Environmental Policy Act, the Clean Air Act and legislation on national parks, endangered species, pesticides, coastal protection, and ocean dumping. He made the environmental activist Russell Train a major part of his Administration, including the second head of EPA. Train spoke correctly when he said that the Nixon era "put into place the basic principles and framework of environmental law".

It's impossible to imagine such a Republican President today. He would, to speak religiously for a party certain it's the guardian of holy political truth, be excommunicated as a true Republican. Today, most Republicans strongly oppose environmental regulation and would abolish or cripple EPA. They decry global warming as a liberal hoax. They'd regard Nixon's wage, price and currency controls as socialism.

Some demand we return to the gold standard. They've pilloried Barack Obama as a socialist for a health bill to the right of Nixon's. Forgetful of Nixon and China, the GOP sought to crucify candidate Obama for saying he would negotiate with Iran.

That Richard Nixon would have no chance to be nominated for national office in the Republican Party of today. The man would be regarded as simply much too liberal, way off the conservative reservation. Who back then wouldn't have laughed at being told he'd have had the best policies of any Republican President since?

It's not just that the Republicans have moved far to the Right: they keep moving. Yesterday's acceptable position can quickly become heretical deviation from new dogma. Thus, John McCain was long distinguished for advocating immigration reform until, threatened from the far Right in a 2010 primary, he pirouetted to the immigrant-bashing now required to be a true Republican.

The Tea Party's success in 2010 moved the Republican Congress even further. It's morphed into the Freedom Caucus in the House, large and strong enough to put a stranglehold on policy. The Right's vicious rhetoric gets worse and worse. Just when it seems the GOP has gone as far rightward as possible, they open a new frontier.

Now, we have President Donald Trump, proud to ally himself with the racist far Right; reactionary health care bills; assaults on immigrants; proposed tax "reform" even more skewed to the rich than the regressive, for-the-most-rich tax cuts of George W. Bush.

How and why has this happened? We look at three reasons: the nature of the times and their dominant issues; the Republicans' skill at shaping perceptions; and their skilled use of the political process.

2. Times for Conservatism

America is a moderately conservative country, cautious about change, with punctuated bursts of liberal reform. From the Civil War until Reagan, conservative years were times of political quietude. No longer. The now dominant conservatism is strident and noisy, determined to undo most of the reforms of over a century.

One explanation for the shrill conservatism is the times. From World War II to the late Sixties, the country was turned upside down. America leapt into world affairs as the dominant power; battled Communism in the Cold War; and endured the traumas of Vietnam and the Sixties' cultural upheavals. Secular materialism hit America hard (years after its impact on Europe) as the contemporary form of self-absorbed, entitled individualism took hold. Though we won the Cold War, after Nine Eleven, strong fears of foreign enemies remain.

The coalescence of these disquieting changes unsettled the American people. The "anxieties and insecurities" caused by "acids of modernity" began to dissolve what Americans found "reassuring and familiar" about culture, religion, workplace and home.[84]

The cultural divide begun in the Sixties scared and angered traditional Americans. Their politics became dominated by their fears for our security, our moral and religious condition and their economic present and future.

The rebellious young declared cultural war, rallying to "sex, drugs and rock 'n roll". They and many others protested the Vietnam War, often raucously. Men burned draft cards, women burned their bras, people burned American flags. Vietnam hawks were boobs and much of the working class — Nixon's "silent majority", later christened Reagan Democrats — were branded racists.

---

[84] Andrew Bacevich, *Washington Rules: America's Path to Permanent War* (Metropolitan Books 2010)

The silent majority accepted the challenge to cultural war. If liberalism was about sexual promiscuity, disdain for patriotism and unwillingness to stand up for the defense of the nation, well, then, many Americans concluded, they better speak up, loudly, for national security and for the values that made the country great.

Self-righteous individualists, the Sixties' protesters had little respect for authority, loved confrontation, were aggressively uncivil and smugly dogmatic and claimed to speak for society's victims. Conservative protestors since have followed this script.

History teaches that when secularity seems to be pushing religion off the stage, there'll be a strong revival of deep faith. This one has been as fervent and long-lived as any in our history. Feeling that liberal America threatens their deepest beliefs, many of the millions who've become evangelical Christians enrolled in the Republican political front of the culture wars.

Economics also drove millions of America to the right. Beginning in the Seventies, the gains in good times mostly went to the already well-off. The economic fortunes of working and middle class Americans — the heart of the silent majority/ Reagan Democrats — began to stagnate or decline. As people felt the economic pinch and saw their prospects decline, they became fearful and angry.

One might think the logical response would be to support liberal policies, as from FDR to LBJ. It was not. By this time, as we'll see, the Republicans had won the perception war, and Democrats had made themselves unattractive, even on economics, to large parts of the New Deal coalition. The economic frustrations and fears of middle America came to be put, not at the feet of FDR's "malefactors of great wealth" and their GOP sponsors, but at high taxes, big government and large deficits, associated with Democrats.

And so, for more than forty years conservatives have ridden a rising tide. On family values: abortion, gay marriage (until recently), pornography, sex education in the schools. On patriotic support for country, flag and our troops. On the Democrats' support for welfare and affirmative action. On concern that taxes are too high, out-of-control deficits threaten to bankrupt the country and government has become much too large and intrusive, corroding our freedoms.

3. The Political Process

Until recently, the GOP has out-thought, out-organized, out-disciplined and out-politicked the Democrats.

Begin with thinking. Conservative activists created think tanks to develop conservative positions. Some are general issue institutions, like the American Enterprise Institute and the Heritage Foundation. Others are devoted to particular sets of issues, like Americans for Tax Reform, Focus on the Family (founded by a leader of the Christian Right), and the Federalist Society (focused on legal issues).

The think tanks have been well-funded, staffed with bright thinkers and politicos. They have had the time and money to develop all manner of positions and issue initiatives and push them with Congress, Republican Administrations and the public. They have provided foot soldiers of the conservative revolution and candidates and staff for Republican Presidents, Senators and Congressmen.

The Democrats have had little of this. While there've been efforts to rethink New Deal ideas, well-suited then but not now, they've been much less well-organized, well-funded and persistent than the GOP's. Progressives have developed fewer new ideas; rarely presented an overall program; and haven't had a strong political apparatus like the one selling Republican ideas.

The Republicans have, until recently, far out-organized the Democrats. They've built a strong national party organization and worked closely with conservative organizations. They've used the best fund-raising techniques, to get large contributions from the rich and small checks from others. They've found, groomed and persuaded electable candidates to run for office and used election laws to their advantage, often to disenfranchise poor, young and other likely Democratic voters. They've developed superb electioneering techniques for public relations and advertising and canvassing voters and getting-out-the-vote. Democrats long lagged far behind, until under Howard Dean (2005-08), the Democratic National Committee developed a strong political organization.

Conservative Republicans have employed strict party discipline to get their way. When they won the House in 1994, Tom Delay was their whip to enforce party discipline, which he did with a vengeance. Known as The Hammer, Delay threatened any GOP Congressmen thinking of voting against the rightist party line with ostracism: no power in the House and a right-wing opponent to take away his seat in the next primary.

Delay could afford to run extremists in primaries because so many Congressional districts were gerrymandered to favor one party. As voters in the Republican primary are more conservative than the overall electorate, they're likely to vote out a "moderate" to elect a strident conservative. And, then, as the district is solidly Republican, that candidate would beat the Democrat in the general election even if he lost moderate voters. The Democrats have their share of one-party districts; but, Democrats don't impose party discipline.

The Republicans' discipline now dominates Congress. The Republicans have mostly voted en masse on big issues since Barack Obama became President. Even the few remaining so-called moderates have usually gone along with the reactionary politics of "no" demanded by their leadership. Few Congressional Republicans any longer search for, or support, acceptable compromise.

Now, with Trump as President and the Republicans in control of both houses of Congress, the Republicans are finding it harder to insist on unanimity. They are learning that it's easier to say "no" than to craft legislation, whose terms divide GOP factions.

The Republicans further benefit because much influential media are dedicated conservatives. Fox is as partisan as possible. (Liberal MSNBC is far less influential.) Talk radio, important to middle America, is dominated by angry rightists like Rush Limbaugh. Many influential television clergy include conservative politics in their evangelical messages. The liberals have nothing comparable.

4. Polarization, Perception and Image

Richard Nixon left his party a rich inheritance of capital earned by the politics of polarization. His Southern strategy used race-coded messages to woo Southern whites; and his appeal to the silent majority's patriotism, traditional morality and opposition to black demands won over many unionized workers and other formerly Democratic moderates. He won a landslide re-election over George McGovern, a good and able man but a "new" Democrat, who, as we soon see, were busily alienating the center of the country.

Until brought down by his crimes, Nixon was close to replacing the New Deal coalition with a Republican majority. Then, briefly, it seemed that, really, things had not changed all that much.

The election of 1980 and the Presidency of Ronald Reagan made evident that a new conservative coalition now dominated American politics. The Watergate hangover was over, and a charismatic, likable, politically astute, deeply conservative man was President. The man was a political genius. No intellect, he was as good at the surface of things as anyone, a wizard at convincingly bringing any topic back to his few basic conservative principles. He made everything seem so clear and simple and right: even his strongest opponents might occasionally find themselves nodding in agreement until they realized just what he was saying.

Though Nixon was very good at polarizing, people saw through disagreeable "Tricky Dicky" even when they liked what he said. Reagan polarized all of the time. He just sounded so good. The man was coated with Teflon: he managed somehow not to be scarred even by the Iran-Contra scandal late in his Administration in which senior staff severely abridged basic Constitutional restrictions.

Reagan was expert at driving wedge issues of race, morality, national security and big government right through the electorate's heart. The country was ready for the messages he delivered so well. He polarized on race: "welfare mothers driving welfare Cadillacs". He polarized on morality, even though he was a remarried Hollywood divorcee dysfunctionally distant from his gay liberal son.

He polarized especially well on government. The country was ready for the anti-government message his pithy phrases ingrained deeply in the American psyche. "Government is not a solution to our problem, government is the problem." "The nine most terrifying words in the English language are, I'm from the Government and I'm here to help." Reagan's most enduring, and unhealthy, legacy has been to persuade so many of us as if it were Gospel that, other than for policing and security, government is bad.

There was something, something fundamental, else. Former First Lady Rosalynn Carter put it well: "I think this President makes us comfortable with our prejudices."[85] Reagan bears much of the responsibility for making Americans feel that it's not bad to have, and to voice, prejudices and intolerance.

Politics (like life) is about perceptions as much as reality. Nixon began and Reagan perfected the public's association of Democrats and liberals with things a majority of the country abhor: welfare mothers driving welfare Cadillacs, demeaning patriotism, immorality, large government, high taxes, etc., etc. They used wedge issues to drive much of the country from liberals in horror.

Their Republican successors have successfully followed their script. They have made "liberal" a dirty word to many Americans. They've made it easy to demean liberal policies and Democratic initiatives with just a, by-now well-understood and accepted, phrase or two. This has mostly worked for decades even when the policy would benefit most of the people they persuade to oppose it. They have successfully cast the national political play so that liberals are big government, high tax, irresponsible advocates for the poor but not for "you". They have

---

[85] In a 1985 interview with Mike Wallace: Mike Wallace, *Between You and Me* (Hyperion 2005), p. 49.

succeeded thus in reducing politics to a few sound bites evoking fear, distrust and dislike of the other side.

As we now see, Democrats spent forty years helping the GOP by doing everything possible to alienate the political center.

B. The Politics of American Liberalism

What were Democrats doing while Republicans were brilliantly pummeling progressive ideas? What alternative messages and vision were liberals offering the American people? Clearly, whatever they did worked poorly.

A vision needn't be, and usually isn't, a detailed political program like all the legislation Lyndon Johnson proposed for his Great Society. More often, visions are a few basic principles, a new direction and tone, perhaps a few essential policies: the New Deal, JFK's New Frontier, the views of Ronald Reagan.

Since Robert Kennedy's death, Democrats have offered the nation no lucid vision, no coherent set of principles and directions.[86] Left to figure out for themselves what liberals stand for, voters have drawn their perceptions from Democratic policies, positions and messages, from the cut of the their collective jib and from portraits drawn by Republicans. Democrats have not been well-served.

We've seen how skillfully the Republicans leapt into the breach to define the Democrats. But, tuned in as they've been to the distress of the times, they could have succeeded so well only because Democratic policies, messages and style have deeply alienated a large portion of the American people.

Let's consider four facets of Democratic self-immolation: shifting in goal from making the American Dream a reality for all Americans to distributive justice to help the poor (and becoming seen as the party of special interests); failing to deal with wedge issues; failing to make the

---

[86] Hillary Clinton's lack of vision hurt her badly in 2016's "unloseable" election.

case for wise regulation, sensible tax policy or controlling big government; and refusing to value, and to talk intelligently and wisely about, the political implications of values.[87]

1. From American Dream to Distributive Justice

Democrats lost the allegiance of much of the middle class because they fundamentally changed their focus. From FDR (and Wilson) to Lyndon Johnson, they were the party of the aspirations of average people. When they made themselves the party of the American Dream, they became the party of middle and working Americans.

At least since Benjamin Franklin and Jefferson's paean to the self-ruling yeoman farmer, America has celebrated the opportunity of each individual to make the most he can of himself. Jacksonian democracy extolled the common man of the middle. Soon thereafter, the Free Soil and free labor movements and the nascent Republican Party opposed slavery because they believed its continuation would block the American Dream for white free laborers. With Wilson and FDR, the Democrats first joined, and then took over, the celebration of the average American.

With the country gripped by Depression, FDR made Democrats the party of the people — working people, the poor, much of the middle class. Wed to don't regulate, pro-big business ideas, the GOP badly mishandled the Depression. The Democrats became the ascendant party by championing the common man as the Republicans became, correctly, identified as the party of big business and the rich. This enabled the Democrats to forge the liberal coalition which dominated American politics from 1932 until 1968.

By the Sixties, the Depression was long over and New Deal policies such as Social Security, legalizing unions and regulating finance had made a great difference. The economic divide of the Twenties had narrowed greatly and working people had good jobs and nice homes in

---

[87] I do not mean to be "holier than thou" as I, too, held some of these positions.

new suburbs. From World War II to the late Sixties, things for average Americans got pretty darn good.

Those in dire need were fewer and most visibly urban blacks (the rural poor were close to invisible). The compassionate liberal impulse to reduce suffering turned to the most needy, the "other America".[88] It was time to help the poor we'd left behind. It was time to do everything possible to bring low-income blacks and white Appalachians and others mired in poverty into the mainstream workers and other middle Americans had recently entered.

And so, by the late Sixties, the Democrats shifted their focus from the average American, making the American Dream a reality for all, to distributive justice to help the poor. Where Democrats/liberals had long supported policies to help both middle/working Americans and people living in poverty, they shifted their focus to the (black urban) underclass. The party of FDR, Truman, Kennedy and Johnson was the party of all the people. Their Democratic successors became the party perceived to be primarily for (and largely only to have sympathy for) the mostly black poor. That turn has been politically disastrous for Democrats. Ironically, by much diminishing the Democrats' power, it's also been disastrous for the poor.

As liberals turned to the plight of poor and black folk, they seemed to lose compassion for middle America. It was a rare liberal Democrat who showed empathy for the pain driving the traditionalist side of the culture wars or who focused on the widening inequality pummeling middle America. To most liberals, traditionalists were jingoist, dogmatic, narrow-minded, selfish and often racist — and usually not all that bright. They were authoritarians telling everyone else how to live and with whom to sleep. And, did liberals ever let their contempt show.

The Democrats' timing was inauspicious. Just as they shifted focus away from middle Americans, those Americans were hit hard: by

---

[88] See Michael Harrington, *The Other America* (Simon & Schuster 1962).

economics and the Vietnam War, the upheavals of the Sixties and other vicissitudes we've studied of modern life. They needed liberals' sympathies and support (especially on economics) more than ever. The distribution of wealth began to disadvantage working people who'd been the main beneficiaries of the New Deal. Pocketbooks began to pinch hard in the Seventies, just when an updated version of FDR-like economic policies might have kept the Reagan Democrats as Democrats. The optimism from beating the Depression, winning World War II and building a contented post-war country quickly turned sour as the the money no longer was so good and as the dislocations of the modern world view and mass culture hit home. Just when the center needed an understanding, progressive voice, the Democrats moved on.

One important cause of the liberal turn to distributive justice came from the realm of political ideas. In 1971, John Rawls published *A Theory of Justice*, the most influential book of political thought of the century. It was widely read and not just by academics. Its core idea quickly became an article of faith among liberal intelligentsia, even if they didn't actually read it.

The success of Rawls' book was no surprise. He was a famous philosopher teaching at Harvard who thought and wrote well and clearly. He came to comforting conclusions in sync with basic principles of liberal democracy. He wrote in the deeply respected tradition of social contract philosophers like Hobbes, Locke and Rousseau deducing basic political principles by discerning what terms (what contract) on which people getting together to form a society for the first time would agree. As Rawls put it, to what provisions of the social contract would people agree in the "original position" of these hypothetical citizens meeting to establish their society? Rawls' first conclusion was comforting to Americans: the primary political virtue to which his citizens would agree is liberty.

Rawls' transformative idea was his second principle, which he called the "difference principle". It was perfectly suited for liberal minds of the time. The difference principle holds that a just society will allow only that level of inequality which will benefit its least advantaged members. Thus, it is ethically just for a surgeon or Microsoft's founder to earn above average income if that much income is necessary to induce him to put his talents to use such that society's least well-off members benefit. But, there is no moral justification for Bill Gates to earn more than that necessary amount.

Standing back with the perspective of over forty years, the difference principle seems quite extreme: that justice imposes an obligation to limit our earnings to no more than what is probably a not-very-high socially justified minimum. This was a massive shift from the old American emphasis on opportunity for all to equality. At the time, the idea held a large swath of progressive in thrall.[89]

The difference principle would undermine the American Dream. The Dream is based on the belief that people are capable of ruling themselves and making the most of their opportunities. For the successful, that includes reaping whatever benefits they can fairly earn from their efforts. For the disadvantaged, though society and government may owe them help to boost them past barriers blocking the road to success, they are responsible, self-reliant actors capable of, once so nudged, improving their lot with effort.

The difference principle rests on a very different sense. The successful would have no moral right to any of their gains except as measured by its restrictive calculus.[90] And, most unhappily, it has a tendency to view the disadvantaged paternally, (almost as if the obstacles they face have dis-enabled them to succeed) rather than people needing a nudge to seize opportunity.

As such ideas became the currency of progressive policy, Democrats abandoned much of the New Deal coalition. Democrats morphed from

---

[89] (By the Nineties, Rawls seemed to have backed down.) Social contract theory rests on the fiction that people can decide how to structure society before it begins. But, as we've always lived in society, the "original position" is a fiction ill-suited as a device to discern basic principles.

[90] This is far more restrictive than the idea that we have social duties, which include to pay progressively scaled taxes.

the party of the American Dream for all to distributive justice for the poor, from opportunity to equality, from the party of the people to the party of the dispossessed. The rights and needs of the poor blotted out regard or empathy for the rights and concerns of middle and laboring Americans. They expressed compassion for criminals but not for victims. And so, they lost millions of middle Americans and handed power to conservative Republicans.

The Party of Special Interests

At the same time, Democrats were transformed for many Americans from the New Deal's party of the people to the party of special interests. Not only of the poor and black but of other groups in the new Democratic coalition: teachers' unions, labor bosses (but, less and less, their members), public employee unions, trial lawyers, women's groups, civil libertarians and environmentalists.

Millions concluded that Democratic policy was designed not to better the entire country but to provide recompense to each part of the coalition for their money, support and votes. The public drew unflattering conclusions when Democrats eschewed reforms opposed by these groups[91]; and supported exorbitant pay and pensions for municipal workers.

Walter Mondale's 1984 speech accepting the Presidential nomination is exemplary. As he set forth the policies for first one group and then another, the benefitted group cheered while the rest quietly waited their turn. No wonder Democrats became seen as politicians of pork rather than the party of the people.

2. Wedge Issues

The Republicans skillfully exploited, and the Democrats lavishly lost, the wedge issues central to the GOP's resurgence. Their approach to "family values", patriotism/ national defense and aiding the black

---

[91] Such as holding teachers to good performance and reining in abuses in medical malpractice and other big cases brought by plaintiff's lawyers.

underclass did much to make "liberal" a dirty word. It did not help that liberals had a way of morally superior preaching.

When poor people made, in the lexicon of the age, "demands", most Democrats said, "Of course. You're needy." The "silent majority" saw liberals and Democrats, safely ensconced in tony suburbs, expecting them to bear the brunt of their pro-black policies.

Liberals believed school busing to achieve racial balance was essential to allow black children to be educated well, unconcerned that the busses mostly ran to and from middle American neighborhoods. Blacks needed "affirmative action" to overcome centuries of slavery and racism though this often meant, and was taken by middle America to mean, quotas to assure blacks of jobs and college admissions in place of middle American whites. When it became clear that the welfare system encouraged mothers to be single, bred a culture of dependence and undermined self-responsibility, liberals denied the evidence. Democrats showed little sympathy for crime's victims, resisting anti-crime policies because wretched circumstances drove urban blacks to steal and murder.

The liberals' response to the conservative "family values" "social agenda" further drove the wedge. Liberals were going to oppose restrictions on abortion, discrimination against gays and such because they highly value tolerance and rights. But, they could've softened the blows with greater sensitivity and by explaining their values. (We consider patriotism and national security below.)

3. Big Government, Regulation and Tax Policy

The size of government has exploded. Liberals correctly believe that a fair, well-governed modern society requires an energetic government; and government is much bigger to administer the welfare state and regulate the complexities of modernity. While conservatives generally oppose a great deal of these domestic undertakings, they believe in a powerful national defense apparatus, which accounts for much of the state's expansion.

Since government programs require bureaucracies, those programs naturally tend to become bureaucratic, that is, inefficient, impersonal, intrusive and frustrating — and unpopular. All those big agencies occupying all those massive public buildings make many more of us queasy than the low tax, anti-government crowd.

Democrats have dealt poorly with public opposition to big government. They have little explained the need for strong government other than for military, intelligence and homeland security. And, they've shown little concern or thought about how to ameliorate the ill effects of government bureaucracies.

The Need for Government Action

Confronting America's worst economic crisis, FDR led the nation to understand the helpful virtues of appropriately active government.[92] He successfully made the case that economic regulation was necessary for public protection and that programs to make society fairer (such as unemployment insurance, Social Security, protections for unions and wage and hour laws) made the country better.

His successors from Truman through Johnson followed in his footsteps: culminating in LBJ's historic civil and voting rights, Medicare and education legislation. They persuaded a majority of the country that society needed government action to redress problems that would not get fixed by themselves. Much good has come from their liberal policies: enhanced medical security, reduced discrimination and bigotry, educational initiatives such as Head Start, the Peace Corps and much more.

But then, most Democrats (Ted Kennedy a rare exception) forgot how to make the case that government action can solve big problems — or to take credit for the benefits of their reforms. Most Democrats pulled their punches: think of Bill Clinton. President Obama did occasionally make the pro-government case.

---

[92] Teddy Roosevelt and Woodrow Wilson had paved the Presidential way.

It's as if the GOP's anti-government pitch left liberals reeling, afraid to buck the Reaganesque tide to argue for strong government. Odd, since George W. Bush expanded government more than any recent American President. Instead of stating clearly, unashamedly and un-defensively why we need regulation and social legislation, they often sound obfuscatingly muddled. (This, though polls consistently show that while a majority dislikes big government, most Americans also wants government to address major social problems.)

Though President Obama haltingly launched a sometimes counter-offensive, liberals have unaccountably failed to persuade un-wealthy Americans of the obvious proposition that Republican economic and tax policies benefit the rich at their expense. Consider George W. Bush's tax cuts for the wealthy. Despite polls that a large majority opposed the Bush cuts and support economic policies which are more liberal than conservative, too many Democrats have gone along with the Republicans or muted their criticisms. Democrats have also failed to address the history of deficits: that they soared under Reagan and the two Bushes, rose barely under Clinton and only rose under Obama to fight the GOP's Great Recession.

In his health care speech to Congress in September 2009, President Obama made the most vigorous, eloquent and persuasive case for strong government to make society fairer of any President since LBJ:

> "One of the unique and wonderful things about America has always been our self-reliance, our rugged individualism, our fierce defense of freedom and our healthy skepticism of government. And figuring out the appropriate size and role of government has always been a source of rigorous and sometimes angry debate....
>
> "That large-heartedness — that concern and regard for the plight of others — is not a partisan feeling. It is not a Republican or a Democratic feeling. It, too, is part of the American character. Our ability to stand in other people's

shoes. A recognition that we are all in this together; that when fortune turns against one of us, others are there to lend a helping hand. A belief that in this country, hard work and responsibility should be rewarded by some measure of security and fair play; and an acknowledgement that sometimes government has to step in to help deliver on that promise....

"You see, our predecessors understood that government could not, and should not, solve every problem. They understood that there are instances when the gains in security from government action are not worth the added constraints on our freedom. But they also understood that the danger of too much government is matched by the perils of too little; that without the leavening hand of wise policy, markets can crash, monopolies can stifle competition, and the vulnerable can be exploited. And they knew that when any government measure, no matter how carefully crafted or beneficial, is subject to scorn; when any efforts to help people in need are attacked as un-American; when facts and reason are thrown overboard and only timidity passes for wisdom, and we can no longer even engage in a civil conversation with each other over the things that truly matter – that at that point we don't merely lose our capacity to solve big challenges. We lose something essential about ourselves."

Democrats need to do more of this.

Dealing with the Problems of Large Government

Unlike Obama in this speech, Democrats rarely deal with the problems of big government. They project that they think big government is always good and don't care about its inefficiencies, costs and intrusions on liberty. They are loathe to consider scaling back this or that program or agency and tend to dismiss attacks on government programs as the ranting of right-wingers, racists and plutocrats (sometimes they are) without dealing with legitimate criticisms. No wonder voters conclude they don't "get it".

Democrats have done little thinking and talking about ways to ameliorate the problem. For too long, they have stuck to the New Deal approach to identify a problem, create a new agency, devise regulations and let the agency fix the problem. (Which sometimes works.) They're rarely willing to sunset a program or agency because the problem has been solved or no longer a high priority or there are better, market-driven ways to find good solutions. They project to the country that they want large government not just where it's needed but everywhere.

Democrats have mostly ignored thinking and talking about ways to improve how government regulates. When an agency is doing a poor job, they may try to find what human beings have acted unwisely. But, they rarely try to deal with the problems inherent in large bureaucracies: how to have effective agencies which aren't captured by the regulated and which act effectively and with the minimum necessary intrusiveness. Democrats would fare better politically if they took on these issues.[93]

4. Refusal to Value Values

America was founded on, and long sustained by, a vision of civic life that placed ethics prominently in the public square. The Declaration of Independence grounded America on "self-evident" truths that "all men are created equal," "endowed by their Creator with certain unalienable rights" to secure which "governments are instituted among men." Lincoln believed the Union was sacred because founded on what was right. He appealed to "the better angels of our nature", urging us to act "with malice toward none, with charity for all, with firmness in the right as God gives us to see the right...."[94]

---

[93] This would include championing more market-based means of regulation, to allow regulatees to figure out how best to meet the regulatory goal (say, the extent of allowed pollution), rather than mandating the means.

[94] Abraham Lincoln, First and Second Inaugural Addresses

Values talk propelled the liberal campaigns of the mid-twentieth century: the New Deal, the civil rights and peace movements, reforms proposed by Jack Kennedy and Lyndon Johnson. In his Presidential campaign, Robert Kennedy urged policies he said called upon America's heritage as a nation committed to justice, a community with obligations to one another. Ronald Reagan appealed strongly to (often much different) values, as have his Republican followers.

The Declaration and Constitution created a nation bound together in a common weal, each of us with equal rights and with responsibilities. Great leaders from the Founders through Lincoln, the Roosevelts and the Kennedys appealed to this historic connection between ethics and politics. Until, after the death of Robert Kennedy, progressives (his brother and, occasionally Obama, excepted), largely abandoned values talk, thus casting aside the application of the basic principles on which America was founded to liberal politics.[95]

The Right launched its resurgence from a platform of conservative values. They've claimed to be the guardians of our heritage of liberty and of public morals. They've succeeded in no small part because liberals have refused to challenge their "values" claims.

Instead of challenging the Right with their own (highly admirable) values, the principles on which America was built, most liberals have run the other way. They've feared that values and politics are a dangerous brew, that public talk of morality supports the Right's social agenda because the Right casts that agenda in terms of its values. Better to base policies on rational thought and good sense.

Many liberals are secular materialists, and secular materialism undermines ethical conviction by teaching there are no certain truths. If one believes that the choice of values is nothing more than a matter of personal preference, policy talk should be based in reason without appeals to morality. Leave morality to religion.

---

[95] This discussion is much influenced by Philip Gorski's brilliant American *Covenant: A History of Civil Religion from the Puritans to the Present* (Princeton University Press 2017).

Liberals eschew applying values to policy issues because they've come to think that values talk equals religious talk. As its an article of contemporary liberal faith that religion has no place in politics, the more the Right inject their values into political debate, the more liberals shudder with horror. As if to make a value-based political argument is to eviscerate the separation of church and state.

This is a fundamental misreading of American history. The Founders established our republic on a foundation of values. That foundation was not, as the Right insists, Christianity. Though the Founders were Christians (though many were, famously, actually Deists) America was not, not at all, established to be a "Christian nation".

Rather, America was built on a foundation of what Philip Gorski calls our unique civic religion of prophetic republicanism.[96] That civic religion is largely a combination of the ethical vision of the prophets of the Hebrew Bible and the ancient tradition of civic republicanism developed by Aristotle and Cicero. Its sacred texts include the Declaration of Independence, the Constitution, the *Federalist Papers* and Lincoln's greatest speeches. It is this tradition which Founders such as George Washington often cited, inter alia, to insist that good citizenship is essential to the success of our government.[97]

Prophetic republicanism contrasts — sharply — with its two competitors for American hearts and minds: religious nationalism and radical secularism. Today's Right preaches religious nationalism. This combines apocalyptic thinking with super-patriotism to see America as God's instrument to assure that good finally and irrevocably triumphs over evil in this world. This emotional engine of the Right, an impossible goal outside the gates of Eden, breeds intolerance, militarism and messianic thinking.

---

[96] See *American Covenant: A History of Civil Religion from the Puritans to the Present*, cited above.

[97] See the discussion in Chapter Twelve, Section A-2 below; also in Chapter Five, Section B-3 above.

Many on the Left insist on radical secularism, based on the two ideas of modernity with which our exploration began, secular materialism and extreme individualism. That belief set would remove not only spirituality but values from the public square.

Both militant Christianity and anti-spiritual materialism are hostile to the prophetic republicanism at America's heart. Neither speaks to "the better angels of our natures" or urges us to act "with malice toward none, with charity for all".

The liberal retreat from values talk betrays our civic religion's promise of ethical republicanism. It cedes the ground to people who reject the values on which our nation is based. To succeed, liberals must build their case on the values of prophetic republicanism. To tell the nation why religious nationalism is wrong. To tell their progressive allies and everyone else that radical secularism is wrong. To make the case that their policies draw on the well of our deepest values and are offered to fulfill those principles.

Our history since Robert Kennedy's death shows that liberals' abandonment of appeals to values has been bad politics. Progressives have thus appeared to values-motivated voters to be indifferent or hostile to public morals. They've given color to the claim that value-free progressive proposals are nothing but pork for special interests. Having allowed conservatives a monopoly on how to apply values to public discourse, progressives have given them an open field to redefine public ethics. They've allowed the hard Right to speak as champions of Christian ethics without challenging them to square their faith with the likes of W's war in Iraq, torture, opposing universal health care, seeking to destroy the safety net for the disadvantaged and opposing environmental protection.

Liberals have seemed hypocrites when the values underlying their compassion for the poor show through. They've thus deprived themselves, and the country, of dialogue by not taking arguments of the other side seriously enough to debate them on their ethical terms.

Barack Obama sometimes eloquently applied his faith and moral precepts to issues.[98] Obama wisely said that if liberals want to succeed, they need to do this, to re-engage in what Michael Sandel has called the "politics of moral engagement".[99]

****

Could liberals have won more elections had they stood by their principles? Or, was the conservative tide too strong to overcome? What about now? Or, does liberal values talk doom liberals?

The "social issues" needn't have sunk the ship. Liberals could, like Robert Kennedy, have respected the beliefs and empathized with the fears of traditionalists without selling out their principles by agreeing to policies they believe they must morally oppose.

American triumphalism is a powerful emotional force and we're going to support our troops strongly. Millions of us are dazzled by our power and believe we've a God-given mission to save the world. While liberals will take hits when they oppose over-the-top aggression (Vietnam, W's needless invasion of Iraq), try to restrain empire and vote to reduce the defense budget, Robert Kennedy (who ran on very liberal principles) provides an instructive example.

Kennedy's great charisma is not the only reason he may have been elected President despite his strong liberalism. He had, and explained, new visions of the use of American power and new ways to address social problems. When he explained why he opposed the Vietnam war to audiences of hawks, he kept their respect, changed some minds and got many votes of people he didn't convert. He did the same talking about policies to help the poor and black to working class whites. He stood on the moral bases of his beliefs, explained how his views fit into his larger, innovative vision and treated his audiences with respect

---

[98] As in his great speech on race in 2008 and his talks of public service.

[99] Michael Sandel, *Justice: What's the Right Thing to Do?*, Farrar, Straus and Giroux (2009), p.268

and empathy. He made them see that he cared about them, even when he advocated actions with which they did not agree.

Liberal leaders since 1968 have expressed nothing like his broad vision of American power and social morality, let alone a suite of workable, innovative policies. They've rarely set forth the moral bases of their positions or challenged the moral bases of the Right.[100] And, they've rarely tried to dialogue with traditionalist voters.

And so, American liberals lost the American center. Democrats win some elections but not because they're liberals. They've become distrusted on values and national security; believed to be weak and addicted to big government and high taxes; and without vision or stated, discernible moral bases for their policies. Too many average Americans believe Democrats don't give a damn about them. Having lost the trust and respect of millions they should have kept, the GOP now controls all three branches of the federal government. Amazingly, Democrats lost to Donald Trump.

Marco Rubio celebrated his 2010 election to the Senate by saying that though "Though the United States is simply the greatest nation in all of human history, ... we know that something doesn't seem right." That "something" he means is the liberal part of America. At least Rubio was articulate. Donald Trump showed that even coherence isn't necessarily required to beat the liberals.

Perhaps the Democrats have just been unlucky. Great leaders come around rarely, and it would've taken great leadership to navigate the treacherous shoals of security and patriotism, race and values, staying true to liberal values while keeping the respect and votes of millions they lost. Jack and Bobby Kennedy were great leaders, but they were killed. Perhaps Ted could have been that leader but he drove his Presidential prospects off that bridge at Chappaquiddick. There has been no great Democratic champion since.

---

[100] There's a difference between values talk and discussing one's faith. Though Ted Kennedy didn't speak of his deep religious faith, no one could doubt his politics were grounded in a passionate moral sense.

CHAPTER ELEVEN: AMERICA'S POLITICAL UGLY SIDE

"America is beautiful, but she has an ugly side."
Neil Young, "Lookin' for a Leader" © 2006

A. The Politics of Polarization

1. Schism in the Polity

Since the Republicans won Congress in 1994, politics have deeply polarized. All those inescapable maps dividing the country into red, conservative and blue, liberal states, dividing us with them. Intense schism has loosened the ties binding us to a common weal and turned "compromise" and "working together" into dirty words.

In 2004 Barack Obama introduced himself to America, hopefully saying, "there is not a liberal America and a conservative America — there is the United States of America. There is not a black America and a white America and Latino America and Asian America — there's the United States of America." As our divisions have swollen since, this hope has vanished from the public square.

The most striking manifestation of the polarization is the utter, and growing, dominance of the Republican Party by the far Right. Though there are moderate and even conservative Democrats in Congress, all, or almost all, GOP Congressmen and Senators are more conservative than every one who is a Democrat.

This represents a sea change from before Reagan and the Gingrich-led takeover of the House. There were plenty of conservative Congressional Democrats (not all from the South) and plenty of liberal and moderate Congressional Republicans[101]. The GOP seriously considered nominating for President a Teddy Roosevelt-style liberal, New York's Governor Nelson Rockefeller.

---

[101] Including such ardent liberals as Senators Jacob Javits of New York, Clifford Case of New Jersey and Charles Mathias of Maryland.

Now, practically all Southern conservatives have long been Republicans. And, the Republicans have long purged not only Rockefeller/Javits liberals but most moderates. Even un-extreme conservatives risk being tossed out in primaries, branded as heretics known as "RINO: Republicans in name only". While less ideological, the Democrats have had litmus tests: abortion, affirmative action, etc. — but without GOP-style voting discipline in Congress.

Section B-1 below explains why a healthy democracy needs to be nourished with reasoned discourse and cannot work if politics is a war to the finish. But, reasoned discourse seems impossible now that our parties are utterly polarized. Balancing and bargaining has become largely impossible between the parties. Let's explore why.

2. The Political Reasons for Polarization

The Republicans' tectonic shift rightward began with Barry Goldwater's nomination in 1964 just as Democrats were moving left. LBJ's success in getting Congress to pass the Civil Rights and Voting Rights Acts drove hosts of Southern whites to the GOP.[102] But, there were still plenty other moderate and conservative Democrats and liberal and moderate Republicans.

The Republicans began to polarize the electorate successfully with Nixon. It worked spectacularly: by early in Reagan's Presidency, the GOP had persuaded most Americans that the parties are ideological opposites and the Democrats the party of "ultra," most disagreeable liberalism. Soon many "Reagan Democrats" followed Southern whites across the aisle, and the GOP became the majority party.

As we saw in the last chapter, the Republicans could take over despite their hard swing to the right for two reasons: their rhetoric was perfectly in tune with the distress of the times and, the Democrats

---

[102] When he signed the Civil Rights Act, Johnson (over-optimistically) told Bill Moyers: "I think we have just delivered the South to the Republican Party for a long time to come." LBJ had no doubt this great legislation was worth the price.

simultaneously both moved left and became politically deaf. Each move to the party's outer flank weakened the middle from which non-polarized politics could be staged.[103]

American progressives, repulsed by flag-waving support of the Vietnam War ("my country right or wrong"), unwisely came to distrust patriotism. Repelled by militaristic self-congratulation, they became uncomfortable celebrating America, somehow seeming to feel that patriotism was inhospitable to liberalism. Conservatives, goaded by Ronald Reagan's infamous statement "government is the problem" forgot (they used to know) that government is essential for more than police and army.

Citing the GOP's years of polarization, Democrats blame the Republicans. With reason, but, the record is a bit more complex. Consider the Senate's review of nominees to the Supreme Court. It wasn't always toxic, and it began with the Democrats.

In 1971, Richard Nixon nominated Clement Haynsworth, Chief Judge of the Fourth Circuit, to the Court. Democratic Senators successfully led a crusade to defeat Haynsworth at the behest of organized labor, claiming Haynsworth was an extremist (his record on labor issues was conservative, but reasonable) and (falsely) hinting at racism. The Court lost an exceptionally distinguished jurist.

Then, in 1987 Ronald Reagan nominated Judge Robert Bork of the District of Columbia Circuit to the Court. Bork was a brilliant, articulate spokesman for very conservative views who was deeply respected by people who knew him, even when they dissented strongly from his radicalism. Bork's nomination raised the difficult question of the extent Senators ought defer to a President's choice whose views they find extreme. To prevail, the Democrats savaged a likable man.

---

[103] Polarization has been exacerbated by the change in media. Most Americans used to get news from three centrist networks. Now, conservatives watch Fox News, liberals MSNBC and others go to web sites which agree with them.

Republicans have never forgiven them, and most Court confirmations since have been partisan, angry and ugly.

3. The Clash of Fundamental Ideas

America is embroiled in culture wars over the ideas of modernity. Politics is a major front in the hostilities. The fight is fierce and unyielding because each side believes its way of life is at stake.

Secular materialism, extreme individualism and the new morality challenge faith in God and traditional ideas about right and wrong. These ideas are at the core of the beliefs of millions of believing Americans whose faith and moral code provide the foundation for, and give meaning to, their lives. The ideas of modernity threaten them deeply. Conversely, millions of other Americans feel liberated by the new morality. They feel deeply threatened by traditionalists' resolve to force a return to what they believe was a benighted, repressive past.

The enfeebling of our national and local communal ties inflames the passionate intensity of the fight. People feel vulnerable and defensive when fundamental values are challenged and are much inclined to resist their change. When we're anchored by strong communal connections, we can more readily accept adjustments because we feel rooted and confident. When, as now, we've lost that anchor, we're more likely to fight in self-defense.

We live in intolerant times of closed-minded moral certainty. Though progressives point to the intolerance on the Right, the problem is not so one-sided. Contemporary individualists tend to be too self-centered to listen to, let alone respect, contrary points of view. After years of schism, we've become all too comfortable living in a country torn asunder.

B. Political Discourse in Modern America

1. The Case for Reason, Civility and Compromise

Politics is naturally partisan, raucous and mean. Each side wants to win and it's often dirty. Yet, allowing for all that, the present state of our politics is most disturbing.

Politics also can be, often has been and ought to be, a noble calling. It has ever attracted men and women who offer public service and propose and implement ways and means to meet social challenges by their lights of the wise and the good. Astute politicians want to win, but not to demonize or eviscerate the other side: not because they're charitable but for four reasons essential to good governance.

The first reason is that a healthy state needs the consent of the governed. Members of an eviscerated opposition are likely, to a small or large degree, to withdraw their emotional and reasoned attachment to a state utterly dominated by people aiming to destroy them politically and subject them to principles they abhor. They may not rebel, but a healthy state needs far more than the sullen acquiescence of a large chunk of its citizens. A state which is utterly dominated by one side which has won a war to the finish suffers the freedom-destroying disease of "tyranny of the majority".

Second, it usually takes cooperation with the other side to get things done. Interests and ideas do not simply divide in two, with everyone always on the same side. Complex societies are, as Madison taught in the Federalist Papers, made up of many factions. Most citizens will belong to multiple factions, the cross-currents of which are central and crucial to the democratic process.

With factions, legislative skill requires mastery of the art of compromise. The interests of the factions can only be addressed and problems solved by brokering diverse interests. To put together a deal to get something done means cobbling together the votes of legislators with different ideas and speaking for different interests. This is not possible when politics is deemed a war to the finish.

When a nation's politics is dominated by two polarized parties, the resultant duality on issues sucks the diversity and multifarious nature of the many factions out of the system. The possibility of shifting coalitions essential to our Madisonian democracy shrivels. Every issue gets reduced to one all-encompassing side or the other. If factional issues and wishes don't fit neatly into this dominant duality, they will either be shunted aside or squeezed unnaturally into the polarized mold.

The legislative process of compromise and deal-making is often unattractive (that's why the art of legislation has been said to be as distasteful as "making sausages"); and the compromises struck are often sub-optimal. Recall Churchill that "democracy is the worst form of government except all the others that have been tried." That leads to the third reason to prefer a democracy of sides which have mutual respect and which are willing to talk and compromise.

This reason takes us back to Madisonian factions. Judith Shklar made the point well in her summary of Madison's reasoning in Federalist Nos. 10 and 51, those cornerstones of American democracy. The subject is how the new American system of government would avoid the ruinous conflict of factions believed to have destroyed Athenian democracy and the Roman republic:

> "Far from having to crush differences of interest or political and religious opinion, diversity was encouraged to flourish in an extended republic [that is, a nation far larger than a small city-state]. The greater the multiplicity of religious sects and of more tangible property interests, the more likely these groups are to form changing and flexible electoral coalitions, none of which has a motive for crushing the others....As every group has a chance to be a part of a majority at some time, but also in the minority at others, none has an interest in oppressing their opponents. The representatives of the people act according to the same expectations. They can, moreover, deliberate calmly and save the people from occasional follies,

and still remain close enough to the electorate to maintain their trust."[104]

That fourth reason is that outcomes with multiple inputs are usually better than decisions unilaterally imposed. That is because no one has a monopoly on wisdom or sees all pertinent perspectives. It helps to explain why to prefer oft-messy democracies to "efficient" dictatorships, even if those are "benevolent".

A healthy democracy requires the practice of the arts both of limited war and of dialogue and compromise. Though politics naturally excites the passions, they require reason, civility and mutual respect if the combatants are to keep society united and effectively address its problems. By this light, American politics are in dire straits.

2. Political Dialogue in Contemporary America

Reason and civility in American politics are, with rare exceptions, a dim memory. Rational and polite dialogue has largely vanished among disputing candidates, among citizens debating issues, between most commentators, abetted by the ever-present spinmeisters. Mutual respect for one's political opponents has largely been replaced by contempt and hatred.

Politics is, these days, most often attack politics. The other side consists of demons, bad people, liars and scoundrels, out to destroy all that is true and good, people who want to hurt "you". Ugly epithets and screaming screeds rule the day.

Television ads usually focus on the shortcomings of the opponent instead of why to vote for the sponsoring candidate. Some time ago, I saw back-to-back television ads by opponents for a local race. The first ad said nothing about its sponsor but showed a most unflattering picture of his opponent with vicious content-free attacks on his character. The message was "vote for me because my opponent is a

---

[104] Judith Shklar, "Montesquieu and the New Republicanism" (1990), in Judith N. Shklar, *Political Thought and Political Thinkers*, p. 258.

very bad person". The next ad was a mirror image of the first. Neither ad identified the office or discussed any issue.

Attack politics do not end on Election Day. They dominate political discourse, much cable news, talk radio and speeches of officials. It is worse on the Right though few leaders are blemish-free. Consider some of the attacks on President Obama. Right wing rallies routinely portrayed the President as Hitler, often with Republican Congressional leaders smiling in approval. A Republican Congressman yells out at the President during a speech to Congress "You lie!" and becomes an instant conservative hero. Etc.

It's gotten so extreme that a large percentage of Americans believe that the church-going President Obama is not a Christian, was not born in America, is a closet Muslim extremist determined to deliver the nation to radical Islam and also, somehow these things are thought to co-exist in one man, a fellow determinedly leading the nation to socialism. Now, whatever one thinks of Obama's persona and policies, this is utter nonsense. And now, the leader of this rubbish has been elected to succeed Obama.

The country is suffering a precipitous decline of intelligent political discourse. It would be healthy if Americans could debate crucial issues as a citizenry who, though with different views, share a common devotion to what's best for the nation. To reason, argue and perhaps even persuade about how to reform the health care system, engage in the world, manage our deficits and energy difficulties and deal with immigration. To do so without demonizing people with different ideas. To be willing every so often to compromise to try to solve a major problem and to accept a solution one wished had been otherwise. This is necessary, but it is not possible in present-day America.

C. American Government Today

The American government is a deadlocked dysfunctional mess. By so dis-serving the nation, it threatens our future as a democracy, as a great power and as bearing any semblance to a "city on a hill".

1. Money Power vs. Citizen Power

The problem begins with money. A democracy enfranchises its citizens so that their collective words, opinions and deeds can be the basis for governing. So that they can self-govern as active citizens engaged in deciding the nation's public choices.

We no longer live in such an America. We've examined one set of reasons for citizen disempowerment, that mass culture, mass media and extreme self-focus have eroded our sense of active citizenship. The other reason is that our politics has been hijacked by money. The wealthy have used a tsunami of wealthy contributions to seize control of our politics and government, and, in the process, washing the soil of democracy into the sea.

Elections have become very expensive, largely to pay for television advertising. Candidates for the Presidency spent $2.6 billion in 2012, much more in 2016. Though candidates have mastered the art of raising money from the small contributions of "average Americans", the enormous resources required to run for President, Governor, the Senate and the House can only be raised by getting many large contributions from wealthy individuals and institutions. Money always talks but never before as loudly as in America today.

This was true before the Supreme Court's *Citizens United* decision opened the floodgates to massive contributions. Overturning a century of precedent and practice, the very conservative Republican majority held that corporations have the same rights of self-expression as people so that any limitation on corporate political contributions is unconstitutional.[105] As predicted, corporate money has flooded into Republican coffers in the elections since 2010.

Money dominates the election of candidates, and then it dominates the processes of government. Congressmen and Senators naturally listen

---

[105] Probably every major Founder would turn over in his grave to learn that the Court held that corporations have the rights of free speech afforded to people.

to contributors who write large checks, and they hope for more when they seek re-election. With two year terms, House members never stop raising money for the next election.

Elected officials say that the only benefit donors derive from large contributions is "access", the ability to press their views in person. Well, few citizens without big, open checkbooks get that special "access". If that were all, it would pose a serious problem that might not be truly dreadful. But, it defies human nature to believe that most officials' positions are unaffected by all that money.

Consider Senator Max Baucus, at the time the powerful Democratic Chairman of the Senate Finance Committee. He was thus a fulcrum of efforts to pass the Affordable Care Act. He kept the legislation favorable to the insurance industry. He's claimed that his crucial position wasn't influenced by that industry's contributing nearly $1.5 million to his 2008 re-election campaign in a lightly populated state he carried with 73% of the vote. Perhaps. If so, he's a man of uncommon inner strength, and his contributors are people of especially poor judgment. If not, all that money given him and other legislators bought America a sub-optimal health care bill.

The need to raise vast sums to run for office coincides with surging inequality. The combination gives wealthy American citizens and institutions a deeply unhealthy sway over the political process, now much exacerbated by *Citizens United*. Since most of them are conservative, the beneficiaries are mostly candidates and ideas of the Right. Money buys influence and the power to shape opinions through marketing techniques and amass concrete political power. Average citizens are overly influenced (frequently against their economic interest) as their voices are drowned out by large contributions. This is plutocracy.

The power of money also distorts the regulatory process. Large regulated institutions spend fortunes to inundate administrative agencies with blizzards of briefs, position papers, expert studies, visits and meetings which ordinary citizens can't match. They're much bigger and richer than the agencies trying to regulate them. Even the most effective public interest advocacy groups don't have the resources to come close to what industry invests in keeping regulations friendly and assuring that regulatory proceedings help, or at least don't damage, their businesses.

There's no solution on the horizon. Institutions rarely reform themselves, and the Court has made reform impossible so long as *Citizens United* remains law.[106]

2. Congress, etc.

To benchmark our government's performance, let's begin with Lincoln and Jefferson.

> Lincoln: The legitimate object of government is to do for a community of people whatever they need to have done, but can not do, at all, or can not, so well do, for themselves — in their separate; and individual capacities."
> Jefferson: "The purpose of government is to enable the people of a nation to live in safety and happiness. Government exists for the interests of the governed, not for the governors."

Is our government satisfying needs we can't do by ourselves? Is it operating for the benefit of the people rather than "the governors"?

Let's begin with a few positives. Since Nine Eleven, the American government has protected our physical safety. Obama kept the Great Recession from becoming a depression. His Administration passed a flawed health care bill increasing coverage and taking baby steps to reform a system choking the nation. It passed a financial reform bill, though industry gutted much of it in the regulatory process. It did good

---

[106] A change in the ideological composition in the Court would likely lead to the overruling of this 5-4 decision.

work on education and reversed some of its predecessor's desecration of the environment.[107]

Few would say much else good about government's performance in recent times. It's largely ignored major pressing problems. It failed to protect the economy from the Great Crash or do anything about the economic slide of a majority of Americans. It's hardly contributed to the public's reasonable hopes for happiness.

Congress uniformly gets poor marks. Though many members are devoted public servants, the culture of the place is pork, privilege and self-preservation. Arrogance, self-righteous preening and entitlement abound. Jack Kennedy wrote *Profiles in Courage* about Senators who'd taken stands which hurt them politically because they were right. Would he profile anyone today other than John McCain (who cast the vote that sunk his party's horrible 2017 health bill).

Congress rarely gets anything useful done. Republicans mostly vote down the proscribed party line. There is virtually no open-minded dialogue, working together across party aisles or compromise. The House is now in the grip of the Freedom Caucus/Tea Party Right which believes that dialogue with Democrats, let alone compromise, is evil. Things in the Senate are only marginally better.

Senators love to style the Senate "the world's greatest deliberative body". Only if "deliberation" means pompous pontificating without getting things done. Legislation tends to languish in the Senate because the Senate is an anti-majoritarian body, whose rules allow a minority to block action. It requires a super-majority of sixty Senators approve most legislation (other than spending bills) which a minority chooses to filibuster.[108] This though the Constitution requires

---

[107] Now in 2017, the Trump Administration and Republican Congress are trying to undo health care, financial reform and Obama's actions protecting people and the environment; to eviscerate the century-old safety net; and to reduce further the taxes of the very wealthy.

[108] Though the filibuster rule has been modified on a few issues, much legislative action still requires a supra-Constitutional super-majority.

a super-majority only to amend the Constitution, and for impeachment, approval of treaties and overriding a President's veto.

Senate rules allow a Senator to hold nominations of public officials without explanation. Senators sometimes "hold" nominations to force the President on something else. Thus, in 2010 Senator Richard Shelby (an anti-government deficit hawk), cynically placed a "blanket hold" on dozens of nominations to force the signing of a contract for a constituent defense contractor and also to have the building of an expensive new federal center in his state authorized.

Gerrymandering is a major cause of governmental malaise, in Congress and state legislatures. State legislatures gerrymander districts to lump Democrats together and Republicans together. Extreme candidates tend to win in these one-party districts because what counts is the the majority party's primary dominated by its ideological base. Gerrymandered districts have allowed Republican leaders to intimidate moderate GOP Congressmen by threatening an arch-conservative opponent in the next primary. Gerrymandering has also enabled the GOP to keep control of the House despite losing a majority of votes for House seats.

California recently enacted an experiment to take the polarizing sting out of gerrymandering. The general election is now contested between the top two vote-getters in the primaries. In a solidly Republican district, the top two vote-getters might be a hard Right who would have won before and a moderate Republican. Now, the moderate Republican would have a good chance to win the general election with the votes of moderates, independents and Democrats. Perhaps this will reduce the number of elected extremists.

Corruption is endemic in Congress, and not because there is much bribe-taking. The corruption is the system's dependence on the corrosive power of money. Because most of the prodigious sums a candidate needs to raise is contributed by very wealthy people and "political action committees" (PACs) of large businesses, trade associations and unions, most elected officials are beholden to moneyed interests in deciding what to support and how to vote.

3. The Presidency

A modern nation needs a strong executive. The American Presidency is a paradox.

On one hand, the President's domestic powers are limited. While the President can do much through the the bureaucracy, most substantial change requires legislation. Here the President is hemmed in by the Constitution's checks and balances, now magnified by Congress' dysfunction. On the other hand, he is the leader of the all-powerful imperial Presidency. In matters of diplomacy, security and war and peace, the President can act with little institutional constraint.

When Theodore Roosevelt took office, the Presidency was weak. Only a few nineteenth century Presidents exercised strong power: Jefferson for the Louisiana Purchase and Embargo Act, Jackson's war on the US Bank and support of the tariff, Polk's waging the Mexican War and Lincoln's waging the Civil War. Then, TR, Wilson, FDR and their successors expanded the President's power to deal with the needs of a newly vast, industrialized and powerful modern nation.

While Presidents must be able to act with vigor, their military and foreign powers have grown out of control, proof of Lord Acton's famous axiom that "power corrupts and absolute power corrupts absolutely".[109] Most dangerous has been the erosion of legal and Constitutional limits on Presidential power in foreign policy and war.

Presidents claim to follow Lincoln, who suspended the sacred writ of habeas corpus for border state citizens believed to be working for the Confederacy. But, modern presidents have far exceeded what Lincoln thought necessary to save the embattled Union. Some examples: Lyndon Johnson tricked Congress into the vague Gulf of Tonkin

---

[109] Lord Acton, quoted in his *Essays on Freedom and Power* (1972)

Resolution, which he used to start a major war. Nixon illegally bombed Cambodia. Reagan illegally diverted funds to the Nicaraguan "contras". George W. Bush lied the nation into a major war[110] and illegally detained and tortured prisoners.

Presidential abuses of power are not confined to foreign affairs. Nixon ignored civil liberties, turned agencies loose on his "enemies list" and led the criminal cover-up of his staff's Watergate break-in. His opinion was, as he unapologetically stated, "When the President does it, that means it's not illegal."[111]

Until Bush the Younger, few Americans thought any President would ever again disdain the limits of the rule of law as much as Nixon. W engaged in secret, illegal torture; lied the nation into war; illegally spied on and wiretapped US citizens; and failed to comply with multiple Congressional subpoenas. He attached illegal "signing statements" when he signed legislation he didn't fully like, that he would only enforce the legislation on his "interpretation" usually to most certainly not what Congress clearly intended. Now, Donald Trump is off to a start likely to be even more despotic than W. We will see in the next chapter that Presidential excesses are one source of the danger that despotism might come to America.

4. Washington During Obama and Trump

The dysfunctions of the American government have never been worse than since the inauguration of Barack Obama. The Republicans in Congress decided that, rather than accept co-responsibility for governing the nation, they would subordinate everything to bringing

---

[110] Bush and his people used three rationales to go to war to topple Saddam Hussein: that he helped Al Qaeda plan Nine Eleven, that he was pursuing nuclear weapons and that he had vast stockpiles of chemical and biological "weapons of mass destruction". They knew the first two rationales were false and that the evidence for the third was unreliable, outdated and considered wrong (as it turned out to be) by the UN inspector.

[111] The Presidency is the biggest bully pulpit in the world with unprecedented ability to sway public opinion, honestly or otherwise.

Obama down, initially to prevent his re-election. Thus they voted nearly unanimously to oppose his every major initiative, even those with which they had some agreement.

The Congressional Republicans were uninterested in bargaining or compromise. Though Obama and the Democrats had won the 2008 election handily, the GOP insisted that it was "our way or the highway". With Senator Jim DeMint, they opposed health care because "If we're able to stop Obama on this, it will be his Waterloo. It will break him." Rather than contributing to solving problems, they only said "no" believing they could thereby re-take the country.

The Republicans invoked the filibuster much more than ever before to kill bill after bill which commanded majority support. In 1965, an aide told LBJ Medicare would pass comfortably as they had at least fifty-five votes. Thanks to the filibuster, that's now an abject defeat.

The 2016 election gave the Republicans control of the Presidency and both houses of Congress. The perfect opportunity, so they crowed, to roll back many of the reforms enacted since the Progressive Era, reduce further taxes on the wealthy, get rid of many of the protections afforded by regulations and eviscerate the safety net for the less advantaged. This, though it would devastate many Americans, including working class whites who are the base of Trump's support. Though, so far, in mid-2017, the GOP seems incapable of agreeing upon the terms of their legislative initiatives.

Because there's almost no effort at dialogue or compromise, the nation suffers. Constructive action is no longer possible and major problems needlessly fester. What will happen to us?

PART THREE: STORMS AND HARBORS

"Oh, a storm is threat'ning my very life today
If I don't get some shelter oh yeah, I'm gonna fade away
War, children, it's just a shot away, it's just a shot away...
Oh, see the fire is sweepin' our very street today
Burns like a red coal carpet, mad bull lost its way."
Mick Jagger and Keith Richards, "Gimme Shelter" © 1969

As the bard said, "you don't need a weatherman to know which way the wind blows."[112] We've seen that what's ailing America is that the bedeviling, bewildering conditions of modernity are attacking our time-honored fundamentals across multiple fronts. It's all the worse because, mixed together, they produce a toxic brew. A brief overview is in order.

Hearts and Minds

Secular materialism, extreme individualism and free market ideology deeply distress us, undermine self-reliance, shatter moral certainties and subvert active, empathetic citizenship. Deeply divided about God and morals, what's right and wrong, how decent people ought to live, our culture wars suppress reason, dialogue and tolerance.

This is inflamed because we're a mass culture, which triggers alienation, disempowerment, isolation and other-directedness, magnified as self-focused "me" culture diminishes our connections. The erosion of our old moral code and the glorification of greed have stoked consumerist fires and spread hedonist pursuits.

Not long ago, most American lives rested on a bedrock of faith, moral code, communal belonging, shared vision and belief in the American Dream. Now, the waves of modernity's punishing punches and of rapid change have pounded bedrock into sand: challenging faith and morals; weakening community ties; deeply dividing our visions; often pushing the promise of the American Dream away. We feel at the mercy of forces we can't influence, let alone control.

---

[112] Bob Dylan, "Subterranean Homesick Blues" © 1965

Economics, Culture and Community

Our mass culture is dominated by vast, impersonal bureaucratic institutions of business and government. They're inherently unfriendly organisms, inflexible, domineering and dehumanizing.

Until recently, local community and a shared sense of national connection were bases of American life. But, we've moved away from old neighborhoods and towns to settle in places where the sense of, and opportunity for, communal connection is much reduced. The culture wars and politics of intolerant extremism have eroded feeling part of a shared national community. Mass media culture has eroded citizenship because big money and television dwarf voters. Sound bites and attack ads encourage us to make political choices on negative emotions and dis-accustom hard thinking about public affairs. Active citizenship is in routed retreat.

The American economy was a cornucopia machine from World War II through the Sixties. But, accompanying mass culture and the era's psychic tumults, the economy stopped living up to its promise. Deregulation stripped away protections from fiscal collapse, fraud and dishonesty, un-safety and shoddy goods. The new knowledge economy put a premium on good education just when its quality fell for most Americans. Inequality bloomed as the market's "creative destruction" has left millions of Americans twisting in the wind.

The American Dream has always been the foundation of our stability and democracy. But for millions on the wrong side of the widening class divide, the Dream has come to be a far distant hope.

Our economic ills flow from the political dominance of free market ideology: low tax rates; reductions in spending on domestic needs; regulatory deregulation; little retraining of displaced workers, etc. This has been made possible by the condition of our politics.

Broken Politics

These toxic elements have fermented a sour cocktail of fury, division and rigidity. Modernity's ideas have split us asunder. The Republicans captured by the hard Right as the Democrats have alienated broad swathes of middle America. Tribal politics — "if your party wants it, I'm against it" — has deadlocked government. The loss of community has eroded the connections among people with different political views. Extreme individualism and loss of community have undermined civic responsibility. Our self-centered individualism shuts ears to disagreeable facts and thoughts.

Tolerance, dialogue, discussion, compromise and mutual respect have largely vanished into the vortices of attack politics. Compromise and bi-partisanship are virtually impossible. Just when it seems the tone of national discourse can't fall lower, it does.

Social trust is gone. But, per David Brooks, "Without social trust, the political system devolves into a brutal shouting match."[113] Can we overcome deep distrust to recover our health? Can we jettison the loathing and disdain poisoning our public square? Though Barack Obama tried, the anger deepened and the chasms widened while he was President. We now have a President devoted to loathing and division. Is social trust possible any longer in America?

Our system requires two healthy parties.[114] While there are still Democratic moderates and moderate conservatives, the Republicans have become a hard Right monolith. Once the home of such liberals and moderates as Nelson Rockefeller and Jacob Javits, the GOP is now angry, reckless and extreme, convinced of its monopoly on wisdom and virtue and its right to remake the nation in its dystopic image. We see below that that leads to decline and mediocrity.

---

[113] *The Social Animal*, p. 319

[114] See Thomas Mann and Norman Ornstein, *It's Even Worse Than It Looks, ibid*, by two highly respected political savants (Ornstein is a prominent Republican) that our system can't function if one party is extremist.

Madison envisioned a republic of factions, negotiating and compromising their way to solutions. But that's gone now that the hard Right's taken over over the GOP. The other side aren't people with different interests and points of view: they're stupid, immoral, even evil. That is what politics became in Germany and Austria before the Nazis. It's what politics has become in America.

America has great strengths: immense resources, human and natural, our freedoms, history and tradition, the values on which we've built a great country. Yet, we're in serious danger of decline because we lacked the political ability to address our addressable problems. Our great democratic experiment could, after so long, fail, our democratic forms hollowed out as we slide into despotism and follow Rome, Babylon and the rest into the archives of history.

We're in the midst of a "perfect storm": modernity's wild, untamed winds, pummeling us from all directions, undermining what are remembered as certainties of a better past. The core ideas of modernity dissolve old beliefs without providing solid grounds for emotional health. A destabilizing mass economy and mass culture serve human needs poorly, weaken community and change too fast for healthy adjustment. All as our politics and government have responded to these changes with angry division and dysfunction.

****

We need healing ideas, antidotes to secular materialism, extreme individualism and free market ideology. As we now see, these ideas are available and rooted in our traditions.

CHAPTER TWELVE: THINKING PAST OUR DOGMAS

"The dogmas of the quiet past are inadequate to the stormy present. The occasion is piled high with difficulty, and we must rise with the occasion. As our case is new, so we must think anew, and act anew. We must disenthrall ourselves, and then we shall save our country." Abraham Lincoln, Annual Message to Congress, December 1862.

"The great enemy of truth is very often not the lie (deliberate, contrived and dishonest) but the myth (persistent, persuasive, and unrealistic). Too often we enjoy the comfort of opinion without the discomfort of thought." John F. Kennedy, Yale Commencement Address, June 1962

The heart of our problem is that we're in the grip of those insidious, failed foundational ideas of secular materialism, extreme individualism and free market ideology. What to do?

The antidote to the first is to return meaning to our lives by accepting that spirituality is real and and the world has a purpose. This does not require adherence to organized religion.

The ideational antidote to excessive individualism and free market ideology is to regain our sense of community. The communitarian thinkers teach that, because we live in societies, we have both individual rights and our communal duties to our fellows.[115]

These are contemporary versions of the ideas on which America was built. The Founders and the generations which followed believed that the world was both spiritual and material and that creation had a purpose.[116] They believed that people were members of communities, not Ayn Rand-type atoms, and that active citizenship was essential for

---

[115] We might also ground ethical principles in the conditions and nature of human life. This would provide a set of shared (and ancient) values to serve as an ethical foundation on which to base dialogue.

[116] Though many were Deists, they all believed in the divine.

a good life. In essence, they were spiritual communitarians. America would be well-served if these ideas became, once again, the lingua franca of our politics.

A. From Secular Materialism To Spirituality

Secular materialism makes sick our hearts and minds. The ancients were right that people need to believe that something beyond themselves gives meaning to the world and their lives.

Thinking faith had no reality but to fill a void in weak human hearts, Marx mocked religion as "the opiate of the masses". His conviction that a just materialist society would make the oppressed content has worked out poorly. Marx' spiritual disdain is shared by many atheists, superior in their certainty that faith and religion are nothing but crutches for the billions who lack their uncommon strength and courage to accept that there is no God, no realm of the spirit. We are alone, even if most of us can't bear the thought.[117]

Is the world so bleak, nothing but particles which now cohere and now clash and now have nothing to do with any others? Is there no purpose to life beyond the laws of science? Philosophers have long sought to prove that God exists. Most thinkers, religious or not, agree that they have, by the laws of Reason, all failed.

The lack of logical proof does not prove there is no God or spirit. Kierkegaard's answer was to accept God with a non-rational leap of faith. There are ways other than that leap to conclude there is a realm of Spirit, a creator God present within the world.

I know from where anti-spiritual people come. For years, I was a rock-ribbed materialist atheist, devout in my unbelief. I couldn't accept ideas of God and Spirit for two reasons: because of the presence of evil and because I thought God and Spirit required suspension of the

---

[117] Some neuroscientists think the human brain is hard-wired to believe in God. Though some think that, if true, this proves spiritual notions are just hard wires' false fantasies, it may rather be that our minds are inclined to believe in what exists.

laws of science. If God, Spirit and paranormal phenomenon (such as miracles) couldn't fit with Newtonian physics, I couldn't accept them. But, over time, the evidence of Divinity and Spirit piled up. As I learned more about modern physics, I found it quite compatible with a non-material spiritual realm.

Central ideas of modern physics — quantum mechanics, the uncertainty principle and field theory — drastically change the Newtonian picture of the world. It turns out that, at the sub-atomic level, matter is neither solid nor measurable, not the fixed, readily calculable material we'd thought it to be. Rather, most of matter is empty space; electrons are simultaneously both particles and waves of light, simultaneously in more than one place. As Einstein taught in his equation, E [energy] =m [mass] (x) c [speed of light] (squared), mass and energy are different aspects of the same thing. One consequence of all this is that it's impossible to tell when or whether that electron is a particle or a wave or just where it is.

As these effects operate at the sub-atomic level, Newtonian principles about the macro-world we inhabit are correct. What modern physics explains is that the micro-world which is the foundation of existence is much different from the mechanical certainty from which philosophic materialism derives.

Sub-atomic physics has also learned something revolutionary about connections between particles. Heretofore, particles were considered separate and distinct, unconnected except able to adhere chemically or attract and repel each other electrically or mechanically. And of course, nothing, nothing whatsoever in the universe, could travel faster than the speed of light.

Recent experiments seem to toss those notions in the dustbin. Photons (tiny sub-atomic particles) which have been in close proximity have been found later to affect each other even when kept utterly disconnected, either by lead (impervious to light) or separated by great distances. In these experiments, an action done to one photon registers with the other — through lead and faster than the speed of light. These experiments are among the bases of new theories that the universe, rather than being utterly empty almost everywhere, consists of multiple fields of information in tiny particles which are readily shared. It seems that, rather than distinct atoms alone in a cold universe, all is connected to all.[118]

For a secular materialist comforted by the certainties of Newton's laws, this is wild and crazy stuff. Yet, it seems to describe the world.

God and Spirit fit easily into a universe whose physical foundation is quantum theory, the uncertainty principle and field theory. Since electrons are simultaneously in more than one place, there can be more than one kind of reality. Rather than a single stable thing, the same physical material is simultaneously in different places doing different things, seen differently by different viewers with different perspectives. The great physicist David Bohm drew one possible conclusion: that reality is a set of holograms, that the world we see, feel and inhabit is one explicate order of many orders implicate in the holographic universe. Because the world we see is far from the only world, a world of Spirit can readily co-exist with the material world in which we live.[119]

Some physicists go further to claim that quantum mechanics requires a superhuman presence. Thus, Amit Goswami argues that because electrons are not in just one place, the world would not cohere without a supreme intelligence to assure that electrons be, and stay, where they need to be. Without a guiding intelligence, this collection of particles would not cohere to be a table nor stay a table from one moment to the next. Rather, it would disintegrate (perhaps to re-form) as the electrons change positions.[120]

---

[118] This fits well with communitarian ideas, see below, about human flourishing.

[119] See David Bohm, *Wholeness and the Implicate Order* (Routledge Press 1980).

[120] See Amit Goswami, *God Is Not Dead* (Hampton Roads Publishing 2008).

Perhaps Goswami is right that quantum physics requires the presence of God; perhaps not. Perhaps Bohm saw the world is in error. Perhaps other authors with spirit-allowing theories haven't gotten it right. The point is that the new physics makes ample room for God, Spirit and paranormal phenomena, that Science needn't trump Spirit after all. You don't have to dismiss Science to have spiritual faith that there's something beyond our material world.[121]

Perhaps, Reason will some day prove that there is a realm of Spirit, that God exists. Until then, it's a matter not of rationality but belief, "feeling" and emotion. To quote one observer, "Religion [I'd say "spirituality" rather than "religion"] does not depend on the success of some speculative theory about the universe. It depends upon the sense of human beings that they can apprehend a personal reality that is other and better than they, and that supports and encourages their own striving for goodness."[122]

There is quite a bit of supporting evidence. Consider this. It may just be lucky chance, but the physical characteristics of the Earth are in so delicate a balance that the slightest variation in any of the chemical and other characteristics of our planet would make complex life impossible.[123] The same is true of the balance of physical forces which allow the Universe to cohere. Does it not cause wonder that the universe came to exist at all, that it was able to develop into the rich world we know, that the laws of physics and biology are as they are so that the universe and life could happen? If Science can't prove a

---

[121] Scientists such as evolutionary biologist Richard Dawkins argue that Science proves atheism because there is no room for action outside of the laws of matter. See, e.g., Richard Dawkins, *The God Delusion* (Mariner Books 2008). This thinking seems to be based on an outmoded mechanistic view of reality.

[122] Keith Ward in Paul Davies and Niels Henrik Gregersen, eds., *Information and the Nature of Reality: From Physics to Metaphysics* (Cambridge University Press 2010), p. 298.

[123] See James Lovelock, *Gaia: A New Look at Life on Earth* (Oxford University Press 1979).

Supreme Intelligence impossible, why is such nan existence not a more plausible explanation than the random effects of the Big Bang's unexplained ancient explosion?

There is much more evidence. Many "paranormal" experiences, which purely material thinking can't explain, have been verified. There are scientifically inexplicable cures, visions from near-death experiences, seemingly impossible powers of such deeply religious people as Tibetan Buddhist monks and Hindu savants. There's the evidence of very similar experiences of great mystics from many traditions and faiths who gain knowledge of a profound, distinct spiritual world. The usual materialist opinion is that all of the people reporting all of these experiences were either delusional or liars. It seems highly unlikely.

I am no mystic. I've not myself been graced with experience of the ineffable. While I have no iron-clad logical proof, evidence of design (such as noted above) and such feelings, experiences and reports make it utterly clear to me that there is a spiritual world, a Divine presence, a purpose to life beyond the here and now, though we mere mortals can merely surmise what that is.

What will a new world view imbued with spirituality look like? Will it be a return to the medieval world view? Will a new spirituality be fundamentalist, harshly dogmatic like our hard religious Right or, worse, like Islamic fundamentalism? Will it throw out the good of Enlightenment values with the bath water of materialism?

That need, and ought, not be. The great Judeo-Christian faiths are based on the belief that (a good) God created the world and imbued it with divinity and purpose, that at the heart of things is love. The great eastern religions are not monotheistic (e.g., Hinduism) or even believe in a God (Buddhism), but they share the belief that the world is divine, purposeful and based on love.

Religion can veer from love and goodness to intolerance, and then from that to violence, when believers become convinced that only their ideas about God are right and that unbelieving blasphemers must be erased. But, that contradicts the core message with which the great religions began and which animate their best thought. Which, to repeat, is that Creation is divine and that all people — even those mistaken blasphemers — share in that divinity.

Consider James Carroll's deliberation on religious violence through the ages in *Jerusalem, Jerusalem*. Carroll concludes with five principles which animate religion because they honor God's Creation. They're as good as any roadmap for how to live a life imbued with faith:

> (1) "Good religion would celebrate life, not death." (2) "Good religion recognizes in God's Oneness a principle of unity among all God's creatures, a unity that is also know as love." (3) "Good religion is concerned with revelation, not salvation": revelation that God is in the world, within ourselves in this life here and now; not salvation from enemies and hell. (4) "Good religion knows nothing of coercion." (5) And, "in the new age, good religion may, paradoxically, have a secular character."

As Carroll explains, "Religion at its best is only a way of knowing that religion [meaning 'organized religion'] is unnecessary" as people find a "conception of the person in relation to a conception of the divine".[124]

Spirituality has implications for how we manage society. It imposes the duty to respect the people created by, or thanks to, God, with human rights, fairness, decent social services, opportunities and a safety net when circumstances go badly awry. And, we have the duty to respect God's creation with ecological care and concern.

****

My personal surmise about the purpose of existence is this: One of the most persuasive arguments against the existence of a good, omnipotent God is that the world is full of evil. Bad things happen to good people,

---

[124] James Carroll, *Jerusalem, Jerusalem* (Houghton Mifflin Harcourt 2011), pp. 310-16.

all the time. How can one square that with belief in an all-powerful beneficent God? Voltaire famously could not, seeing the horrific Lisbon earthquake of his time as proof that there can be no such God. The man-made horrors common to modern times are much worse. So I had thought for many years.

I've reconsidered. God could not create a world which was all good because that would not allow for life in any form we can imagine. Everyone would then be God-like, perfect. There'd be no basis for striving, for doing all that constitutes an active life. Everything would be like the last cantos of Dante's *Divine Comedy* with all engaged in the single activity of praising God.

Creation required that God separate matter from His Divine Existence. Had God not separated matter from Himself, all existence would be God: not a universe as we know it, but every thing wholly faultless and good. That is, to create the world, God had to shatter part of His Divinity. But, God connected His Creation to Himself by putting a piece of His Divinity into every thing.

I surmise that the purpose of the world is what Judaism calls "tikkun olam", to repair the thus-broken world so that it, we, can approach ever closer to the Divine. If mankind or whatever creatures might succeed us ever reach that state, that would be the end of history, probably something like the conclusion of the *Divine Comedy*. For life as we know it then to resume would require a new Creation.

Of course, this surmise could be as wrong as wrong can be. Regardless, it is now evident to me is that we humans aren't just randomly evolved collections of particles living in the cold, lonely empty universe of philosophic materialism. Life is more than a chance occurrence where nothing really matters. There's a spiritual world and a Divine purpose to life.

So most people have believed until the modern age. Modern materialism has left holes in secular hearts. We need healing. For that, it's essential to return to a belief in spirituality and the holiness and purpose of life. The good news is that it is highly likely that this will be a return to something true.

B. Communitarian Ideas and Capabilities

1. Communitarian Thought

Descartes, the fountainhead of individualism, believed we humans are autonomous individuals separate and distinct from the societies in which we live. Communitarians start from the quite different premise that as we necessarily live in societies, our nature cannot be isolated from, but is entwined with, community life. It's the better way to think about the human condition.

Different communitarians make more, or less, room for the importance of the individual within her community. Some — call them "strong" communitarians — define what's good by what's best for the community as a whole. The needs and wants of individuals take a back seat to the community's collective wants and needs.

Rousseau apotheosized what he called the "general will", what's deemed best for the overall community, to which individual wants and needs are to be subordinated. The general will trumps the individual: what's best for the entire community must prevail whatever its effects on some people.[125] Rousseau's (and the Utilitarian) view emphasizes man's social role at the expense of his individuality. Unsurprisingly, totalitarians are fond of the general will because it subordinates individual rights to social duties, a long swing of the pendulum from extreme individualism to social control.

The thinking which can cure us Americans is of "soft" communitarians who value both sides of humanity: her personhood and her social being. This kind of balanced thought goes back to Aristotle, who, because his standard of ethical value was the good of the polis, was an ancient communitarian. Like soft communitarians, Aristotle would

---

[125] In this, Rousseau resembles the Utilitarians for whom we must maximize the greatest good for the greatest number, regardless of the effect on individuals.

have opposed the notion of a general will because, for him, the power of society and state existed not for its own sake but because a strong community is essential for people to thrive.

John Dewey similarly defined freedom as participation in the common life of society. His ideal was, as he said in Liberalism and Social Action, to establish "an entire social order possessed of a spiritual authority that would nurture and direct the inner as well as the outer life of individuals." For Dewey, the individual isn't an atom-like cog but a realized person capable of good citizenship.

Present-day "soft" communitarians such as Alasdair MacIntyre, Michael Sandel, Michael Walzer and Charles Taylor blend the communal aspect of human life with deep respect for each person and her rights as a unique individual.[126] They teach that life's meaning comes from our connections with others. As Taylor explains in Sources of the Self, the way people relate to each other is what gives significance and meaning to the choices they make.

The basis of these communitarian ideas is that we unique individuals live together in societies. Though distinct individuals, we are social beings, all in this together. Each person's identity blends her distinctive personhood and the characteristics of her communities. As we soon see, this is, in fact, how our minds work.

Per Aristotle, man is a social animal. Human nature is rounded: both individual and communal. In the Middle Ages, people bent their individuality to society's rigid rules. The extreme form of today's individualism conversely ignores the social half of our humanity. As an unrestrained individual cannot live a good, useful and satisfying life, the individualism of our day was bound to sicken us at heart.

---

[126] Central works include Alasdair MacIntyre, *After Virtue* (Notre Dame Press 1981); Michael Sandel, *Liberalism and the Limits of Justice* (Cambridge University Press 1982); Charles Taylor, *Sources of the Self* (Harvard University Press 1989); and Michael Walzer, *Spheres of Justice* (Basic Books 1983). See also Wilson Carey McWilliams, *Redeeming Democracy in America* (Kansas University Press 2011) for superb background from America's founding.

MacIntyre makes clear that we aren't isolated individuals:

> "For I am never able to seek for the good or exercise the virtues only qua individual....I inherit from the past of my family, my city, my tribe, my nation, a variety of debts, inheritances, rightful expectations and obligations. These constitute the given of my life, my moral starting point. This is in part what gives my life its own moral particularity."[127]

Rather than atoms bouncing separately around the cosmos we are, in Sandel's phrase, "bound up with membership and belonging":

> "[W]e all approach our own circumstances as bearers of a particular social identity. I am someone's son or daughter, someone's cousin or uncle; I am a citizen of this or that city, a member of this or that guild or profession; I belong to this clan, that tribe, this nation. Hence, what is good for me has to be the good for one who inhabits these roles."[128]

Communities owe people rights and people have duties to their communities. We have the rights of free people: free expression, freedom from arbitrary state action, etc. We also have the duties of citizens: to participate in political life by voting and otherwise; to give the community needed service; to pay fair taxes to support the common good, and so forth.

People are neither rootless atoms nor personality-less ants or bees. Each of us is a unique individual with his own persona, who can only live and thrive in society. We are, in significant part, our connections to other people. We need simultaneously to respect and honor our individuality and our social identities, our surfaces and our depths, to aim at personal goals in the context of our social connections.[129]

---

[127] *After Virtue*, p. 220.

[128] *Justice: What's the Right Thing To Do* (Farrar, Straus and Giroux 2009), p. 222

[129] Such a life is at odds with the idea that the market ought to be king.

It's well past time to have the pendulum swing back to the middle. To believe again in responsibilities as well as rights, to see the world as more than just what's there for me. To remember that being an active democratic citizen is necessary for psychic health, essential to a good life. The Founders built America on a balance between society and the individual. The communitarian vision of the good life provides the contemporary version of that essential balance.

2. Rights Derived from Human Capabilities

"Human capabilities" thought supplements communitarian thinking by defining some of what society owes its members. Martha Nussbaum and Amartya Sen argue that society has an ethical duty to enable each person to maximize her "human capabilities", which are the aspects of a person's life which enable her to thrive.[130]

In Nussbaum's expression, capabilities are what a person is "able to do and to be," "a set of (usually interrelated) opportunities to choose and to act....the alternative combinations of functionings that are feasible for her to achieve." "[T]hey are not just abilities residing inside a person but also the freedoms or opportunities created by a combination of personal abilities and the political, social and economic environment."[131] Capabilities include longevity; bodily health and physical integrity; living in circumstances in which one can use her abilities and senses; and having some control over her circumstances through economic and political activity. Capabilities thinkers make the case that each person has the right, inherent in human dignity, to a life in which she can exercise her capabilities.

Notice a crucial distinction between the "me culture's" sense of

---

[130] See, e.g., Amartya Sen and Martha Nussbaum, *The Quality of Life* (Clarendon Press 1993); Martha Nussbaum, *Creating Capabilities: The Human Development Approach* (Harvard University Press 2011); Amartya Sen, *The Idea of Justice* (Harvard University Press 2009).

[131] Nussbaum, *Creating Capabilities*, p. 20.

rights and rights derived from "capabilities". Contemporary self-absorbed individualists think about rights passively, as things I ought to be given. The capabilities about which Nussbaum and Sen speak are different: the rights not to receive docily, but to be able to do. They are provided as the necessary means to enable an active life, making as much of oneself as she can. The key question is "What is each person able to do and to be?" What is owed is "substantial freedom to choose and act...opportunity to select".[132]

The difference is between expecting hand-outs and expecting the opportunity to go out and get it. It's the difference between entitlement and the ability to reach for the American Dream.

3. Extreme Individualism and the Mind

There is much neurological evidence, recently developed, that the human mind differs greatly from the image of the extreme form of individualism. As we have seen, that image is that I am me, you are you, and, though we may intersect in society, what makes me who I am is wholly inner to me and to my nature and experiences. I thus am, in essence, a human atom.

Thinkers and artists since Nietzsche and Conrad have seen we humans in a different light. Our minds blend both what comes from within and what we take from others. That is, we are fundamentally connected "in a web of other souls in such a fundamental way that one soul feels, responds to and supplements" other souls "in a shared feeling of solidarity that ... is constitutive of a community". Not always but often, especially when under external threat.[133]

As Lawtoo's book shows, neurological researchers have found that the brain's neurons are much susceptible to the effects of others, both others who are personally in our lives and others from the

---

[132] Id., pp. 18, 20, 24, 25.

[133] Nidesh Lawtoo, *Conrad's Shadow: Catastrophe, Mimesis, Theory*, pp. 124-25 (Michigan State University Press 2016). See also, e.g., Conrad works he discusses and Nietzsche, *Beyond Good and Evil*, e.g. sec. 12.

past. This latter means that who we each is includes the cultures and traditions we imbibe as we live.

C. Values and the Grounds of Ethics

People will always disagree about what is right, fair and just. A good society debates and decides public questions with intelligence and civility, but these are now in short supply in America. A shared set of moral principles would give us a framework for public discourse that would facilitate civil and principled debate. While our religions and traditions provide sets of values, revealed by God or sanctioned by history, we are too diverse for any one of them to command anything like universal assent.

Is there a non-faith set of values which might gain wide agreement about how best to frame our political discussions? A basis for thinking morally that doesn't depend upon your religion or mine, upon the history of our cultures or upon the personal preference that this philosopher appeals to you and that one to me? There is. It is to find the values best suited to us given the nature of our human lives. What follows is a brief sketch of this path to common values.

This first step is to set forth the basic parameters of our lives. We know, without substantial dissent, core facts about who we are[134]; the

---

[134] We are diverse, unique and complex social beings of body and spirit, reason and emotion, products of nature and nurture, sharing a common humanity, loving life, wanting to better our lives, neither all "good" nor all "bad".

conditions of human life[135]; and the nature of human thinking.[136] These are the traits, characteristics and circumstances which shape human lives. They are, as such, the "grounds of ethics".

The second step examines the moral implications of these grounds of ethics. In light of human nature and life, what values will best lead us to live as well as possible? We find that if we take the values which follow as our guides, we will produce lives and societies as healthy and rich as circumstances allow. Because they are based on the human condition, these values have been prized by all manner of societies and are logical and congruent with how we think about right and wrong. They feel right.

The values we deduce from the grounds of ethics are these: To relate to humanity as a whole with tolerance, respect, justice, solidarity, generosity and charity.
- To be reliable and accountable, caring, honesty, loyal, kind, loving and merciful and compassionate with others.
- To be humble, patient and detached, dignified, diligent and persistent, courageous, committed and passionate.
- To be open-minded, flexible and skeptical; to learn from experience and from different points of view and to know ourselves and the world; and to have a sense of reverence, respecting the non-rational and the mystical.

---

[135] Life is immensely complex, intertwined and difficult and constantly changing. It is strong, fragile and finite; imperfect; full of conflict and cooperation; necessarily lived within limits and based on the past.

[136] The mind is immensely complex, engaging reason, emotion, physical drives and spirituality; deeply influenced both by innate traits, abilities and tendencies and by experience, though we can know but a little about all this. We use only a bit of our mind's richness, and can never escape one's own perspective, so that we can never be certain of the "truth".

- To follow the three overarching values of the Golden Rule, to live in the mean; and to balance competing values in the light of facts and circumstances.[137]

By providing a familiar moral framework for debate, these values are good guides to good politics. They promote reasoned, respectful discourse by active, humane citizens, mindful of the Golden Rule, encouraged to tolerance, mutual respect, open minds, the humility to think "I'm not always right" and the courage to make hard choices when necessary. Because we share a common set of moral principles, we can focus disagreement on how best to weigh and apply our shared values to the question of the moment. It could be a large step back to healthy politics and good government.

---

[137] These values harmonize well with communitarian and capabilities ideas and with the return to spirituality discussed above.

CHAPTER THIRTEEN: DEMOCRACY FOR THE USA

"It's coming from the sorrow in the street,
The holy places where the races meet;
From the homicidal bitchin' that goes down in every kitchen
To determine who will serve and who will eat.
From the wells of disappointment where the women kneel to pray
For the grace of God in the desert here and the desert far away:
Democracy is coming to the U.S.A."
Leonard Cohen, "Democracy" © 1992

A. What Kind of a Country Do We Want?

What kind of country do we want? How can our country make it possible that Americans have good lives?

We want a country that works: providing the basis for material well-being and allowing us to feel morally good. We want a nation able to face up to, and competently address, its major problems. We want a nation which offers what we've long called the American Dream, so that, with pluck and effort, one can make a better life for herself and her family, so her children have better opportunities than her own.

No one can thrive outside of a society which makes success possible. Bill Gates and Steve Jobs could not have prospered in North Korea. As Elizabeth Warren has often said, no one gets rich on his own: she needs the support of a community and of public services.

We want a society in whose values and ideals we believe. We want a nation in which we are proud to answer: "What kind of country are we?" We, or most of us, want an America which tries to live up to our ideals: the city on a hill. We've seen that means to want a society which looks to communitarian ideas and away from secular materialism to a sense of spirituality. We (ought to) want a society of active citizens, imbued with self-interest, rightly understood, as a balance between personal and social wants and needs.

We want a nation whose people have the moral and social capital a successful democracy requires. To reprise David Brooks, we have lost, and must rebuild, our old social and moral capital based on strong communities and moral consensus.[138] We want a political system which can, for all our inevitable disagreements, deliver sound solutions to pressing problems. We want a "national greatness agenda".[139] What ought that to be?

America's agenda is long — and urgent, because our dysfunctional politics have long thwarted solutions to pressing problems. This is unsustainable. The problems won't fix themselves. They are, however, solvable with will and wisdom. But, unless we Americans seize the day and seize it soon, this mighty nation of great promise will go the way of other empires which came, saw, conquered and declined. America today faces, as Barack Obama repeatedly said during his 2008 Presidential campaign, what Martin Luther King called "the fierce urgency of now".[140]

An agenda to return America to health requires vigorous government action. How could it be otherwise in a complex, modern society, when markets are insufficient for many needed tasks? We need to get over the knee-jerk reflexivity of our vehement anti-government mood. Ronald Reagan was wrong. Government is not the problem: it is an essential part of any solution. Our challenge of policy is to define government's role wisely.

---

[138] David Brooks, *The Social Animal, ibid*, p. 334.

[139] David Brooks, "A National Greatness Agenda", *New York Times*, November 10, 2010. See also Tom Friedman, "!00 Days", *New York Times*, June 21, 2011.

[140] Martin Luther King, "I Have A Dream", Address at the Lincoln Memorial, August 28, 1963

B. Some Thoughts About Policies

"Well, God is in His heaven
And we all want what's His
But power and greed and corruptible seed Seem to be all that there is."
Bob Dylan, "Blind Willie McTell" © 1983

That seems too much like our country today. Despite recovery from the Great Recession, America is in crisis. We're so angry and divided that we avoid even trying to solve urgent, fundamental problems. It seems like a vicious circle with no exit. The divisive anger breeds more dysfunctional politics which block solutions. As the problems worsen, frustration feeds the irate belief that a demonic other side is responsible for the crisis. "They" are ruining the country and making my life worse. The chasm widens and the crisis deepens.

So, is the richest nation in human history condemned to slide into mediocrity, its great promise returned unredeemed? If not, what ought we do? America has grave problems and huge assets: free institutions, vast resources, a flexible economy, an enterprising people. Destructive decades have weakened the assets, but they're still available, if only we stop frittering them away.[141]

To thrive, America must address pressing economic issues; reduce its sprawling and unaffordable empire; tackle global warming and other environmental degradation which threaten healthy human life with the rest of the world; restore the vanishing American Dream and reduce inequality; and promote, and so restore, active citizenship among the people. A few words about these issues.[142]

---

[141] See, e.g., Fareed Zakaria, *The Post-American World*, *ibid*; and David Brooks, "The Crossroads Nation", *New York Times*, November 8, 2010.

[142] This book's first edition contained detailed policy suggestions in its Chapter 15.

1. Economic Policies and Regulation

Much as the libertarian Right wishes it weren't so, we need a sound regulatory regime to protect us from carelessness and greed. Disliking government interference, we haven't found a good path through the free market/regulatory thicket, to find how best to forestall another crash, limit cheating in commerce and prevent unsafe and harmful goods.

The kind and level of regulation should fit the circumstances: tightest for great risks (like mining accidents and air traffic control) and shaped to fit particular markets.[143] It should, where it can, set the required ends rather than the means of compliance: to incent regulatees to devise how best to accomplish the public objective.

America is deeply in debt. Unlike individuals, economically successful nations can prosper with a great deal of debt. But, there are limits and we've increased what we owe willy-nilly like a child building a sandcastle as the tide's rushing in. We've reached the point where we ought to heed the incoming tide.

America's "sovereign debt" is what's owed creditors who've financed federal budget deficits with loans and to whom we pay a great deal of interest.[144] The radical Republicans have made the sovereign debt a political football to try, by refusing to increase the debt limit to pay bills already incurred, to force drastic reductions in domestic spending.

---

[143] Where present regulation is too tight, relax it. Where it's overly relaxed, unrelax it. Where it's overdone or mal-administered, change it. If bureaucratic creep ossifies the process, change method, rule or administrators. Be eternally vigilant to prevent the regulated from controlling the regulators.

[144] Public "deficits" also include the extent to which Medicare and Social Security funds are estimated to be insufficient to meet future obligations. These are projections which change if future tax payments differ from estimates, if program terms are changed or, as to Medicare, if health care costs rise faster or slower than is assumed. We can manage these "deficits" with modest changes and otherwise essential control of health care spending.

Though too high, our debt needn't be reduced at once, so long as we adopt a sound deficit-reduction plan now. That should include stiff cuts in excessive spending on defense and agricultural subsidies (which now mostly benefit large agri-businesses).

2. The American Empire

America's been an empire since World War II, though we don't own other peoples' territories. We bestride the globe like a colossus, employing our enormous power to try to shape the world to our wishes. Though it's supposed to make us secure and it's seductive when it seems to bring glory, the plain fact is that our vast empire is ruining our health. We don't need nearly what we spend on defense, intelligence and domestic security. We simply cannot afford it.[145]

America built up an enormous defense and intelligence establishment to defeat Communism. We were told to expect a very large "peace dividend" once the Soviet Union fell. Instead, we spend even more on our empire and have many more troops, contractors and bases abroad than at the height of the Cold War.[146]

We simply can't afford the trillions (as much as the rest of the world combined) we spend on empire, bloating excessive deficits and starving domestic needs. Rome declined because it overextended. If the full scope of our empire was necessary for our protection, we'd face a Hobson's choice: defend against foreign threats but ignore domestic problems or the opposite. But, though we need plenty of bases, military forces, weapons and the like, we simply don't need so many to be secure.[147] The idea is to tame the lion of empire, not

---

[145] See Andrew Bacevich, *Washington Rules: America's Path to Permanent War, ibid.*; Chalmers Johnson, Dismantling the Empire: America's Last Best Hope (Metropolitan Books, 2010) and William Pfaff, The Irony of Manifest Destiny: The Tragedy of America's Foreign Policy (Walker & Company 2010)

[146] We've also massively privatized military and intelligence functions, at great expense, losing control and quality.

[147] A major reason for so massive an empire is our dependence on foreign oil.

dismantle our power; to scale back our ambition to police the world and try to control so much of what other nations do.[148]

The costs of empire are much more than financial. Quite famously, Dwight Eisenhower — General Eisenhower — took the occasion of his farewell address as one of America's most popular Presidents to warn of the military-industrial complex:

> "In the councils of government, we must guard against the acquisition of unwarranted influence, whether sought or unsought, by the military industrial complex. The potential for the disastrous rise of misplaced power exists and will persist. We must never let the weight of this combination endanger our liberties or democratic processes. We should take nothing for granted. Only an alert and knowledgeable citizenry can compel the proper meshing of the huge industrial and military machinery of defense with our peaceful methods and goals, so that security and liberty may prosper together."

The militaristic leviathan Ike feared is here. It's coarsened our discourse, led to arrogance and hubris and undermined core values of human dignity and respect and bred a tolerance of torture.[149]

3. Global Warming and Healing the Environment

This is the most urgent problem of all. The evidence, and the consensus of scientists, is overwhelming that the Earth is warming precipitously and that industrial man is the, or at the least a major,

---

[148] Terrorism is our worst immediate threat. But, combatting terrorists isn't so much a military matter as requiring sophisticated and determined police action.

[149] It induces our leaders to assume God-like powers. Hear Karl Rove: "We're an empire now, and when we act, we create our own reality. And while you're studying that reality ... we'll act again, creating other new realities, which you can study too, and that's how things will sort out. We're history's actors...and you, all of you, will be left to just study what we do.' Ron Suskind, "Faith, Certainty and the Presidency of George W. Bush", *New York Times Magazine,* October 17, 2004

cause. We are despoiling air, water and land and using resources at a rate far greater than the Earth's ability to recover and replenish. Unless we act quickly and decisively, we'll irrevocably foul our nest and run out of resources on which we've come to depend.

Discussion of climate change and environmental degradation ought to be, needs to be, about "how to fix" not "whether". This discussion must include reducing energy use and changing its sources. Despite the Right's insane faith that global warming is a myth,[150] we must act now to keep the planet from becoming an inhospitable furnace, running out of natural resources and further degrading our air, water and land. If we humans don't learn to live as best we can in symbiosis with the Earth and act forcefully now, we will condemn ourselves to suffer climate catastrophes which will displace billions and wreak havoc on civilization. Or worse.

As we act, we must balance the speed and economic impact of reducing emissions to try not to damage the economy. While new energy-saving technologies and alternative energy sources should boost the economy, we don't yet know by how much and it'll take time. Though we need to act quickly, action which throws world economies to the mat won't be adopted.

Animals know not to foul their nests. Any sane society will respect the environment, if not out of love and care for God's creation then to avoid disaster.[151] Having put our home in peril, it's suicidal to be other than an environmentalist. To quote Thoreau, "What's the use of a fine house if you haven't got a tolerable planet to put it on?"

---

[150] One definition of insanity is the inability to distinguish fantasy from reality.

[151] Strong environmentalism ought to be a handmaiden of Biblically-based faith. God gave man care and stewardship of the Earth for his life, health, sustenance and prosperity. We're to care for and replenish Her gift, not lay it waste. God gave man rule over Nature (to "subdue it") to benefit from its glorious bounty by managing Her Creation well, not by despoiling the divine gift.

4. Restoring the American Dream: Inequality and Fairness

The American Dream's always been the American birthright — the promise of opportunity at the core of our greatness, the main reason the poor and huddled masses fled across the oceans to a strange new world. But, it's gone terribly wrong.

Beginning in the Seventies, the Dream has receded for millions of ordinary Americans. We're now more deeply divergent economically, and the divide is widening, than since the eve of the Great Depression. Education and opportunities for the majority on the wrong side of the curve have weakened. The quality of "social goods" provided by government (health care, education, infrastructure...) declines as we starve public spending. Life in the middle, let alone below, keeps getting harder.

It's no wonder people have become cynical about leaders and institutions. Mass democracies depend on the connections of national community, which require a sense of fairness and shared sacrifice. But, our increasingly unbridgeable class divide — far greater than accounted for by differences in talents, effort and circumstances — corrodes that sense. Democracy can't thrive when the bottom two-thirds or ninety percent feel they can't make it.[152]

The goal is an America in which inequality returns to post-World War II levels, a country not egalitarian but fair, in which people can make what they will of their abilities. That requires policies: (1) which attack the class divide directly through fair tax and employment policy and (2) which provide good, ample "social goods" — education, health care, infrastructure and a safety net.

There's a wide range of fair tax policies. The present American tax code is not one of them. A just and fair tax code has graduated rates, so

---

[152] Our class divide is a vicious circle undermining the economy's foundations. As millions lack opportunity to contribute amply, the economy sub-performs, providing less to spend on the social goods needed to provide those opportunities. And so it goes.

that the better-off, who benefit the most from society, pay a larger proportionate share of society's costs. Though the American tax code is graduated on paper, the array of deductions and credits are such that it's not in practice. As constructed, it does not ameliorate but contributes to rising inequality.[153]

"Social goods" are goods and services which the unaided market does not, or is unlikely to, provide well. Many social goods are essential to good lives. Because they make life better in ways markets don't adequately value, only government can amply provide them for everyone at good quality and affordable cost.

This means significant government involvement to provide good education, health care and such essential infrastructure as roads, bridges, airports and train stations. We've underinvested in education and infrastructure for years and our health system provides mediocre care (except at the top) at by far the greatest cost in the world. We must address all this wisely and well.[154]

We also need to improve our social safety net substantially. Many people suffer catastrophes. There's no moral failure in losing one's health or having his job vanish and be unable to find new work. Apostles of the libertarian church of the free market insist that government do nothing about this, that those who need help are in that difficulty because of their moral failure. As Ayn Rand had her hero say, "The only good which men can do to one another and the only statement of their proper relationship is—Hands off!"

That's a poor answer. We live connected in societies. We have moral duties, starting with the Golden Rule. The question is not whether, but

---

[153] Justice and sound economics also require that we ameliorate the ravages of unemployment and underemployment by trying to have the economy provide ample good jobs and retraining those whose skills are no longer in demand.

[154] Other social goods include environmental protection, defense and police protection and cultural resources like libraries, museums and public television.

what, to do. We've become miserly to the downtrodden. We ought to do more. The welfare system ended under President Clinton was a poor scheme, encouraging fathers not to live with their families and fostering a culture of dependence. We need to find better ways to provide a safety net when people precipitously fall. We owe our fellow men and women a social minimum below which people in a rich nation shouldn't have to live.[155]

5. Promoting Good Citizenship

The Founders rested their hopes on our being a nation of active citizens, passionate, informed and opinionated, deeply engaged in issues and politics. The paradigm has been the seven hours-long complex debates about slavery between Stephen Douglas and Abraham Lincoln across rural Illinois in the Senate election of 1858.

How different now! Though we have much more schooling, we prefer sound bites to analysis and reasoned discourse; millions of us are shockingly ill-informed about our history; and we have virtually no patience for extended argument.

We need policies to induce its people to return to the active participation in public affairs which a healthy democracy needs. These include (1) making it easier to vote, rather than enacting restrictions promoted by Republicans to shrink the franchise for their electoral benefit and (2) reducing big money's dominance over politics and government. Another idea is to require a year of national service, whether in the military, teaching in poor schools (as in Teach for America), or working on infrastructure projects, in the health care system or in the Peace Corps.

---

[155] A fairer nation is in the interest of the well-to-do because they need a healthy community to thrive other than in the very short run.

CHAPTER FOURTEEN: DEMOCRACY CAN FAIL: ARE WE WILLING TO PAY THE COST OF FREEDOM?

"Find the cost of freedom, buried in the ground Mother Earth will swallow you, lay your body down."
Stephen Stills, "Find the Cost of Freedom" © 1970

These may be fine policies. But, are approaches anything like them possible? Instead, might American democracy fail?

Most Americans would find that a silly question (at least before Donald Trump). We're a freedom-loving people deeply devoted to liberty. We have a revered Constitution to assure democracy and guarantee against despotism. Yes, we have our faults and dysfunctions. But, despotism in America??? "It can't happen here."

That's the title of Sinclair Lewis' Thirties' novel imagining such a happening. Philip Roth did it better sixty years later in The Plot Against America. Each portrayed mass hysteria electing a Nazi-era fascist President. The Founders understood that despotism could arrive via the ballot box.

American democracy has resiliently adapted eighteenth century arrangements to vast changes. But, it'd be folly to feel secure. Forces and circumstances are undermining our democracy of, by and for the people. Unless checked, they'll undermine it further.

Ask a different question: is our success assured? Will we be thriving in 2040? Grave doubts sensibly abound. Deeply divided, we avoid dealing with hard issues. The ties which bind have badly frayed. Our inability to solve our problems threatens our world leadership. Many fewer of us still believe the future will be better than the present.

We have the ways and means to fix our problems. Fail and the circle is vicious: unsolved problems subvert active citizenship and stir up despotism. Which further weakens active citizenship and makes problem-solving less likely.

A. What a Strong, Democratic Nation Needs

1. Solving Its Major Problems

The human condition is that everyone has problems. Successful people deal with theirs. A nation that doesn't is bound to decline.

Some problems are insoluble. The multi-ethnic Hapsburg and Ottoman Empires couldn't survive the eruption of nationalism even had they been well governed. By 1945, Britain lacked the resources to maintain its empire. States fall because they can't stop invaders.

Not all nations are doomed to decline. Perhaps the Roman Empire was, perhaps not. Had it'd been as well managed in the third century as under the great emperors from Trajan to Marcus Aurelius, if it had followed Marcus Aurelius' lead to scale back its empiric ambitions, it might have thrived much longer than it did.

America is certainly not doomed to decline. We have the resources, open and entrepreneurial culture, people and institutions to thrive and thrive. Our success doesn't depend on being the sole great power as we were after the fall of Soviet Communism: a unipolar planet's an unnatural condition. America can still provide our people with prosperity and security, can still be the "city on the hill" If.

In his splendid book, The Post-American World Fareed Zakaria explains America has everything needed to flourish, so long as it overcomes its do-nothing politics to deal with its problems:

> "A set of sensible reforms could be enacted tomorrow to trim wasteful spending and subsidies, increase savings, expand training in science and technology, secure pensions, create a workable immigration process, and achieve sufficient efficiencies in the use of energy. Policy experts do not have wide disagreement on most of these issues, and none of the proposed measures would require sacrifices reminiscent of wartime hardship, only modest adjustments of existing arrangements. And yet, because of politics, they appear

impossible. The American political system has lost the ability for large-scale compromise, and it has lost the ability to accept some pain now for much gain later...." (p. 211.)[156]

It's urgent we overcome our political dysfunctions to regain the will to get at our problems. If we don't, we'll needlessly go the way of Rome and the Ottomans. We've only so much time to start. Barack Obama explained he ran for President "because of what Dr. King called 'the fierce urgency of now.' Because I believe that there's such a thing as being too late, and that hour is almost upon us."

2. Active Citizens Sharing Values and Vision

Per the Founders, a democratic nation needs a community of active citizens broadly sharing basic values and a vision of the aspirations of their nation. We once had that, and somehow need to get it back.

Start with shared values. The culture wars have disunited us over core beliefs. We disagree, with vehemence and contempt, about the role of government and all manner of public policies. The other side isn't just misguided: it would lead us into either authoritarian theocracy or perdition. With politics so polarized, there's little mutual respect, dialogue or willingness to compromise, which is aggravated by our drift into class division.

American democracy's always rested on a shared vision of the American Dream and self-government. On being the great "city on the hill", imbued, perhaps by God, with a special mission to the world. Americans still want to believe in their Dream and to be self-governing little "d" democrats. They still want to envision America as the "city on the hill". But, these great visions are being eclipsed by drift, division and malaise. The idea of self-government has become remote; and millions of the less-than-privileged find it difficult to believe any more in the Dream.

---

[156] (Norton 2009). Zakaria excluded health care from his "easy-to-fix list".

As George Washington said, it's "the basis of our system, that every citizen who enjoys the protection of a free government owes not only a proportion of his property, but even of his personal services to the defense of it." But, we've lost that willingness to sacrifice when needed. It's also been weakened in three other ways.

The first is disrespect for leaders. Democratic self-government requires citizens to believe that good can come from politics and government. But, Americans have become cynical about, and developed contempt for, their officials. In 2010 the New York Times described results of focus groups of voters across the spectrum:

> "These voters did not hate politicians. They simply saw both parties, along with the media and big business, as symptoms of the larger societal ailment. And this underlying perception, that politicians in Washington conduct themselves just as childishly and with the same lack of accountability as the kids throwing chicken casserole in the lunchroom, may well be the principal emotion behind the electorate's propensity to vote out whoever holds power....
>
> "Modern presidents win elections by promising to reform Washington....But once they are elected, they find themselves sucked into the capital's partisan culture, caught up in familiar debates while the people who supported them struggle with a growing sense of chaos. And so the voters rebel again."[157]

The second reason is our obsession with material gain. Recall Tocqueville's observation, apt today, that an overly heightened "taste for physical gratifications" will cause people to be "carried away, and lose all self-restraint, at the sight of the new possessions they are about to lay hold upon." They "lose sight of the close connection which exists between the private fortune of each of them and

---

[157] Matt Bai, "Voter Disgust Isn't Only About Issues," New York Times, October 6, 2010

the prosperity of all" and the "discharge of political duties appears to them to be a troublesome annoyance, which diverts them from their occupations and business".[158]

The third reason is widespread hatred of government. Ever since the anti-federalists opposed the Constitution, some Americans have much distrusted, disliked and wanted to limit government. That strain is now more virulent than ever, as millions of us reject with fury any solutions to problems involving actions by government.[159]

Tocqueville explained the danger which intolerance of active government poses to democracy:

> *"A nation which asks nothing of its government but the maintenance of order is already a slave at heart-the slave of its own well-being, awaiting but the hand that will bind it."*[160]

Like the Founders, Tocqueville knew that the alternative to engaged citizens is control by the few:

> "When the bulk of the community is engrossed by private concerns, the smallest parties need not despair of getting the upper hand in public affairs. At such times it is not rare to see ... a multitude represented by a few players, who alone speak in the name of an absent or inattentive crowd: they alone are in action whilst all are stationary; they regulate everything by their own caprice; they change the laws, and tyrannize at will over the manners of the country; and then men wonder to see into how small a number of weak and worthless hands a great people may fall."[161]

---

[158] *Democracy in America*, vol.2, pp. 140-41.

[159] The irony is that a wise active government would improve most of their lives because the low-tax, low-regulate regime they prefer favors the wealthy.

[160] *Democracy in America*, vol.2, pp. 141-4 (emphasis supplied)

[161] *Democracy in America*, vol.2, pp. 142.

B. Dangers Facing America

1. The Threat of Decline

"For the Romans did in these cases what all wise princes should do: they not only have to have regard for present troubles but also for future ones, and they have to avoid these with all their industry because, when one foresees from afar, one can easily find a remedy for them but when you wait until they come close to you, the medicine is not in time because the disease has become incurable."
Niccolò Machiavelli, *The Prince* speaking when the Romans governed well. (emphasis supplied).

America's greatness and power are not inevitable. If America drifted downward to second class, who knows what would follow.

Nothing lasts forever. But it's not the tides of time which ought to trouble us. We should tremble because, despite vast resources and advantages, we're letting our imperiling problems slide. To repeat:
- We need to address the ecological crisis of environmental degradation and climate change that threatens healthy human life on Earth.
- We need to reduce our debilitating dependence on oil.
  We need to address the widening disparity in income and wealth and restore the prospect of the American Dream for all of us.
- We need to improve our education and health care, get health costs under control and rebuild our neglected infrastructure.
- We have the means to reduce unsustainable deficits and attend to our urgent domestic needs, if we make wise policy choices wisely.
- We spend much too much on military and related intelligence. We need a strong national defense and active foreign policy. But, that doesn't require spending all those trillions which bloat our budgets and starve domestic needs.

These are soluble problems, if we have the intelligence and will. So far, we have not. There's no reason for America to go the way of the Habsburgs and Roman Empire. What's required is that American leaders and the American people work together to solve America's problems. If we do, we will thrive. If we fail, we'll decline. As has been said, we are in a time of "the fierce urgency of now".

2. The Threat of Despotism

There are three possible outcomes should America decline. We might wake up from the slumber sleep in time to restore the nation. We might lethargically fade slowly. Or, we might turn to despotism.

Our continuation as a democracy is no more inevitable than our evergreen prosperity. The city on the hill could drift to despotism inside the outward trappings of Constitutional government. The circle could be vicious: the more the drift, the more the political division and frustration, then the worse the problems get.

Democracy means more than the election of officials under a well-written Constitution. The Soviet Union famously had a splendid Constitution. Many dictatorships hold elections which are not free: candidates are proscribed; the state manipulates the election process; fraud deprives the people of their will. We still don't know whether, or the extent to which, this occurred because of Putin's Russia in 2016.

The idea of American democracy means much more than those essential free elections. It is encapsulated in that vague term "self-government". This doesn't mean that individual citizens personally make legislative decisions, as in a New England town meeting. That's not possible in a large polity. Self-government connotes that each citizen has the right to have a say and the ability to have his ideas count in the political process.

Recent decades have been harsh to self-government in America. The marriage of mass culture and politics has diminished the voices of most people. The power of money has given wealthy people and powerful institutions disproportionate influence. Five conservative Republican Supreme Court Justices handed the 2000 election to George W. Bush in a decision few observers thought had any logic or support in precedent other than "our guy wins".

The poor performance of America's national government imperils self-government. The ideological extremism of the GOP prevents compromise. Congress is incapable of action on most major issues. If there's a sound balance between the heavy hand of bureaucracy and effective regulation, America hasn't found it. The non-legislative powers of the imperial Presidency threaten democracy. The Bill of Rights meant little to Richard Nixon and George W. Bush. They seem to mean nothing to Donald Trump.

The Presidency has become so vast and opaque that it's hard to see bad deeds. The conservative Court is disinclined to check the imperial aspects of Presidential power. Presidents wage war with as little consultation with Congress as they can get away with. Anything less, we've long been assured, would cripple our security in a hostile world.

All this has happened without any man on horseback or change in the outward appearance of the Constitution and the institutions of government. While thinkers, leaders and pundits occasionally declaim how far we've drifted from democratic government, as yet, their alarms haven't made it into our auditory canals. Though Donald Trump's behavior is beginning change that.[162]

Tocqueville observed that citizens in a democracy naturally hold the contradictory feelings of loving power but not those who hold it.[163] They are, he said,

> "constantly excited by two conflicting passions; they want to be led, and they wish to remain free: as they cannot destroy either one or the other of these contrary propensities, they strive to satisfy them both at once.... They combine the principle of centralization and that of popular sovereignty; this gives them a respite; they console themselves for being in

---

[162] While Trump's not the proverbial military dictator, he does have strong despotic tendencies.

[163] *Democracy in America*, vol. 2, p. 296

tutelage by the reflection that they have chosen their own guardians."[164]

This natural form of cognitive dissonance can be held in precarious balance but it isn't easy. That balance requires that people believe "they have chosen their own guardians" and hold leaders in some respect. As we've seen, circumstance endangers the first condition and the second condition is in routed retreat. It's not hard to imagine that a people who esteem power and disrespect officials might yearn for a charismatic supreme leader. That may be what many of the voters who supported Donald Trump sought.

The Founders assumed the government they were creating would be full of the partisan wrangling natural to free humans. They bet their experiment that, underneath the normal rancor, the people would share a commitment to a shared nation, tolerance, reason and compromise. These perquisites to self-governing freedom are now hard to find, displaced by intolerance, fury and irrationality. For parts of the Left and most of the Right, things must be "my way or the highway". A dangerous authoritarian impulse was bubbling beneath the surface even before the election of Trump.

Dis-ease, fury and inclination to the authoritarian are fueled by the slipping away of the American Dream. The disappointment of raised expectations breeds scapegoating, anger, intolerance and impatience. American patriotism is immensely strong. If the world's gone wrong, it can't be the fault of our great nation. It must be the fault of "others" — if not foreign enemies or despised minorities, perhaps those people on the other side. Whoever's responsible for the mess needs to be put in his place.

Millions of Americans are fed up with the rancor, partisanship and failure to address hard issues. Many yearn for leaders to act like leaders, for issues to be well-debated, for compromises to be made and for solutions enacted. That's one reason so many independents voted

---

[164] *Democracy in America*, vol. 2, p. 319

for Barack Obama in 2008. But, anger, partisanship and our dysfunctional politics has, so far, made that impossible.

The electorate is swung by (some) independents. The disappointed independent middle has become very volatile: heavily for Bush and the Republicans in 2002 and 2004, strongly Democratic in 2006 and 2008, then veering sharply back to the right in 2010, Democratic two years later, Republican since.

They expect leaders to get at solving the country's problems, and when they don't see that happening, they vote the bums out and vote back in the ones they've already found wanting. However understandable the frustration, the extent of the volatility is irrational, like the behavior of the anonymous mass of a mob. If the nation's elected leaders can't make progress at their job of enacting solutions to the country's ills, it's far from beyond the pale that the authoritarian undercurrent could erupt through the skin.

So, of course, it could happen here. The strong man could ride in on horseback. Or, it might be a weak blowhard who's only political skill is the art of demagoguery. It might be a small group, not one man. It needn't be a revolution at all. It could keep our constitutional forms, emptied of meaning, the way Augustus transformed Rome from republic to empire while leaving the trappings of republic in place and claiming just to be a citizen.

Both Tocqueville and John Stuart Mill worried that democracy could fall prey to soft despotism. They worried that citizens, reduced to sheep-like dependency, enervated by ease and grown accustomed to delegating hard thought to those in charge, lose political will. In such a state, the appearances of democracy (voting, institutions, stated if eroded rights...) would remain, as the citizens surrender real power — without awareness they've done so.

If a majority clamored loud and long enough for a strong leader, it could happen. Some President could anoint his successor, the electorate voting him in while the old President, not needing the title, exercised the real power. Or, the Twenty-second Amendment, limiting

Presidents to two terms could be repealed for a popular leader. Hard as it is to imagine, there could be a (bloodless) coup.

Or, what seems more likely, despotism might, like Carl Sandburg's fog, "come on little cat feet", quietly unnoticed. Until, as in the Rome of Augustus, democracy becomes enshrouded in mist. If, perversely, one wanted to boil a frog, if you threw him into boiling water, he'd jump out of the pot. Instead, you'd put him in a pot of warm water and slowly increase the heat bit by bit, allowing him to get comfortable in the increasingly warm water until he drowses off. When the temperature gets high enough, the sleeping frog boils.

American democracy hasn't yet found antidotes to the poison eating at our democracy. Citizenship has become less active, the money power dominates and American democracy has adapted poorly to mass culture. Are we drifting, will we drift, passively into a polity with the trappings but not the substance of democracy? It could happen here. It need not, if we seize the day.

CHAPTER FIFTEEN: HOPE

A. Prognosis

"I think that we can do better in this country."
Robert Kennedy, said often, especially in his 1968 campaign

"Hey Jude, don't make it bad.
Take a sad song and make it better."
John Lennon and Paul McCartney, "Hey Jude" © 1968

Our ship of state is grounded. There are sound practical solutions to our problems, based on ideas and attitudes which go back to our roots. We have the ways and means to get back on track. But, we're not. Not yet. How ill is this patient?

Are we terminally untreatable? Do we have it in us to get off the shoals and sail to open water? Or, as it's easy to imagine, are we condemned to decline into mediocrity? The answer — preliminary, tentative and in danger of being over-optimistic — is that, with a good deal of feasible change, America can return to health.
Some of what ails can't be changed, though unfortunate effects can be ameliorated. Some can be changed with wise policies and better politics. Some require what's most difficult of all: changes in ideas and attitudes.

What Can't Be Changed

America is neither going back to a pre-industrial society nor rejecting capitalism. Any America one can sensibly imagine will be a capitalist mass society, full of large bureaucratic institutions of business, government and culture. Even if a greater percentage of people work in small organizations, big organizations will continue to have immense importance. Most people will probably live in large cities and their suburbs. The economy will be susceptible to capitalistic "creative destruction". Though the Internet might open up culture, the mass media aren't going away.

Living in mass society, we will have to deal with bigness. To be effective, large organizations will need to learn wiser and more people-friendly ways, to ameliorate the stifling effects of bigness. This won't be easy and no matter what, we will have to learn to live as well as possible as parts of a series of masses.

What Good Politics and Better Policies Can Change

America will need good policies, such as those sketched in the last chapter, to deal with our urgent problems so that we can prosper and thrive. With wisdom and will, we can successfully address runaway health costs; enormous deficits; our unaffordable role as policeman of the world; immigration; crumbling infrastructure. We can probably still avoid the catastrophe of global warming if we act boldly, wisely and quickly.

This is what well-governed nations do: to empower their government to do, as Lincoln said, "whatever they need to have done, but can not do, at all, or can not, so well do, for themselves — in their separate; and individual capacities."[165] The question is whether we can heal our broken politics to take the steps we need to take. Polarized politics aren't inevitable. The system can keep equilibrium if voters punish parties when they go off the deep end.

Of Ideas and Attitudes: Getting to Healthier Social Psyches

We humans are capable of self-destruction, and political healing won't come just because it's wise and necessary. People naturally resist disruptive change. We naturally cling to comfortably habitual ideas and arrangements, even when they aren't so good. Better safe than sorry, keep the devil we know than strike out for potentially (only potentially!) better shores. All this is magnified as our politics are badly broken because our social psyches are badly wounded. We've seen that the forces of modernity are causes of our malaise:

---

[165] Fragment, July 1, 1854

secular materialism, extreme individualism and free market ideology, the contemporary economy, mass culture and the pace of change. They've shaken America's foundations, dismaying traditional and secular Americans, poisoning our culture and politics, destroying our sense of community and citizenship and making us feel disempowered, alienated, other-directed and unsettled.

So, to get healthy again, we must regain solid foundations by regrounding ourselves in ideas and beliefs which provide security and comfort. When solidly grounded, we humans can duck more punches and stand when punches fall, equipped to avoid and to surmount feelings of disempowerment, alienation and other-directedness. Feeling more at home, we'll be less angry and more inclined to want to work together to solve problems. It is a pleasant prospect.

But, far from certain. Might, instead, America be in a doom loop, a downward spiral with no exit? The history of the last several decades is not comforting. Things have gotten worse, and then worse again.

B. Getting to Success

Our politics is desolate. Is this, from the saddest of great songs, the picture of our future?

> "And I don't know a soul who's not been battered.
> I don't have a friend who feels at ease.
> I don't know a dream that's not been shattered or driven to its knees.
> But it's all right, it's all right
> We've lived so well so long.
> Still, when I think of the road we're traveling on
> I wonder what went wrong.
> I can't help it, I wonder what went wrong.
>
> And I dreamed I was dying.
> And I dreamed that my soul rose unexpectedly
> And looking back down at me
> Smiled reassuringly.

> And I dreamed I was flying
> And high up above my eyes could clearly see
> The Statue of Liberty sailing away to sea.
> And I dreamed I was flying.
>
> We come on the ship they call the Mayflower.
> We come on the ship that sailed the moon.
> We come in the age's most uncertain hour and sing an American tune.
> But it's all right, it's all right
> You can't be forever blessed.
> Still, tomorrow's going to be another working day
> And I'm trying to get some rest.
> That's all I'm trying to get some rest."
> "American Tune" © Paul Simon © 1973

It's easy to feel lost, that we're no longer "forever blessed". Is "the Statue of Liberty sailing away to sea"? Can it be that time is ticking on some awful explosion? Will the dream and promise of America, a dream and promise that, for all our imperfections, our history has often redeemed just vanish, to become but a dim memory? Perhaps, but that need not be.

It briefly felt after Obama's first election in the midst of the Great Crash that the country had reached a Rooseveltian moment, that bold solutions to pressing problems had suddenly become possible. But, though he did much good, Obama was not up to being transformative; and, the Right seized the void to resurge more radical than ever. That moment, perhaps illusory, when the change we desperately need seemed there for the grasping, passed.

Though we're still sliding downhill, there are, even in the Presidency of Donald Trump, several bases for optimism.

The first is that America has great strengths from which can spring the resilience, wisdom and courage we need. We Americans have always been a strong and supple people, blessed to live in a land of milk and honey. We're an open society in a land of exceptional natural resources. We've a great tradition of freedom, democracy and can-do, entrepreneurial spirit. However divided, we still share devotion to our nation. With improved education and decent opportunity, we could, again, thrive as informed, active citizens.

It's too soon to write off America. We've before risen with pluck to meet the challenges of difficult times. There could come a point of no return when we've let too much good soil wash away. Yet, organisms, people and societies have great recuperative powers. It's a good bet that there's enough left in the American tank to permit the country to regain its health.

The second reason for optimism is the law of the pendulum. If a pendulum doesn't swing so hard that it breaks, it will, even after a long one way swing, return to the center (hopefully not to swing too far in the other direction). The pendulum of American politics might swing away from rancorous division, with which polls show most of us are fed up. It's not beyond the pale that enough voters will demand healthy changes — and stick to their guns through several elections. The traumas of the Great Crash and now the election of Donald Trump and the Trump-GOP efforts to run the country for the benefit of the wealthiest Americans have moved many of us to embrace new thinking and support major reforms.

The third, and most significant, reason for optimism is that world views are not permanent; and we seem to be in a period of transition. Secular materialism has, it seems, passed its peak. Like our ancestors as the medieval world of faith was dissolving but before the modern materialistic world had emerged, we stand on the edge of a new world. It's started to be born but it's too soon yet to see its colors and contours.

Unless the new era is as harsh as the vision of the Right, as closed and intolerant as the Middle Ages, there'll be no reason to mourn the passage of the modern world view.[166] For a long time, it served humanity well; but that time has passed. It's a good guess that the new world will be more spiritual and less individualist. Perhaps Americans are becoming more receptive to the ideas we need: spirituality, an ethics of responsibility, communitarian thoughts. If not now, will they be soon, while there's still time to fix our broken nation? It's possible.

1. A Politics of Success

No person, no faction, no group has a monopoly on wisdom. Each side of the political aisle stands for an important truth. Listen to Daniel Patrick Moynihan, "The central conservative truth is that it is culture, not politics, that determines the success of a society. The central liberal truth is that politics can change a culture and save it from itself." A well-governed nation needs times of un-extreme progressive and times of un-extreme conservative government.

What America needs now is an extended period of liberal ascendancy. The conservative ascendancy has been long, and problems have built up which their solutions can't fix. The extreme right-wing policies of today's Republicans can only deepen our crisis. For now, it's up to the liberals to try to fix America. Is a liberal ascendancy feasible?

Liberals have had a bad time since 1968. Franklin Roosevelt made the Democrats the natural governing party. From FDR through LBJ, the Democrats proposed, sold to the electorate and enacted the great progressive reforms of the New Deal and Truman, Kennedy and Johnson: Social Security, Medicare, the Civil Rights and Voting Rights Acts, strong financial regulation, fair tax policies. The one Republican President, Dwight Eisenhower, was a moderate conservative with no interest in repealing the New Deal. So long as we don't want to throw out the baby of humanitarian ideals with the bath water.

---

[166] So long as we don't want to throw out the baby of humanitarian ideals with the bath water.

The country prospered. Millions rose into the middle class, disparities of wealth and income narrowed sharply and the few recessions were mild and short-lived.

And, then, as chronicled in Chapter Ten, it all fell apart. The conservatives counter-attacked with brilliant strategy and adept élan. Long after Ronald Reagan's election, the Republicans skillfully dominated American politics and dictated the national agenda. They have offered a narrative, vision and message which have resonated well with the feelings, fears and thoughts of a majority of Americans. They have preached and preached and preached their values, persuading very many Americans that they're the party of morals and ideals, while the Democrats are a soulless collection of liberal interest groups. They've mastered modern political organization and have ruthlessly dispatched anyone in their way.

They became the natural rulers of the land. In charge (and dominating debate even when Democrats held power), they've enacted and enforced de-regulation and tax policies favoring the rich. Their policies (abetted by some Democrats, including Bill Clinton) brought on the Great Crash and the Great Recession. They've prevented the adoption of policies to address climate change, declining levels of education and affordable, quality health care for all. Largely ignored for years, these problems have grown like tumors, harder to cure now than when the Republicans took over.

But, it's a great mistake to blame only the Republicans. The Democrats let them take the field. They stopped speaking in terms which articulated the worries and values of most Americans. With the exception of Dwight Eisenhower, the Republicans from Herbert Hoover through Barry Goldwater were out of step with the country. Then, it became the Democrats who projected a vision of America that did not attract, and often repelled, the majority. Not that all of their ideas were unpopular: many were what people wanted. It was that the package was quite uncongenial.

Are progressives fated, as the Right proclaims, forever to be the minority, disrespected and despised by most of the country, capable of winning some elections, but never able to sustain power or use it for progressive ends? They are unless they learn the lessons of what went wrong; develop a powerful vision of America's future; find ways and means to explain that vision which appeal to a majority of Americans; and connect their policies to their vision.

Nearly five decades ago, liberals disconnected from middle America. They need to reconnect, to attract more voters to liberal values. For all that time, many progressives regarded the silent majority as hopelessly chauvinistic, bigoted and foolish, that millions of voters who sustained the New Deal coalition had for one reason or another (prosperity, racism, militarism...) gone over to the dark side.

There's been and is racism, militarism and the economic conservatism of prosperity, but blaming them for the Republicans' rise is too facile. Chapter Ten chronicles how liberals changed their basic message to emphasize ideas, values and feelings much disliked by a majority of the country. The past need not be prologue. There is a progressive message, a progressive vision of America which can resonate with, and get the support of, most Americans. It has the great virtue of being what America now needs.

Success requires strong leaders able to articulate a compelling vision and set of policies in ways which resonate with most Americans. Men and women able to gain support and lead the country to get things done. But, liberals have long suffered from weak leadership.

Democratic Presidents, Presidential candidates and Congressional spokesmen since Robert Kennedy have mostly failed to provide strong leadership. Ed Muskie might have, but he was done in by Nixon's dirty tricks. Ted Kennedy tried, but he lost too much stature after Chappaquiddick. Bill Clinton had the skills, but, for whatever reasons, didn't make the grade. Despite his promise, Barack Obama didn't lead as well as he seemed likely to do.

Had political skill been sufficient, Bill Clinton could've been a transformative President. But, unlike Reagan, he lacked a big picture vision with which to explain "here's the future America I see". Faced with an increasingly right-wing, unscrupulous GOP determined to destroy him, the best he could do was "triangulate", chasing the Republicans for deals more and more their way as they got more and more conservative.

Barack Obama campaigned as if he had a vision of a better America. He won the White House with eloquence, a message of hope and national renewal and an ability to teach about difficult issues. Once inaugurated, he largely silenced his eloquence and message of hope; time and again he unsuccessfully tried to compromise with a party dedicated to destroying him. He failed to use his bully pulpit to teach what's wrong, why it's wrong and how to fix it. He offered little in the way of vision and only rarely explained how his policies promote, and his opponents' policies retard, sound values. And, so, he squandered one of those rare transformational moments when crisis opened America to turning in a new and hopeful direction.

The upshot is that liberals desperately need strong leadership, like the Roosevelts, the Kennedys and Lincoln: "a leader to bring our country home; re-unite the red, white and blue before it turns to stone."[167] A leader with a vision based on our values, with eloquence, political skill, charisma, and the will to use them, to compromise where wise and to fight hard when not. Millions of us hoped, thought, we had elected that leader in Barack Obama. For all his many virtues, it wasn't him. Who will it be?

2. Visions of What America Can Be

We can't passively wait for great leaders. When one coms along, we must be ready. For now, progressives' urgent task is to define the America they envisage and policies to get there. While, as times have changed, the policies will differ from the New Deal and the Great

---

[167] Neil Young, "Lookin' for a Leader" © 2006

Society, they will seek to manifest the same vision which propelled the Democratic ascendancy from FDR to Robert Kennedy's murder. That vision is a just society in which most Americans have a real shot at the American Dream.

Republicans have a vision for America. They trumpet its appealing parts — self-reliance, low taxes, freedom from interference, patriotism. But just what would their America be like? Republican rhetoric disguises their harsh perversion of the American Dream.

Republicans would reduce even further taxes on the very wealthy, greatly increase spending on defense and security and reduce deficits by shrinking the rest of government drastically. They'd get rid of most of our limited safety net and eviscerate public services by privatization (Social Security and Medicare) or plain old slashing funding (such as for Medicaid). Everyone would be free to take care of himself without government interference or assistance. The Ryan budget and Mitt Romney's election plans would go far towards their ambition "to get [government] down to the size where we can drown it in the bathtub."[168] Donald Trump would go even further.

Every American would be on her own. There'd be little regulation, and people would have the opportunities their circumstances allow. If they make it, they'd have lots of money, and pay few taxes as government wouldn't do much beyond defense, police and fire work. If they don't, well too bad for them. They're probably slackers.

The gulf in income and property between the best off few and everyone else would continue to widen, sharply. The people at the top would have access to, and money to afford, good education and health care and to have a fine retirement. Not so much everyone else. They'd be left slim pickings by an unregulated market and minimalist state, as the well-off would get most good opportunities.

Government would offer little, if any, help for the disadvantaged: a

---

[168] The stated goal of Grover Norquist, the powerful (among Republicans) founder of Americans for Tax Reform.

person with disabling disease, unemployment or other catastrophe would have to do the necessary for himself and his family or find charity somewhere. (Recall the Republican cheers at a 2012 Presidential debate that an uninsured man be left to die because he couldn't pay to enter the emergency room.) No Golden Rule for public life.

Security concerns would dominate public discourse and enemies dealt with harshly. If civil liberties erode, that'd just be the price of buying public safety. The American empire would continue to try to make the world in our free market democratic image, often militarily. Fed by military muscle-flexing, we'd frequently celebrate militaristic patriotism.

Environmental issues would be off the table, global warming officially a hoax, while the real warming of our planetary home would proceed apace. Politics would be overwhelmed by billions spent by the likes of Karl Rove and the Koch Brothers to hold on to power so as to keep the country properly free.

The well-off would avoid crime behind the gates of their guarded communities. Abortion and gay marriage and civil unions would be outlawed. America would be declared a "Christian country".

We'd be a nation in the spirit of Ayn Rand's dyspeptic hero: "The only good which men can do to one another and the only statement of their proper relationship is—Hands off!" For all but the well-off, the nation would bear an uncomfortable resemblance to Hobbes' state of nature, that condition of "war of every man against every man," of "continual fear... and the life of man, solitary, poor, nasty, brutish" (if perhaps not "short"). The sense of community and active citizenship on which the Founders built America would vanish.

This is an unappealing vision unless you both don't care about others and are, or expect to become, rich, to afford private schools, first class health care and the keys to a gated community. Though, before long, global warming and other environmental ills would make life quite uncomfortable even for the 1%. Because we'd let our major problems continue to slide, America would decline.

This is a horrible prospect, and liberals have let conservatives off the hook by not exposing the nature of the America of Republican dreams. Liberals need to offer their very different vision focused on the American Dream, based on the hopes and values which have been made America great. A compelling vision on which to take the fight for America's future and soul to the Right.

That vision is to make America again a nation in which every person has real opportunity to earn the means to a better life. To have the good education and good health care which make that possible. To afford decent housing and have the opportunity for a decent retirement. To provide economic justice for the middle class and the poor, so that they pay taxes commensurate with income in a system which fairly apportions the burdens of government and public services. To run government with fiscal responsibility so what's spent and tax breaks which are offered serve the public interest. To have an economy which is well, but not overly, regulated, protecting us against unbridled market excesses: fraud, abuse, dishonesty, unsafe products and the consequences of untrammeled greed.

The goal of this America will be for each person to have the means to achieve the American Dream himself. Government'll help by providing good public services, fair tax policy and retraining and other programs to provide decent opportunity to everyone. It'll be an America that prizes self-reliance. The vision is that in such an America, as after World War II, by making society more fair and substantially increasing opportunity, inequality will again reduce.

This America will care for the poor and disadvantaged without losing sight of the needs of Americans in the middle. It'll provide a decent safety net and have special programs to alleviate poverty and help people pull themselves up to success. But, liberty would trump economic equality, so long as basic social arrangements are fair and opportunities are available for all. It will be an America whose primary goals have moved from Rawlsian distributive justice to the ability to exercise one's capabilities.

It'll be an America which has a strong national defense but no longer seeks imperial dominion over the world. We'll have the weapons, armed forces and bases we need for security, which'll be much less than today. It'll be a nation of which to be proud and to feel patriotic: not only in necessary military actions, but in the values we'll be living at home, proud to revive Detroit and Cleveland instead of trying to remake the Middle East in our image.

Liberals will offer hope instead of fear, connected community instead of Hobbes' state of nature. They'll respect middle Americans and their values: not by abandoning tolerance, coddling racism or claiming climate change is a delusion propagated by grant-seeking scientists. Rather, they'll stand up for progressive beliefs and values as they engage in respectful dialogue with those which differ.

Think of how, in 1968, Robert Kennedy got the esteem and votes of millions of the "silent majority". He didn't pander, nor disrespect the values of those who disagreed with him. Rather, he firmly stated why his compassion and other values compelled him to urge this and that course of action. He offered reasoned argument, informed by what he believed to be right. He got the votes of many of that silent majority, some by persuasion as to what ought to be done, some because he earned their respect despite their disagreements.

Since his murder, most liberal leaders have shied away from large visions of what America ought, can come to, be. This is a great mistake. Bobby's vision excited millions. It was essential to the very real possibility that, had he not been killed, he may have been elected President. As he said at the end of his speeches (paraphrasing George Bernard Shaw), "some men see things as they are and ask 'why'. I dream of things that never were and ask 'why not'." It is past time for liberals to articulate what ought to be.

The liberal vision will have a deep respect for all forms of spirituality and faith. It'll be of a nation which really is based on democratic values, whose citizens accept as willingly as George Washington that their citizenship brings duties as well as rights.

This liberal vision will appeal to people disaffected by what's not right with modernity. It will be based on eternal values, not secular materialism. It'll call for old-fashioned individualism of self-reliance and social responsibilities. It'll look to a fairer America, with much more opportunity for all than the cramped country thrust upon us by decades of conservative policies. It'll provide bases for resurrecting a national community. It will offer people a comfortable political home, as FDR did, giving us confidence our leaders are pursuing values and policies which can improve our world.

This book has attempted to understand the causes bedeviling America. You can only fix what first you understand. This liberal vision is of American greatness, worthy of great progressive leaders from the Roosevelts to the Kennedys. It is a path to healing.

It is based on the American Dream, on what attracted the huddled masses across the ocean. It's the promise of that dream — a nation blessed not just with resources but with splendid values, offering opportunities for all — which has made America a special nation. It's a great and realistic dream, and it is past time to revive it. Over forty years ago Paul Simon sung, wistfully at the time, "We come on the ship they call the Mayflower. We come on the ship that sailed the moon. We come in the age's most uncertain hour and sing an American tune". This vision offers the possibility that America can once again make harmonious the American tune, can once again, as the city on a hill, be a beacon to its citizens and to the peoples of the world.

FINIS: November 11, 2017

SOURCES AND INFLUENCES

I could not have written this book without the wisdom and inspiration of other works, only some of which are cited in *Difficult Times*. Though this is a work of non-fiction, I begin with literature because great novels and plays from Aeschylus to Philip Roth have been my best teachers.

The plays which mean the most to me are those of Aeschylus (especially the *Oresteia*), Sophocles (particularly the Oedipus plays and Antigone) and of Euripides (especially the *Bacchae*); the tragedies and histories of Shakespeare; *Faust* and other plays of Goethe and Eckermann's *Conversations with Goethe*; and the plays of Ibsen.

The novels which have most opened my mind are Stendhal's *The Red and the Black*; Balzac's *Lost Illusions*; those of Dickens (particularly *Hard Times*); George Eliot's *Middlemarch*; Melville's *Moby Dick*; Tolstoy's *Anna Karenina* and *War and Peace*; Dostoevsky's *The Possessed* and *The Brothers Karamazov* (for me, the two best of novels); the great Germans of the early twentieth century: Thomas Mann (especially *The Magic Mountain*), Hermann Hesse (*The Glass Bead Game* above all), Hermann Broch (especially *The Sleepwalkers*) and everything by Kafka; the works of Joseph Conrad, particularly *The Heart of Darkness* and *Nostromo*; Ford Madox Ford's *Parade's End*; Albert Camus' *The Plague* (and his essay *The Rebel*); Fitzgerald's *The Great Gatsby*; Faulkner's *Absalom, Absalom*; and much of the work of Philip Roth, especially *American Pastoral* and *The Human Stain*. While I don't often read poetry, Yeats, Rumi, Frost and, supremely, Rilke belong on this list.

The philosopher who has meant the most to me is Nietzsche. While I have grown more skeptical of some of his teaching than I used to be, he remains the best mind I have encountered, full of startling insights and deep wisdom. My favorites of his books are *The Gay Science*, *Also Sprach Zarathustra* and *Beyond Good and Evil*.

The other vital works of philosophy and religion for me are Aristotle's *Nicomachean Ethics*; *Genesis*, *Deuteronomy*, the social justice teachings of the Prophets and *Job*; Spinoza's *Ethics*; Kant's *Groundwork of the Metaphysic of Morals*; the essays of Emerson and of Isaiah Berlin; Martin Buber's *I and Thou*; John Rawls' *A Theory of Justice*; Ronald Dworkin's *Justice for Hedgehogs*; the works of the communitarians Alasdair MacIntyre, Michael Sandel, Charles Taylor and Michael Walzer, and not only those cited in footnotes 126 and 128; and the works of Martha Nussbaum and Amartya Sen on capabilities cited in footnote 130.

I have learned much by reading history. The history, social science and science books which have done the most to guide me as to how and what I think about ideas in this book are Thucydides' *The Peloponnesian War*, *The Federalist Papers*; Alexis de Tocqueville's *Democracy in America* and *The Old Regime and the French Revolution*; Jose Ortega y Gassett's *Revolt of the Masses*; Harry Jaffa's books about Lincoln; Arthur Schlesinger's *Crisis of the Old Order*; David Halberstam's *The Best and the Brightest*; Taylor Branch's *Parting the Waters*; *The Last Patrician* (about Robert Kennedy) by Michael Knox Beran; Mancur Olson's *The Rise and Decline of Nations*; Hyman Minsky's *Stabilizing an Unstable Economy*; Fritjof Capra's *The Tao of Physics*; and David Bohm's *Wholeness and the Implicate Order*.

I would be remiss not to mention two other large influences. The first are great leaders: Abraham Lincoln, George Washington, Thomas Jefferson, Franklin Roosevelt, Jack and Robert Kennedy, Martin Luther King, Earl Warren and Hugo Black, Vaclav Havel, Nelson Mandela and the Dalai Lama. The second is great music. I have grown and learned much by listening to classical music from Handel and Bach to Mahler, particularly Mozart and Beethoven. And, it will not surprise the reader of Difficult Times that I embrace a good deal of the music of the best artists who began work in the Sixties, none more than Bob Dylan and the Beatles.

www.ingramcontent.com/pod-product-compliance
Lightning Source LLC
Chambersburg PA
CBHW060503090426
42735CB00011B/2092